Human Well-Being Research and Policy Making

Series Editors

Richard J. Estes, School of Social Policy & Practice, University of Pennsylvania, Philadelphia, PA, USA

M. Joseph Sirgy, Department of Marketing, Virginia Polytechnic Institute & State University, Blacksburg, VA, USA

This series creates a dialogue between well-being scholars and well-being public policy makers.

Well-being theory, research and practice are essentially interdisciplinary in nature and embrace contributions from all disciplines within the social sciences. With the exception of leading economists, the policy relevant contributions of social scientists are widely scattered and lack the coherence and integration needed to more effectively inform the actions of policy makers.

Contributions in the series focus on one more of the following four aspects of well-being and public policy:

- Discussions of the public policy and well-being focused on particular nations and worldwide regions
- Discussions of the public policy and well-being in specialized sectors of policy making such as health, education, work, social welfare, housing, transportation, use of leisure time
- Discussions of public policy and well-being associated with particular population groups such as women, children and youth, the aged, persons with disabilities and vulnerable populations
- Special topics in well-being and public policy such as technology and well-being, terrorism and well-being, infrastructure and well-being.

More information about this series at http://www.springer.com/series/15692

Mariano Rojas

Well-Being in Latin America

Drivers and Policies

 Springer

Mariano Rojas
Universidad Internacional
de La Rioja (UNIR)
Logroño, Spain

Universidad Popular Autónoma
del Estado de Puebla (UPAEP)
Puebla, Mexico

ISSN 2522-5367   ISSN 2522-5375   (electronic)
Human Well-Being Research and Policy Making
ISBN 978-3-030-33497-0   ISBN 978-3-030-33498-7   (eBook)
https://doi.org/10.1007/978-3-030-33498-7

This Springer imprint is published by the registered company Springer Nature Switzerland AG
The registered company address is: Gewerbestrasse 11, 6330 Cham, Switzerland

With the aspiration for public policy and the social organization to foster the conditions for people to lead a life they are satisfied with.

Contents

List of Figures

List of Tables

Chapter 1
Latin America and Well-Being

Abstract The well-being situation of Latin Americans can be considered as favorable, and it contrasts to the many problems in the region as portrayed by socio-political and economic indicators. Latin America is commonly characterized as a region with weak political institutions, high corruption, high violence and crime rates, very unequal distribution of income, and high poverty rates. The high life satisfaction reported by Latin Americans indicates that there are other drivers of well-being which have not received the deserved attention. The Latin American case shows that the abundance of person-based interpersonal relationships is an important driver of well-being; policy-makers and governments from other regions of the world should incorporate this driver into their policy framework.

Keywords Latin America · Well-being · Life satisfaction · Happiness · Culture

1.1 High Well-Being in Latin America

Latin Americans report high well-being levels. Life satisfaction is, on average, high in Latin America; of course, there are differences across countries and along socio-demographic groups, with some population segments reporting relatively low life-satisfaction levels. Positive-affect scores in the region are substantially high both in comparison to other countries in the world and to what income levels in the region would predict. Latin Americans do also evaluate their life higher than what their income levels would predict. The main message from Latin America is that there is more to life than income and that there is something to learn from the Latin American case about what the drivers of well-being are and about the way development is conceived and policy is designed for.

Currently used development indicators neglect important aspects in life which are of relevance for people's well-being. Well-being measures are relevant in addressing development debates and strategies because they appropriately incorporate people's values. These measures recognize that the human experience of being well is universal, but they allow for heterogeneity across regions and ages in the relationship between this experience and its drivers. Heterogeneity emerges from historical processes that shape culture and influence values. Hence, the book argues that well-being

© Springer Nature Switzerland AG 2020   1
M. Rojas, *Well-Being in Latin America*, Human Well-Being Research and Policy Making,
https://doi.org/10.1007/978-3-030-33498-7_1

is better measured by relying on people's own assessment rather than on sets of indicators defined by experts and international organizations.

The well-being situation of Latin Americans can be considered as very favorable; it contrasts with the situation presented by commonly used socio-political and economic indicators. These indicators often portray a situation of weak political institutions, high corruption, high violence and crime rates, very unequal distribution of income, and high poverty rates in many Latin American countries. The book recognizes that these problems do exist; it also shows that these recurrent problems do in fact depress the well-being of Latin Americans. It is demonstrated that the life satisfaction of Latin Americans could be higher if these problems were properly solved. However, the book shows that by focusing predominantly on these problems scholars and policy makers get a misleading impression of life in Latin America. Furthermore, the exclusive focus on problems could lead scholars and policy makers to neglect some relevant well-being drivers and it could induce policy makers to undertake wrong policies by lacking a more integral and complete view of the life and well-being of Latin Americans.

It is also important to remark that even on the basis of commonly-used development indicators not everything is problematic in Latin America. For example, per capita income is not low and there is reasonable provision of public goods and an acceptable provision of health and education services in most Latin American countries.

The book shows that high life satisfaction in Latin America is neither an anomaly nor an oddity. It is explained by the abundance of person-based interpersonal relationships which have been frequently sidelined in favor of income measures in the development discourse. The book shows that relationships are important for people's well-being; and that high-quality interpersonal relations are abundant in Latin America. Lessons for public policy and for the conception of development are presented.

1.2 Relevance of Latin American Well-Being Research

The 20th century was dominated by the idea that high income was sufficient for people to enjoy high well-being. The paradigm of development as economic growth emerged as a consequence of this idea, and the attainment of ever increasing levels of income became the main goal of public policy and development strategies. Other notions of progress have been developed, but they end up being closely associated to income and to the main goal of attaining economic growth; this is the case of notions such as: income inequality, income poverty, multi-dimensional poverty, and asset deprivation.

Economists worked during the 20th century in the development of models of economic growth. These models induced policy makers and development organizations to place their attention in concepts such as: competitiveness, productivity, physical capital, savings, foreign investment, natural capital, human capital, and social capital.

The paradigm of development as economic growth led to the construction of national income accounts to keep track of the evolution of the gross domestic product (GDP) and related concepts.

Research carried out during the last decades of the 20th century showed that economic growth is not sufficient to generate people's well-being (Easterlin 1974; Rojas 2019). Greater income may contribute to greater well-being, but it is neither necessary nor sufficient for high well-being, and it also depends on the way it is used. Hence, it is recognized that income may be an instrument for people's well-being, but income is not a final aim and its capacity in generating well-being needs to be assessed rather than assumed. In addition, at the beginning of the 21st century it is widely accepted that there are environmental limits as well as social and human limits to economic growth; thus, the goal of attaining ever increasing levels of income may come accompanied with high well-being costs which income accounts do not accurately appreciate.

Well-being research shows that there are many drivers of people's well-being; such as: income, health, recreational activities, interpersonal relationship at the family level as well as in the neighborhood and at the workplace, and many others (Glatzer et al. 2015; Rojas 2016). The expansion of the number of well-being drivers is good news for policy makers who now have more instruments at their disposal and who can implement creative policy combinations to aim at the final goal of increasing people's well-being. A new paradigm is emerging around the concept of well-being; there is a paradigm shift from the notion of development as economic growth—which predominated in the 20th century—to the notion of development as well-being—which is expected to predominate in the 21st century.

The paradigm shift makes it necessary to intensify research on the drivers of well-being by taking advantage of information from different regions of the world. It becomes necessary to inform policy makers about the many options countries have to increase people's well-being. Research about the well-being situation in Latin American may contribute to this task. High well-being in most Latin American countries shows that policy makers and development strategists may have something useful to learn from the Latin American case. The region shows that it is possible to enjoy high well-being levels and to do so at a lower cost to the planet—and to the well-being of future generations. Latin America is no paradise and, indeed, many problems do exist; however, the region also allows for studying some drivers that contribute to people's well-being and that are neglected by research carried out in other regions of the world; of particular importance is the quantity and quality of interpersonal relations. The Latin American case shows that person-based interpersonal relations constitute an important driver of people's well-being which policy makers and development strategists would like to familiarize themselves with in order for public policy and development strategies to have greater well-being impact.

1.3   The Latin American Region

1.3.1   Latin America: Not Just a Geographical Region

One could think of Latin America as a collection of countries that happen to be in the same geographical region; however, Latin America is much more than this, it is a distinct culture. Of course, there is considerable intra-regional heterogeneity as well as substantial similarities with other regions of the world, but it is possible to think of a Latin American culture with a clearly recognized way of life where close interpersonal relations and the enjoyment of positive affective states predominate (Beytía 2016, 2018; Rojas 2012a; Yamamoto 2016). The Latin American culture emerged from particular historical processes, and some of its features are relevant in explaining the well-being of Latin Americans (Rojas and García-Vega 2017).

1.3.2   The Latin American Region

The Latin American category usually includes those countries in the American continent where romance languages are predominant. On the basis of this vague definition the region incorporates Brazil—where Portuguese is the official language—and eighteen countries where Spanish is an official language: Argentina, Bolivia, Chile, Colombia, Costa Rica, Cuba, Dominican Republic, Ecuador, El Salvador, Guatemala, Honduras, Mexico, Nicaragua, Panama, Paraguay, Peru, Uruguay, and Venezuela. Puerto Rico, another state where Spanish is spoken, is not usually included due to its status as unincorporated territory of the United States; however, it is recognized that Puerto Ricans have a Latin American character. On the basis of a romance-language criterion Haiti—where French is widely spoken—could also be considered as being part of the region; however, its history and culture are very different from those of the Spanish and Portuguese-speaking countries.

It is important to note that many indigenous languages are also widely spoken in the region; this reflects the existence of large indigenous populations in countries such as Bolivia, Ecuador, Guatemala, Paraguay, Peru, and Mexico.

The region goes from the northern 32° parallel to the southern 56° parallel (not considering Antarctic territories). It comprises a population of about 635 million people living in a geographical area of about 19.5 million km². In terms of population size the largest countries in the region are, by far, Brazil and Mexico, with population figures of 212 million and 132 million people, respectively. Colombia, Argentina, Peru and Venezuela can be considered mid-size countries, with populations in between 50 and 30 million people.

Latin America is not a high income region, and no Latin American country would be classified as developed on the basis of its per capita income level. Commonly used indicators point towards the existence of many social problems, such as: corruption and lack of transparency, high income inequality and poverty rates, and high crime and victimization rates (Casas-Zamora and Carter 2017; Gasparini and Lusting 2011; Jaitman 2017; O'Donnell 1999; Puchet et al. 2012; Rojas 2012b; World Bank 2011).

As expected, Latin America is a diverse region; there are significant inter-country differences, as well as substantial intra-country disparities. However, there is a general idea of the region as a single entity, and most people in the region can identify themselves as Latin Americans.

1.3.3 The Latin American Culture

The Latin American identity is not defined by language alone or by sharing a geographic space in the world. The Latin American identity points towards a culture that has emerged from historical processes which are common to all countries in the region. With the emergence of well-being research and the gathering of well-being reports it has become visible that the Latin American way of life is associated with high well-being. The emerging data from Latin America shows that, on average, life satisfaction is high in the region; with positive affect being outstandingly high and life evaluation being above what income levels in the region would predict. It seems that the set of social and economic indicators which are commonly used in development studies do not provide a complete picture of the well-being of Latin Americans.

It is the collision of major civilizations which gave rise to the Latin American nations, as well as three centuries of colonization by Spain and Portugal. The European civilizations—mostly Spaniards and Portuguese—collided during the 15th and 16th century with the large pre-Columbian indigenous civilizations which existed in the region. The collision of these major civilizations was not a peaceful process; it is a history of battles and impositions, of treason and ambition, of conquering and colonization, of being forced to adapt to rapidly changing social and political circumstances and to understand unfamiliar points of view. The large indigenous populations were neither exterminated nor segregated, and over time Europeans and indigenous groups mixed, creating "mestizo" (racially mixed ancestry between American Indian and European—usually Spanish or Portuguese).[1] Many Indians died as a consequence of the new illnesses brought by Europeans, and many others died as a consequence of unhealthy working conditions. But it was not in the interest

---

[1]Bushnell et al. (2017) mention the following factors promoting the mixing of Europeans and Indians in Latin America: The relatively scarcity of Spanish women in the new territory induced male Spaniards to quickly mix with indigenous women. Inter-ethnic mixing was no alien to Spanish conquerors and colonizers as a result of the recent history of coexistence of Moors and Christians in the Iberian Peninsula. The idea of accumulating wealth before marrying was common among Spanish men, and the custom of having illegitimate children was already widely spread in Spain at the time of conquest and colony. In addition, the indigenous civilizations had social hierarchies, with many male and female Indians enjoying high social status.

of the conquerors to exterminate the local populations, and some religious congregations fought for the incorporation of the indigenous groups into the new society (Díaz del Castillo 1955; Estrada 2009; Las Casas 1945, 1951, 1967; León-Portilla 2014). It was clear that the Europeans were the conquerors, but the society emerging from this process incorporated the cultural background of both the conquerors and the conquered. A majority of the Latin American population is considered to be "mestizo" and there are large indigenous populations in countries such as Mexico, Guatemala, El Salvador, Ecuador, Peru, and Bolivia. For example, in Guatemala, about 50% of the population speaks an indigenous language, whereas another 40% are considered mestizo.

It has been more than 500 years since the beginning of the conquest. Latin American culture has evolved during the 300 years of the colonial age and the 200 years of the independence age. Many factors intervened in the shaping of the current Latin American culture, and the blending of the values and worldview of the indigenous people with those of Spaniards and Portuguese is a significant one (Bonfil 1994; de Imaz 1984; Larraín 1994; Morandé 1990, 1991; Zea 1971, 1985). It is important to remark that the blending of values and worldviews does not necessarily imply the complete integration of Europeans and indigenous groups; many studies show that even today there is some segmentation on the basis of the skin color (Ortiz Hernández et al. 2018).

Coexistence with—rather than domination of—nature was a central value of many indigenous cultures. This value contributes to generate a society that is not as interested in changing the social and natural context as it is in living within it (Ángel Maya 1995, 2002, 2006; Noguera and Pineda 2011), which leads to a society that has a slower pace of life and that is not so focused on transforming and mastering nature—and in generating economic growth—as it is in living and enjoying life within the existing conditions (Acosta 2008; Gudynas and Acosta 2011). In addition, the extended-family values of the conquerors blended with the communitarian values of indigenous groups—where relatives tend to live together and to be in close contact (Arizpe 1973; Esteinou 2004; Gonzalbo 1996, 1998; Gonzalbo and Rabell 1996; Rojas and Chávez 2019). These trends promoted the emergence of societies where interpersonal relations were highly valued, with the corresponding abundance of person-based interpersonal relations. In these societies the purpose of the relationship is not motivated by an external task that needs to be performed but by the joint enjoyment of life through the existence of close, warm, genuine and enjoyable relations. It could be said that this historical process leads to societies where the purpose of the relationship is the relationship itself.

The culture that has emerged in Latin America can be characterized by Díaz-Guerrero (1979, 2007), Díaz-Loving et al. (2008), Germani (1965), Rojas (2012c):

– The focus on the nurturing of warm and close interpersonal relations with relatives and friends.
– The centrality of the family—both nuclear and extended.
– An affective regime that values and encourages the experience and manifestation of emotions.

- The existence of relatively weak civic relationships (those relations beyond family, friends, neighbors, and colleagues).
- A relative disregard for materialistic values.
- Weak political institutions.

It can be stated that the Latin American culture has a human-relations orientation or, to be more precise, that it is a relational-oriented culture. These cultural features play a central role in explaining well-being in Latin America (Ateca-Amestoy et al. 2014; Martínez and Castillo 2016; Mochón and de Juan Díaz 2016; Rojas and García-Vega 2017; Velásquez 2016; Yamamoto 2016). Culture plays a role in the relevance of affective and evaluative aspects in life, in how these affective and evaluative aspects correlate, and in the importance some drivers have in explaining them. Affective experiences of being well are highly relevant in explaining Latin Americans' satisfaction with life; in addition, there is a low correlation between affective and evaluative aspects in the region. Hence, the variables which are most often used by researchers to explain life evaluation play a lesser role in explaining affective states in Latin America. In consequence, in order to explain well-being in Latin America it becomes necessary to have a perspective that goes beyond the socio-economic indicators which are commonly used in the literature. This book emphasizes the relevance of person-based interpersonal relations as a major explanation of high well-being in Latin America; research shows that it may also be an important well-being driver in other regions of the world.

1.4 The Structure of the Book

The book is organized in 13 chapters. Chapter 2 briefly presents the conceptual framework of the book, while Chap. 3 makes an in-depth discussion of the conceptualization of well-being followed by the book. Chapter 4 provides a general overview of the well-being situation in Latin America. Chapter 5 deals with the relationship between income and well-being in Latin America, while Chap. 6 gets into the role of income inequality and Chap. 7 into the role of income poverty. Chapter 8 introduces the relational wealth concept and shows that the quantity and quality of interpersonal relations constitutes a major driver of people's well-being. Chapter 9 studies the role of education as a driver of well-being. Chapter 10 gets into the well-being consequences of crime and violence in Latin America. Chapter 11 makes a rapid exploration of the consequences of corruption. Chapter 12 proposes a reconceptualization of development; it discusses the shift from a paradigm of development as economic growth to one of development as well-being. Chapter 13 makes some final comments on the importance of the well-being approach for policy making.

References

Acosta, A. (2008). El buen vivir, una oportunidad por construir. *Ecuador Debate, 75*, 33–47.

Ángel Maya, A. (1995). *La fragilidad ambiental de la cultura*. Bogotá: Editorial Universidad Nacional Instituto de Estudios Ambientales IDEA.

Ángel Maya, A. (2002). El retorno de Icaro; Serie La Razón de la Vida X. *Pensamiento ambiental latinoamericano 3*. Bogotá: ASOCAR, IDEA, PNUMA, PNUD.

Ángel Maya, A. (2006). *Ataraxia*. Cali: Universidad Autónoma de Occidente.

Arizpe, L. (1973). *Parentezco y economía en una sociedad nahua*. México: Colección SEP-INI.

Ateca-Amestoy, V., Cortés Aguilar, A., & Moro-Egido, A. (2014). Social interactions and subjective well-being: Evidence from Latin America. *Journal of Happiness Studies, 15*, 527–554.

Beytía, P. (2016). The singularity of Latin American patterns of happiness. In M. Rojas (Ed.), *Handbook of happiness research in Latin America* (pp. 17–29). Berlin: Springer.

Beytía, P. (2018). The efficiency of subjective well-being: A key of Latin American development. In G. Bula & M. Masaheli (Eds.), *Latin American perspectives on global development*. Cambridge: Cambridge Scholars Publishing.

Bonfil, G. (1994). *México Profundo. Una civilización negada*. México, D.F.: Editorial Grijalbo.

Bushnell, D., Lockhart, J., & Kittleson, R. A. (2017). History of Latin America. In *Encyclopedia Britannica*. Retrieved from www.britannica.com/place/Latin-America.

Casas-Zamora, K., & Carter, M. (2017). *Beyond the scandals: The changing context of corruption in Latin America*. Rule of Law Report, The Inter-American Dialogue.

de Imaz, J. L. (1984). *Sobre la identidad iberoamericana*. Buenos Aires: Editorial Sudamericana.

Díaz del Castillo, B. (1955). *Historia verdadera de la conquista de la Nueva España*. Madrid: Espasa-Calpe.

Díaz-Guerrero, R. (1979). *Estudios de psicología del mexicano*. México, D.F.: Editorial Trillas.

Díaz-Guerrero, R. (2007). La evolución de la cohesión familiar. In R. Díaz-Guerrero (Ed.), *Psicología del mexicano 2: Bajo las garras de la cultura*. México, D.F.: Editorial Trillas.

Díaz-Loving, R., Rivera, S., Reyes, I., Rocha, T., Reidl, L., Sánchez, R., et al. (2008). *Etnopsicologia mexicana: Siguiendo la huella teórica y empírica de Díaz-Guerrero*. México, D.F.: Editorial Trillas.

Easterlin, R. (1974). Does economic growth improve the human lot? Some empirical evidence. In P. A. David & M. W. Reder (Eds.), *Nations and households in economic growth* (pp. 89–125). Academic Press.

Esteinou, R. (2004). El surgimiento de la familia nuclear en México. *Estudios de Historia Novohispana, 31*, 99–136.

Estrada, A. (2009). Naturaleza, cultura e identidad. Reflexiones desde la tradición oral maya contemporánea. *Estudios de Cultura Maya, 34*, 181–201.

Gasparini, L., & Lusting, N. (2011). The rise and fall of income inequality in Latin America. In J. A. Ocampo & J. Ros (Eds.), *The Oxford handbook of Latin American economics*. Oxford: Oxford University Press.

Germani, G. (1965). *Política y sociedad en una época de transición de la sociedad de masas*. Buenos Aires: Editorial Paidos.

Glatzer, W., Möller, V., Camfield, L., & Rojas, M. (2015). *Global handbook of quality of life. Exploration of well-being of nations and continents*. Berlin: Springer.

Gonzalbo, P. (1996). *Historia de la familia*. México: Instituto Mora y Universidad Nacional Autónoma de México.

Gonzalbo, P. (1998). *Familia y orden colonial*. México: El Colegio de México.

Gonzalbo, P., & Rabell, C. (Eds.). (1996). *Familia y vida privada en la historia de Iberoamérica*. México: El Colegio de México y Universidad Nacional Autónoma de México.

Gudynas, E., & Acosta, A. (2011). El buen vivir o la disolución de la idea del progreso. In M. Rojas (Ed.), *La medición del progreso y del bienestar: propuestas desde América Latina*. Mexico City: Foro Consultivo Científico y Tecnológico.

Jaitman, L. (2017). *The costs of crime and violence: New evidence and insights in Latin America and the Caribbean*. Washington, D.C.: Inter-American Development Bank.

Larraín, J. (1994). La identidad latinoamericana. Teoría e historia. *Estudios Públicos, 55,* 31–64.

Las Casas, B. (1945). *Brevísima relación de la destrucción de las Indias.* México: Secretaría de Educación Pública.

Las Casas, B. (1951). *Historia de las Indias,* t. 2. México, D.F.: Fondo de Cultura Económica.

Las Casas, B. (1967). *Apologética historia sumaria,* t. I. México: UNAM.

León-Portilla, M. (2014). *Visión de los vencidos. Relaciones indígenas de la conquista.* México: UNAM.

Martínez, J., & Castillo, H. (2016). "Like the zompopito": Social relationships in happiness among rural and indigenous women in Nicaragua. In M. Rojas (Ed.), *Handbook of happiness research in Latin America* (pp. 113–127). Berlin: Springer.

Mochón, F., & de Juan Díaz, R. (2016). Happiness and social capital: Evidence from Latin American countries. In M. Rojas (Ed.), *Handbook of happiness research in Latin America* (pp. 143–161). Berlin: Springer.

Morandé, P. (1990). Latinoamericanos: Hijos de un diálogo ritual. *Creces, 11*(11–12), 8–16.

Morandé, P. (1991). La síntesis cultural hispánica indígena. *Teología y Vida, 32*(1–2), 43–45.

Noguera, A. P., & Pineda, J. A. (2011). Medición del progreso de la sociedad. de las cuentas a los cuentos ambientales: propuesta de otra manera de pensar-nos en clave de Comunidad Abyayalense en expansión vital. In M. Rojas (Ed.), *La medición del progreso y del bienestar: Propuestas desde América Latina.* Mexico City: Foro Consultivo Científico y Tecnológico.

O'Donnell, G. (1999). Polyarchies and the (un)rule of law in Latin America: A partial conclusion. In J. E. Mendez, G. O'Donnell, & P. S. Pinheiro (Eds.), *The (un)rule of law and the underprivileged in Latin America* (pp. 303–337). Notre Dame: Notre Dame: Notre Dame University Press.

Ortiz Hernández, L., Ayala, C. I., & Pérez-Salgado, D. (2018). Posición socioeconómica, discriminación y color de piel en México. *Perfiles Latinoamericanos, 26*(51), 215–239.

Puchet, M., Rojas, M., Salazar, R., Valdés, F., & Valenti, G. (Eds.). (2012). *América latina en los albores del siglo XXI: Política, sociedad y economía.* México: Facultad Latinoamericana de Ciencias Sociales.

Rojas, M. (2012a). El bienestar subjetivo en América Latina. In M. Puchet, M. Rojas, E. Salazar, F. Valdés, & G. Valenti (Eds.), *América latina en los albores del siglo XXI: Política, sociedad y economía* (pp. 187–207). México: Facultad Latinoamericana de Ciencias Sociales.

Rojas, M. (2012b). Quality-of life research in Latin America. In K. Land (Ed.), *Handbook of social indicators and quality-of-life research* (pp. 529–545). Berlin: Springer.

Rojas, M. (2012c). Happiness in Mexico: The importance of human relations. In A. Selin & G. Davey (Eds.), *Happiness across cultures: Views of happiness and quality of life in non-western cultures* (pp. 241–252). Berlin: Springer.

Rojas, M. (2016). *Handbook of happiness research in Latin America.* Berlin: Springer.

Rojas, M. (Ed.) (2019). *The economics of happiness: How the Easterlin Paradox transformed our understanding of wellbeing and progress.* Berlin: Springer.

Rojas, M., & Chávez, P. (2019). Subjective well-being of the P'urhépecha people: Between tradition and modernity. In C. Fleming & M. Manning (Eds.), *Routledge handbook of indigenous wellbeing* (pp. 330–341). Abingdon: Routledge.

Rojas, M., & García-Vega, J. J. (2017). Well-being in Latin America. In R. Estes & J. Sirgy (Eds.), *The pursuit of human well-being.* Berlin: Springer.

Velásquez, L. (2016). The importance of relational goods for happiness: Evidence from Manizales, Colombia. In M. Rojas (Ed.), *Handbook of happiness research in Latin America* (pp. 91–112). Berlin: Springer.

World Bank. (2011). *Crime and violence in Central America: A development challenge.* Washington, D.C.: The World Bank.

Yamamoto, J. (2016). The social psychology of Latin American happiness. In M. Rojas (Ed.) *Handbook of happiness research in Latin America.* Berlin: Springer.

Zea, L. (1971). *La esencia de lo americano.* Buenos Aires: Pleamar.

Zea, L. (1985). *El problema de la identidad latinoamericana.* México: Universidad Nacional Autónoma de México.

Chapter 2
Conceptual Framework of the Book

Abstract Well-being is an experience people have and not an academic construct. Well-being as reported by people can be used to identify the relevant drivers in a particular population as well as to assess the success of public policy. The well-being reported by citizens is the central criterion to know whether policies are making an impact not only on the dashboard of indicators but, fundamentally, on the experience of being well citizens have.

Keywords Experienced well-being · Happiness · Affect · Life evaluation · Reported well-being

2.1 Well-Being as the Experience of Being Well

This book approaches well-being as a human experience; thus, well-being is not an academic construct but the experience of being well people has (Rojas 2017). In this sense, the book recognizes that it is in human condition to experience well-being and that well-being is experienced by concrete persons. In addition, it is recognized that each person is the authority to make a judgment regarding her well-being situation. In consequence, the book will measure well-being on the basis of the report made by people on this regard.

Human beings have different kinds of essential experiences of being well: Affective experiences associated to emotions and moods, evaluative experiences associated to achievements and failures, sensory experiences associated to pleasure and pain, and flow experiences. People also use this information to make a synthesis regarding how well their life is going on; this synthesis constitutes an overall assessment of people's life and it is usually expressed in terms of being satisfied with life.

Hence, well-being refers to the life-satisfaction synthesis people make as well as to the affective, evaluative, sensory, and flow experiences they have.

People can also provide reports on satisfaction in specific domains of life, such as: satisfaction with family relations, with health, with economic situation, and with job. This information is useful to further understand the overall life-satisfaction report people make.

© Springer Nature Switzerland AG 2020

M. Rojas, *Well-Being in Latin America*, Human Well-Being Research and Policy Making, https://doi.org/10.1007/978-3-030-33498-7_2

The approach recognizes that the experience of being well is inherently subjective; this is: the experience is not independent of the person experiencing it; in other words, it is impossible for the experience to take place without the concrete person whose human condition allows her to experience well-being. The experience is inherently subjective and this is the reason for asking people rather the presuming their well-being; the experience emerges as a consequence of many drivers which can be approximated on the basis of objective variables.

The approach states that the role of the scholars is not to judge a person's well-being but to study the experience of being well which concrete people have. Thus, the role of the expert is to propose theories and implement research techniques to understand what the relevant factors explaining well-being are.

The approach also states that well-being is universal but that the importance of explanatory factors may differ along persons and across regions. With a few exceptions—such as alexithymia and anhedonia—all human beings are able of experiencing affective, evaluative, sensory, and flow experiences; they are also able of making an overall synthesis. In consequence, it can be stated that well-being as the experience of being well is universal and comparable across persons. Nevertheless, people do differ in their life trajectories, personality traits, and brain architecture; people do also grow up within a given culture which influences their aspirations, norms, standards of evaluations, and values. Thus, substantial differences in the relevant drivers explaining people's experience of being well may take place within and across countries.

Income constitutes an interesting illustration. Income can be considered as an objective variable which can be compared across persons and countries. However, well-being comparisons across persons and countries cannot be based on income because, due to its objectivity, it cannot incorporate the inherent subjectivity of well-being. Income's importance as a driver of well-being depends on the values people hold; relational-oriented people attach less importance to income—and derive less well-being from it—than materialistic-oriented people.

Well-being makes reference to the experience of being well as well as to the overall life-satisfaction synthesis people make. It is a great advantage for the study of human well-being that people can report these experiences and the overall synthesis. It is important to recognize that the report of the experience is not the experience itself, and that this report provides general information about the experience without fully portraying it or supplanting it. The matter of well-being studies is the experience, and the report is just an approximation to this experience. Some questions are commonly used by researchers in order to gather information about this synthesis people make, such as the well-known life-satisfaction question and the day-before questions regarding affective experiences.

The common distinction between objective and subjective variables is of little relevance in the study of well-being. Objective variables may be appropriate to measure attributes of objects—such as some of the drivers of well-being—but they could be deceiving when aiming to measure something which is intrinsically subjective—such as the experience of being well. If the phenomenon is inherently objective—such as the dimensions of a house or the amount of income earned—then objective variables are appropriate, but if the phenomenon is inherently subjective—such as the experience of being well—then subjective variables are suitable.

Research shows that well-being is prosocial; this is: experiencing well-being and positively contributing to the well-being experienced by others are highly and directly correlated. The correlation emerges from the fact that those actions and events that contribute to experiencing well-being—such as interacting with others, following social norms, working in activities that others value, and so on—usually contribute to the well-being of others.

2.2   Information on Well-Being from People's Report

The book follows the approach of relying on people's report to assess their well-being. The basic postulate is that well-being is an experience people have and, in consequence, each person is in a privileged situation to make and report an assessment regarding her well-being experience. In other words, it is proposed that each person is the authority to judge her life.

The literature uses different questions to enquire on overall assessments of life people make. The overall assessment of life is usually captured with the response to questions like: "Taking everything in your life into consideration, how satisfied are you with your life?" or "Taking everything in your life into consideration, how happy are you?" There are also questions to explore satisfaction is specific domains of life; for example: "How satisfied are you with your economic situation?" "How satisfied are you in your relationship with your family?" "How satisfied are you with your health condition?" "How satisfied are you with your job or occupation?" and so on. These questions allow for further understanding of the life satisfaction or happy life assessments people make.

The approach also asks questions about essential experiences of being well; such as affective experiences: "Have you experienced (negative emotion) a lot recently?" "Have you experienced (positive emotion) a lot recently?"; as well as to pose phrases people can agree or disagree to assess their evaluate experiences, such as: "So far I have gotten the important things I want in life", "In most ways my life is close to my ideal."

The basic principle is that well-being makes reference to the experience of being well people have and that each person is the authority to make this judgment because she is in a privileged situation to do it. Hence, the best way of knowing a person's well-being is to directly ask her on this regard.

2.3 On Drivers and Policies

The experience of being well depends on many factors in a person's life; for example, her family composition; her relationship with parents, siblings, and friends; her job and attached responsibilities; the characteristics of the workplace; her economic situation; the economic situation in her country; safety conditions in the neighborhood; housing situation; commuting time; personal and social uncertainty about the future; own aspirations; physical and mental health condition; access to recreational infrastructure; access to health services; possibilities of self-determination; political situation in the country; kind of education received; and many other factors. Thus, well-being depends on a very large list of factors; it is possible for the relevant list of factors and for their importance in triggering well-being experiences to vary across population segments and along cultures. It is also possible for differences across persons to exist; however, general patterns can be identified and general main drivers do exist.

The identification of the main drivers of well-being requires the implementation of quantitative techniques to find out what factors are relevant in explaining people's well-being. Hence, rather than guessing which factors are relevant, the approach finds their relevance on the basis of how these factors relate to people's satisfaction with life. Quantitative techniques also allow for the study of synergies and trade-offs in the relationship between drivers and well-being. It is also possible to study the mediating role some factors may play, either boosting or mitigating the well-being impact of other drivers. Hence, the life-satisfaction report is combined with quantitative techniques to find out what drivers are relevant as well as to study the nature of their relationship to well-being.

A different level of analysis focuses on explaining not well-being but the drivers of well-being; in this case it is important to find out which policy instruments have an influence on these drivers. Drivers such as neighborhood safety, commuting time, economic situation, and family relationships depend on many factors and some of them could be influenced by policy instruments. For policy making reasons it is important to study how those instruments under the control of policy makers are related to people's well-being. Of course, the drivers of well-being are also affected by stochastic factors; policy makers have to recognize that not everything is under control and that the relationship between policies and well-being is not a deterministic one. However, well-being research helps in generating useful knowledge to design better policies.

2.4 Actors for Well-Being

The pursuing of well-being involves many actors: international organizations, national governments, local governments, private firms, national institutions, and non-governmental offices. However, there is a central actor which must guide and also circumscribe the behavior of the other actors: people themselves. If people's experience of being well is not taken into consideration then the pursuing of well-being risks becoming a game among organizations and governments and well-being risks becoming a construct of scholars and policy-makers rather than an experience people have. Such a game could end up focusing on the interests of the players rather than on the interests of the beneficiaries of public policy.

2.5 The General Message of the Book

- Well-being is an experience people have. It is not an academic construct, and the role of experts is not to assess the well-being of others but to understand it.
- Daily life involves affective, evaluative, sensory, and flow experiences of being well as well as an overall synthesis people make about how their life is going on, which people usually assess in terms of being satisfied with life.
- The best way to know a person's well-being is to directly ask her. People can report their situation and this report provides the best possible information on their well-being experience.
- Academicians have an important role to play. Researchers must find out what the drivers of well-being are for particular populations and countries; they must also study the relationship between policy instruments and people's experience of being well. Universities should be encouraged to create Well-Being Centers to generate the required knowledge for the design and evaluation of well-being policies.
- Policy makers do also have an important role to play in the design of policies and in their implementation and evaluation. It is important to gather and keep track of well-being information in order to evaluate and enhance social programs and public policies. Familiarity with the well-being approach would help policy makers in taking full advantage of the larger set of instruments at their disposal.
- A holistic view is required in order to understand well-being. Well-being happens to concrete persons—of flesh and blood—and not to simplified agents. By placing concrete persons at the center of policy making, the well-being approach promotes a person-centered perspective in the design, implementation and evaluation of public policy.
- There are many aspects in the daily life of concrete persons; their economic situation is important but it is not the only important aspect. Hence, it would be a big mistake to confuse consumers with persons, as well as to confuse purchasing power with well-being. This book argues that the focus on economic aspects should not come at the expense of other important aspects in people's lives. In particular, the book argues that the quantity and quality of interpersonal relations deserves further attention.
- The well-being approach expands the number of instruments and of options which policy makers have to aim at influencing people's well-being. This implies for a more efficient use of public resources.

- It is fundamental not to confuse the drivers of well-being with well-being itself. Policy actions take place in the space of drivers—and in the lower space of policy instruments—however, it is important to keep track of people's well-being in order to know which drivers are relevant, how relevant they are, and what is the nature of their relationship to well-being.
- Development is not about economic growth but about people being satisfied with life. Economic growth is insufficient to generate well-being and it takes place at a high cost to the environmental. A new paradigm of development as well-being is emerging and this requires for a new narrative; in fact, a new development discourse is emerging. It is very important for development agencies and international organizations to begin adopting this new narrative.
- The well-being approach is pluralistic; it allows for taking into consideration the values of different cultures. This is very important in a world which is becoming globalized but where values and traditions prevail and contribute to the identity and sense of purpose. It is also very important for governments of plurinational States.
- The likelihood of success of social and foreign-aid programs increases when these programs match the intrinsic motivations people have. This match is ensured when policies are designed to impact on people's well-being.
- Life satisfaction is a variable that provides good information regarding the overall assessment of life people make. When databases lack the life satisfaction variable—as it has been the case with most recent Gallup World Polls—many researchers have opted to focus on evaluations of life rather than on the affective state. This is a mistake because people's affective state constitutes a substrate of information which is very relevant for life satisfaction. Policy makers should not ignore the affective space, in special in those cultures where affect plays an important role in explaining life satisfaction.
- Policy actions usually rely on the attainment of specific intermediate goals, such as: income, height and weight, assets, schooling, and so on. Well-being allows for assessing the importance that these intermediate goals have as well as for identifying trade-offs and synergies in this space of intermediate goals.
- The well-being approach calls for a focus on the whole population; this is a difference with respect to the deprivation approaches which focus on particular segments of the population while disregarding the situation of the rest of the population.
- It is important to not to forget that the private sector and the third sector (foundations, non-governmental organizations) can also contribute to increase well-being; for example, by taking actions leading to greater job satisfaction, and making high-impact investments.

Reference

Rojas, M. (2017). The subjective object of well-being studies. In G. Brule & F. Maggino (Eds.), *Metrics of subjective well-being: Limits and improvements* (pp. 43–62). Berlin: Springer.

Chapter 3
Well-Being and Its Conceptualization

Abstract It is in human condition to experience well-being; persons have many essential experiences of being well and are also able of making a well-being synthesis, usually in terms of being satisfied with their life. Human beings can also report their satisfaction in specific domains of life. The experience of being well is essential to human beings because it allows them to ponder vital decisions and to undertake particular actions. The best way of knowing these experiences of being well is by directly asking people.

Keywords Essential experiences of being well · Evaluative well-being · Affective well-being · Sensory well-being · Life satisfaction · Domains-of-life satisfaction

This chapter addresses conceptualization issues in the study of people's well-being. The chapter states that the object of well-being studies is the experience of being well people have; as such, the object of study is inherently subjective because it cannot exist without the specific person who is experiencing it. Thus, subjectivity in well-being studies does not emerge from the reporting of the experience but from the experience itself; well-being is an experience that happens to persons and not to objects. Of course, objective variables can be used to measure many explanatory factors of well-being; however, these explanatory factors—and the variables measuring them—should not be confused with the experience of being well.

The justification for understanding well-being as the experience of being well people have rests not on its relevance to the work of researchers but, fundamentally, on its relevance to people themselves. People are aware of their experience of being well and, for them, this experience is important both as a final aim and as a motivational drive.

The understanding of well-being as the experience of being well people have constitutes a new tradition in the study of well-being. Long-standing traditions have relied on academically constructed notions of well-being. These notions tend to reflect the goals and motivations of those who propose them, but not necessarily

---

This chapter borrows from Rojas (2007, 2017).

© Springer Nature Switzerland AG 2020

M. Rojas, *Well-Being in Latin America*, Human Well-Being Research and Policy Making, https://doi.org/10.1007/978-3-030-33498-7_3

the goals and motivations of people themselves. It is for this reason that top-down traditions do not necessarily generate the same enthusiasm in people as they generate in those who propose them.

3.1 Well-Being as the Experience of Being Well

3.1.1 Essential Experiences of Being Well: Human Condition

It is in human condition to experience well-being; hence, the experience of being well is not unfamiliar to any human being. Well-being is so embedded into human life that people do not need a PhD degree—not even an elementary-education diploma—to hold long talks about it and to report what they experience.

People can have many kinds of essential experiences of being well; they are called essential because human condition suffices for these experiences to take place. Four kinds of non-exclusive essential experiences have been considered in the literature: sensory, affective, evaluative, and flow experiences (Pavot and Diener 1993; Rojas and Veenhoven 2013). These essential experiences constitute the substrate of information people use in making an overall assessment of their well-being situation. It is these essential experiences as well as the overall synthesis people make which constitute the object of well-being studies.

3.1.2 Evaluative Experiences. Failure and Achievement

Human beings are able of processing information in such a way as to assess whether their life meets their own standards, aspirations and goals; the experiences of failures and achievements emerge from these assessments. The distance between goals and accomplishments as well as the importance the person confers to these goals—their values and standards of evaluation—determines the intensity of the experiences of failure and achievement (Eid and Diener 2004; Gilboa and Schmeidler 2001).

People's goals and aspirations are important in explaining their evaluative experience of being well, and many factors do intervene in their formation, such as: Personality, nurturing conditions, life trajectory and, of course, surrounding conditions—such as the geography and historical developments—that shape the culture and values of a nation (Akerlof and Kranton 2000; Jones et al. 2003; Parducci 1995). Social comparisons are also crucial in the formation of people's evaluation norms (Festinger 1954; Steffel and Oppenheimer 2009; Stutzer and Lalive 2004; Suls and Wheeler 2000). In addition, other people, governments, and private companies may intentionally undertake actions to influence a person's aspirations and her norms of evaluation (Cialdini 2006; Packard 1957).

There is research on how the gap between own aspirations and attainments relates to evaluative experiences of being well. Stutzer (2004), McBride (2010), and Clark et al. (2015) study the income gap; as income aspirations raise the evaluative experience declines and this reduces people's well-being. There is little research on the impact of non-income aspirations in life satisfaction. Michalos (1985) proposes the existence of multiple discrepancies—income, health, and others. However, it is important to remark that the evaluative experience of being well makes reference to the achievements and failures which people experience and not to the factors triggering them—such as possessions and events—or to the factors that intervene in the evaluation process—such as aspirations, norms and values.

3.1.3 Affective Experiences. Joy and Suffering

Affect constitutes a second kind of experience of being well which is in human condition. Emotions are associated with psychophysiological states and biological reactions (Larsen and Fredrickson 1999; Murphy et al. 2003). People are familiar with affective experiences such as sadness, joy, boredom, anger, wonder, hope, regret, loneliness, jealousy, love, affection, depression, anxiety, anguish, tranquility, excitement, fear, depression, hatred, panic, pride, shame, and many others. These experiences are part of the daily life of most people.

It is common to make a distinction between emotions and moods: emotions are transient in nature and they are usually triggered by particular events, while moods tend to endure over longer periods of time (Frijda et al. 2000; Pfister and Böhm 2008). Psychologists have studied the affective experiences and, without great originality, have classified them as positive and negative; there is no doubt that this classification reflects their immediate association to the experience of being well (Bradburn 1969; Bryant et al. 2011; Crooker and Near 1998). In the long run some negative affective experiences could end up being fruitful from a well-being perspective, and some positive ones could end up being unfruitful. However, in general, people are motivated to undertake actions that lead to experiences of joy (positive affect) while they withdraw from the events associated with experiences of suffering (negative affect).

The importance of affect in people's lives can be grasped by paying attention to the lyrics of the most popular songs; emotions such as love, sadness, and fear are frequent in these songs. People are aware of the emotions and moods they. Emotions do also play an important role in driving human behavior (Loewenstein 2000; Loewenstein and Lerner 2003).

3.1.4 Sensory Experiences. Pleasure and Pain

Human beings have five senses that allow them to relate in different ways to the environment. The sight, smell, taste, touch, and hearing allow for a lot of possible sensory experiences which can be classified—in different degrees—as pleasurable or painful (Domínguez et al. 2016; Warburton and Sherwood 1996). Sensory experiences involve many features, such as: intensity, location, life interference, frequency, duration and predictability; as a matter of fact, some researchers state that a simplified view of sensory experiences as mere pain and pleasure would be very limited (Williams et al. 2000; Wilson et al. 2009).

Sensory experiences are an integral part in the life of all human beings: people know that injections hurt, and that pain is expected from a visit to the dentist. Mobile phones are designed in such a way as to give pleasing tactile, auditory and visual experiences. Music gives hearing experiences that can be classified by people as pleasant or unpleasant. The fashion industry is based on visual, tactile and olfactory experiences, while the wine industry is based on taste, smell and visual experiences. Large pharmaceutical companies know that patients' adoption of some medical treatments depends not only on their clinical benefits but also on the sensory experiences of pain or pleasure which accompany treatments.

3.1.5 Flow Experiences

Flow makes reference to short, intense and energizing experiences people have; these experiences are associated with actions that imply whole involvement (Csikszentmihalyi 1990). Some features associated with the experience of flow are: complete and intense concentration in the present—rather than in the past or in the future—complete awareness about the current action, alteration of the subjective experience of time, and intrinsic—rather than extrinsic—motivation so that the performance of the activity itself constitutes its main reward (Nakamura and Csikszentmihályi 2001).

Flow experiences may happen out of many different events; for example, as a consequence of practicing spiritual rituals, pastime activities, listening to a symphony, dancing, or even chatting with a friend.

3.1.6 Essential Experiences Overlap and Are Intertwined

The typology of essential experiences allows for a better understanding of people's well-being; however, this classification does not imply for evaluative, affective, sensory and flow experiences to be independent of each other. Experiences are intertwined and they do overlap in intricate ways. As a matter of fact, all experiences emerge from a common source: the concrete human being experiencing them. This implies for a holistic understanding of human well-being.

Persons do experience evaluative, affective, sensory and flow experiences simultaneously; however, people are able of distinguishing among them. For example, sensory experiences may emerge from biopsychosocial factors that also explain evaluative and affective experiences (Gatchel et al. 2007), and the latter could also influence the former (Elliott et al. 2003; Lame et al. 2005). Synergies and trade-offs may also take place; for example, flow experiences could interfere with the realization of activities that foster other essential experiences of being well. Essential experiences of failure and achievement, suffering and joy, pain and pleasure, and flow do overlap (Eich et al. 2000; Fiedler and Forgas 1988; Forgas 1991, 2000). A particular event or action may trigger many kinds of experiences; for example, hunger may be associated with a sensory experience of pain (headache, stomach pain), with an affective experience of irritation, and with an evaluative experience of failure (Rojas and Guardiola 2017). However, it is convenient to distinguish among these experiences not only because it allows for a better understanding of well-being but also because people are able of doing so. For example, research shows that free meals provided to people in hunger may help in reducing their sensory experience of pain and their affective experience of irritation, but may not be useful in lessening their evaluative experience of failure.

3.2   The Overall Well-Being Synthesis

The capacity of making a well-being synthesis on the basis of these essential experiences of being well is also in human condition (Diener et al. 2000; Eid and Diener 2004; Oishi et al. 2003; Rojas and Veenhoven 2013). Humans can make overall assessments such as: 'I like the life I have', 'I am happy', 'I am satisfied with my life', 'I am O.K. with myself', and 'My life is going well'.

In many cases an event triggers evaluative, affective and sensory experiences that come together in generating a well-being synthesis. If an event triggers evaluative experiences of achievement, positive affect experiences and no negative ones, and pleasing sensory experiences then it is very likely for this event to positively contribute to the overall synthesis a person makes—such as her life satisfaction. Meanwhile, an event which generates an evaluative experience of failure, which involves negative emotional states and no positive ones, and which is associated with experiences of pain or disgust tends to reduce a person's well-being, and this is reflected in her overall synthesis—such as lower life satisfaction (Rojas 2017).

It is important to remark that the importance given to these essential experiences in making a global synthesis may vary across people; some people may give more importance to sensory experiences while others may base their synthesis fundamentally on the affective experiences or on the evaluative ones. Thus, the overall synthesis is not a sum or average of the essential experiences people have, and a single formula does not apply to everyone.

3.2.1 Domains of Life and Life Satisfaction

It is also possible to understand the overall synthesis of her life a person makes in terms of her satisfaction in specific domains of life. The domains-of-life literature states that a person's life can be approached as a general construct of many specific domains, and that life satisfaction can be understood as the result of satisfaction in these specific domains of life (Cummins 1996; Headey et al. 1984; Headey and Wearing 1992; van Praag and Ferrer-I-Carbonell 2004; Rojas 2006, 2007; Rojas and Elizondo 2012; Veenhoven 1996).

The enumeration and demarcation of the domains of life is arbitrary; it can go from a small number to an almost infinite recount of all imaginable human activities and spheres of being. On the basis of a meta-study of the literature Cummins (1996) argue for a seven-domain partition: material well-being, health, productivity, intimacy, safety, community, and emotional well-being. Argyle (2002) mentions domains such as money, health, work and employment, social relationships, leisure, housing, and education. Day (1987) considers thirteen areas, among them: family life, working activity, social activity, recreation, personal health, consumption, ownership of durable commodities and properties, self, spiritual life, and country's situation. Flanagan (1978) mentions 15 components, among them: economic well-being, physical well-being, health well-being, relationship with relatives, having and raising children, relations with spouse, relations with friends, community and social activities, political activities, passive and active recreational activities, personal development activities, work. Headey and Wearing (1992) use leisure, marriage, work, standard of living, friendships, sex life, and health.

Most of the research focuses on the study of satisfaction in one domain of life; for example, job-satisfaction studies, as well as on the relationship between this domain and life satisfaction. Some research has studied satisfaction in multiple domains of life (Andrews and Withey 1976; Campbell 1976, 1981; Campbell et al. 1976; Zapf and Glatzer 1987). A most recently there have been several studies addressing the relationship between satisfaction in many domains of life and life satisfaction; for example:

van Praag et al. (2003) study the relationship of satisfaction in different domains of life (health, financial situation, job, housing, leisure, and environment) and satisfaction with life as a whole. Rojas (2006, 2007) studies the relationship between life satisfaction and satisfaction in the following domains of life: health, family relations, economic, job, friends, free time, and community. The main idea is that satisfaction in these domains of life is useful in understanding life satisfaction.

3.2.2 Well-Being and Human Behavior

The overall synthesis people make provides useful information about their well-being situation; it also constitutes important information people use to take important life decisions. People are prone to take those actions that they expect to contribute to their overall well-being as well as to avoid those actions that are expected to put it at risk. Important life decisions are weighted on the basis of their expected impact on the overall well-being synthesis. For example, work decisions such as quitting from a job or working in a specific firm are made on the basis of job and life satisfaction information (Clark et al. 2012); migration decisions and changes in place of residence are made on the basis of life satisfaction information (Helliwell et al. 2018); and purchasing a house also involves community, economic and life satisfaction information. Of course, expectations may be wrong, and when the mistake is revealed people may regret their decisions; but it is the pursuing of greater well-being which inclines people to follow some paths in life while rejecting others. For example, recent studies show that life satisfaction influences voting behavior; people are more likely of voting to the official party if they are satisfied with life; likewise, unsatisfied people are more likely to vote for populist movements (Liberini et al. 2017a, b; Martínez Bravo 2016; Ward 2019).

3.2.3 Do not Confuse Drivers of Well-Being with the Experience of Being Well

It is a common mistake in the study of well-being to end up confusing the drivers of well-being with well-being itself.

This confusion has led some scholars to end up defining well-being as the access to some drivers that are presumed to be of relevance in triggering the experience of being well. This tradition is reinforced by the wrong idea of using objective variables to measure well-being. For example, there is a tradition of understanding well-being as having access to potable water, electricity, food, clothes, cars, jewelry, electronic gadgets, houses, high income, and so on. Hence, it is common to rely on vectors of variables which are assumed to portray the situation of potentially relevant factors. Different techniques in handling large vectors of variables are implemented, such as the construction of composite indicators; however, it is important to remember that neither the large vector of variables nor the composite index constitute well-being. The understanding of these measures as well-being poses the risk of making of well-being an attribute of the objects rather than an experience of the persons, and it also neglects the important role people play in the transformation of mere objects into experiences of being well (Rojas 2017).

It is crucial to clarify that the experience of being well is in people's failures and achievements, in their enjoyment and suffering, in their pleasure and pain, and in their flow state. It is incorrect to appraise well-being in the space of drivers that may trigger it; thus, it is wrong to understand well-being as a collection of assets, objects, and events that may trigger the evaluative, affective, sensory, and flow experience of being well. Access to potable water or electricity, the ownership of a larger house or a car, education, medical facilities, urban infrastructure, safety, and many other factors are relevant because they have the potential of triggering experiences that contribute to people's well-being. This is very relevant for public policy and for development debates; policy takes place in the space of drivers, but policy is relevant only if the changes taking place in the space of drivers do really impact on the space of experiences of being well people have and on people's satisfaction with life. It is always important to keep track of information regarding well-being in order to assess what drivers are relevant and whether policy is really contributing to the final goal of increasing the experience of being well people have.

3.3   On the Measurement of Well-Being: Life-Satisfaction Conception

Veenhoven (1984) states that well-being can only be measured on the basis of a person's answer to a direct question about her well-being; there is no room for speculation based on a person's possessions, facial expressions or other observable behavior. How to know the overall assessment a person makes? It is common to pose a life-satisfaction question of the form: "Taking everything in your life into consideration, how satisfied are you with your life?" or "Taking everything in your life into considerations, how happy are you with your life?" These questions ask people to provide an overall assessment; they are not exactly identical and they provide slightly different information. Most researchers and international organizations are working with the life satisfaction question because it has been shown to rely on evaluative, affective and sensory information. The response scale may be numerical (usually going from 0 to 10) or categorical (usually going from extremely unsatisfied to extremely satisfied) (Diener et al. 2013; OECD 2013; Rojas and Martínez 2012).

There is ample research on measurement methods and on noise introduced by survey design (Ferrer-I-Carbonell 2002; McClendon and O'Brien 1988; Schwarz and Strack 1991, 1999). There is also substantial knowledge on the consequences of working with different response scales (Ferrer-I-Carbonell and Frijters 2004; Kahneman and Krueger 2006; Lyubomirsky and Lepper 1999). There is also research on how overall assessments of well-being are made (Crooker and Near 1998; Eid and Diener 2004; Rojas and Veenhoven 2013). This allows for the design of questionnaires that gather good information regarding the experience of being well people have; it is very useful information that can be compared across countries (Diener and Suh 2000; Veenhoven 1987).

There are also many instruments to gather information on specific experiences of being well and on satisfaction in specific domains of life (Diener et al. 1985; Watson et al. 1988). These instruments have been widely used and tested (Diener et al. 1999). In fact, researchers are working on developing a national account system to keep track of well-being in countries (Cummins et al. 2003; Diener and Tov 2012; Diener et al. 2015).

It is also possible to run qualitative surveys which provide in-depth information on people's experience of being well (Martínez and Castillo 2016).

References

Akerlof, G. A., & Kranton, R. E. (2000). Economics and identity. *Quarterly Journal of Economics, 115*(3), 715–753.

Andrews, F. M., & Withey, S. B. (1976). *Social indicators of well-being*. New York: Plenum Press.

Argyle, M. (2002). *The psychology of happiness*. New York, NY, US: Routledge.

Bradburn, N. M. (1969). *The structure of the psychological well-being*. Chicago: Aldine.

Bryant, F. B., Chadwick, E. D., & Kluwe, K. (2011). Understanding the processes that regulate positive emotional experience: Unsolved problems and future directions for theory and research on savoring. *International Journal of Wellbeing, 1*(1), 107–126.

Campbell, A. (1976). Subjective measures of well-being. *American Psychologist, 31*(2), 117–124.

Campbell, A. (1981). *The sense of well-being in America*. New York: McGraw-Hill.

Campbell, A., Converse, P. E., & Rodgers, W. L. (1976). *The quality of American life*. New York: Russell Sage Foundation.

Cialdini, R. B. (2006). *Influence: The psychology of persuasion* (Rev. ed.). Harper Business.

Clark, A., Kamesaka, A., & Tamura, T. (2015). Rising aspirations dampen satisfaction. *Education Economics, 23*(5), 515–531.

Clark, A. E., Georgellis, Y., & Sanfey, P. (2012). Job satisfaction, wage change and quits: Evidence from Germany. *Research in Labor Economics, 35,* 499–525.

Crooker, K., & Near, J. (1998). Happiness and satisfaction: Measures of affect and cognition? *Social Indicators Research, 44,* 195–224.

Csikszentmihalyi, M. (1990). *Flow: The psychology of optimal experience*. New York, NY: Harper and Row.

Cummins, R. (1996). The domains of life satisfaction: An attempt to order chaos. *Social Indicators Research, 38,* 303–332.

Cummins, R., Eckersley, R., Pallant, J., Van Vugt, J., & Misajon, R. (2003). Developing a national index of subjective wellbeing: The Australian unity wellbeing index. *Social Indicators Research, 64,* 159–190.

Day, R. L. (1987). Relationships between life satisfaction and consumer satisfaction. In A. Coskun Samli (Ed.), *Marketing and the quality of life interface*. New York: Quorum Books.

Diener, E., Emmons, R., Larsen, A., & Griffin, R. (1985). The satisfaction with life scale. *Journal of Personality Assesment, 49*(1), 71–75.

Diener, E., Inglehart, R., & Tay, L. (2013). Theory and validity of life-satisfaction scales. *Social Indicators Research, 112,* 497–527.

Diener, E., Napa-Scollon, C. K., Oishi, S., Dzokoto, V., & Eunkook, M. S. (2000). Positivity and the construction of life satisfaction judgments: Global happiness is not the sum of its parts. *Journal of Happiness Studies, 1*(2), 159–176.

Diener, E., Oishi, S., & Lucas, R. E. (2015). National accounts of subjective well-being. *American Psychologists, 70*(3), 234–242.

Diener, E., & Suh, E. M. (Eds.). (2000). *Culture and subjective well-being*. Cambridge, MA: The Massachusetts Institute of Technology (MIT) Press.

Diener, E., Suh, E. M., Lucas, R. E., & Smith, H. L. (1999). Subjective well-being: Three decades of progress. *Psychological Bulletin, 125,* 276–302.

Diener, E., & Tov, W. (2012). National accounts of well-being. In K. C. Land, A. C. Michalos, & M. J. Sirgy (Eds.), *Handbook of social indicators and quality of life research* (pp. 137–156). New York, NY: Springer.

Domínguez, B., Montero, G., & López, M. (2016). Pain, emotions, and social-well-being in Mexico: Challenges and future trending. In: M. Rojas (Ed.), *Handbook of happiness research in Latin America* (pp. 489–514). Berlin: Springer.

Eich, E., Kihlstrom, J., Bower, G., Forgas, J., & Niedenthal, P. (2000). *Cognition and emotion.* Oxford: Oxford University Press.

Eid, M., & Diener, E. (2004). Global judgments of subjective well-being: Situational variability and long-term stability. *Social Indicators Research, 65,* 245–277.

Elliott, T., Renier, C., & Palcher, J. (2003). Chronic pain, depression, and quality of life: Correlations and predictive value of the SF-36. *Pain Medicine, 4*(4), 331–339.

Ferrer-I-Carbonell, A. (2002). *Subjective questions to measure welfare and well-being.* Discussion paper TI 2002-020/3, Tinbergen Institute.

Ferrer-I-Carbonell, A., & Frijters, P. (2004). How important is methodology for the estimates of the determinants of happiness? *The Economic Journal, 114,* 641–659.

Festinger, L. (1954). A theory of social comparison processes. *Human Relations, 7,* 230–243.

Fiedler, K., & Forgas, J. (1988). *Affect, cognition and social behavior.* Toronto, Canada: Hogrefe.

Flanagan, J. (1978). A research approach to improving our quality of life. *American Psychologist, 33,* 138–147.

Forgas, J. (1991). *Emotion and social judgment.* Pergamon Press.

Forgas, J. (2000). *Feeling and thinking: The role of affect in social cognition.* Cambridge: Cambridge University Press.

Frijda, N., Manstead, A., & Bem, S. (2000). *Emotions and believes: How feelings influence thoughts.* Cambridge: Cambridge University Press.

Gatchel, R., Peng, Y., Peters, M., Fuchs, P., & Turk, D. (2007). The biopsychosocial approach to chronic pain: Scientific advances and future directions. *Psychological Bulletin, 133*(4), 581–624.

Gilboa, I., & Schmeidler, D. (2001). A cognitive model of individual well-being. *Social Choice and Welfare, 18,* 269–288.

Headey, B., Holmström, E., & Wearing, A. (1984). The impact of life events and changes in domain satisfactions on well-being. *Social Indicators Research, 15,* 203–227.

Headey, B., & Wearing, A. (1992). *Understanding happiness: A theory of subjective well-being.* Melbourne, Australia: Longman Cheshire.

Helliwell, J., Layard, R., & Sachs, J. (2018). *World happiness report 2018.* Sustainable Development Solutions Network.

Jones, T., Rapport, L., Hanks, R., Lichtenberg, P., & Telmet, K. (2003). Cognitive and psychosocial predictors of subjective well-being in urban older adults. *The Clinical Neuropsychologist, 17*(1), 3–18.

Kahneman, D., & Krueger, A. (2006). Developments in the measurement of subjective well-being. *Journal of Economic Perspectives, 20*(1), 3–24.

Lame, I., Peters, M., Vlaeyen, J., Kleef, K., & Patijn, J. (2005). Quality of life in chronic pain is more associated with beliefs about pain, than with pain intensity. *European Journal of Pain, 9*(1), 15–24.

Larsen, R., & Fredrickson, B. (1999). Measurement issues in emotion research. In D. Kahneman, E. Diener, & N. Schwarz (Eds.), *Well-being: The foundations of hedonic psychology* (pp. 40–59). Russell Sage Foundation.

Liberini, F., Oswald, A. J., Proto, E., & Redoano, M. (2017a). *Was Brexit caused by the unhappy and the old?* Discussion paper No. 11059, IZA Institute of Labor Economics.

Liberini, F., Redoano, M., & Proto, E. (2017b). Happy voters. *Journal of Public Economics, 146,* 41–57.

Loewenstein, G. (2000). Emotions in economic theory and economic behavior. *American Economic Review, 90,* 426–432.

Loewenstein, G., & Lerner, J. (2003). The role of affect in decision making. In R. Davidson, K. Scherer, & H. Goldsmith (Eds.), *Handbook of affective sciences.* Oxford: Oxford University Press.

Lyubomirsky, S., & Lepper, H. (1999). A measure of subjective happiness: Preliminary reliability and construct validation. *Social Indicators Research, 46,* 137–155.

Martínez, J., & Castillo, H. (2016). "Like the zompopito": Social relationships in happiness among rural and indigenous women in Nicaragua. In M. Rojas (Ed.), *Handbook of happiness research in Latin America* (pp. 113–127). Berlin: Springer.

Martínez Bravo, I. (2016). The usefulness of subjective wellbeing to predict electoral results in Latin America. In M. Rojas (Ed.), *Handbook of happiness research in Latin America* (pp. 613–632). New York, NY: Springer Press.

McBride, M. (2010). Money, happiness and aspirations: An experimental study. *Journal of Economic Behavior & Organization, 74,* 262–276.

McClendon, M., & O'Brien, D. (1988). Question order effects on the determinants of subjective well-being. *The Public Opinion Quarterly, 52*(3), 351–364.

Michalos, A. C. (1985). Multiple discrepancies theory (MDT). *Social Indicators Research, 16,* 347–413.

Murphy, F., Nimmo-Smith, I., & Lawrence, A. (2003). Functional neuroanatomy of emotions: A meta-analysis, cognitive. *Affective, and Behavioral Neuroscience, 3*(3), 207–233.

Nakamura, J., & Csikszentmihályi, M. (2001). Flow theory and research. In C. Snyder, E. Wright, & S. Lopez (Eds.), *Handbook of positive psychology* (pp. 195–206). Oxford: Oxford University Press.

OECD. (2013). *OECD guidelines on measuring subjective well-being.* Paris: OECD Publishing.

Oishi, S., Schimmack, U., & Colcombe, S. (2003). The contextual and systematic nature of life satisfaction judgments. *Journal of Experimental Social Psychology, 39,* 232–247.

Packard, V. (1957). *The hidden persuaders.* Longmans: Green and Co.

Parducci, A. (1995). *Happiness, pleasure, and judgment: The contextual theory and its applications.* Psychology Press.

Pavot, W., & Diener, E. (1993). The affective and cognitive context of self-reported measures of subjective well-being. *Social Indicators Research, 28,* 1–20.

Pfister, H., & Böhm, G. (2008). The multiplicity of emotions: A framework of emotional functions in decision making. *Judgment and Decision Making, 3*(1), 5–17.

Rojas, M. (2006). Life satisfaction and satisfaction in domains of life: Is it a simple relationship? *Journal of Happiness Studies, 7*(4), 467–497.

Rojas, M. (2007). The complexity of well-being: A life-satisfaction conception and a domains-of-life approach. In I. Gough & J. A. McGregor (Eds.), *Researching well-being in developing countries: From theory to research* (pp. 259–280). Cambridge: Cambridge University Press.

Rojas, M. (2017). The subjective object of well-being studies. In G. Brule & F. Maggino (Eds.), *Metrics of subjective well-being: Limits and improvements* (pp. 43–62). Berlin: Springer.

Rojas, M., & Elizondo, M. (2012). Satisfacción de Vida en Costa Rica: Un Enfoque de Dominios de Vida. *Latin American Research Review, 47*(1), 78–94.

Rojas, M., & Guardiola, J. (2017). Hunger and the experience of being well: Absolute and relative concerns. *World Development, 96,* 78–86.

Rojas, M., & Martínez, I. (2012). *Measurement, research and inclusion in public policy of subjective wellbeing: Latin America.* México, D.F.: Foro Consultivo Científico y Tecnológico.

Rojas, M., & Veenhoven, R. (2013). Contentment and affect in the estimation of happiness. *Social Indicators Research, 110*(2), 415–431.

Schwarz, N., & Strack, F. (1991). Evaluating one's life: A judgment model of subjective well-being. In F. Strack, M. Argyle, & N. Schwarz (Eds.), *Subjective well-being: An interdisciplinary perspective* (pp. 27–47). Pergamon Press.

Schwarz, N., & Strack, F. (1999). Reports of subjective well-being: Judgmental processes and their methodological implications. In D. Kahneman, E. Diener, & N. Schwarz (Eds.), *Well-being: The foundations of hedonic psychology* (pp. 61–84). Russell Sage Foundation.

Steffel, M., & Oppenheimer, D. (2009). Happy by what standard? The role of interpersonal and intrapersonal comparisons in ratings of happiness. *Social Indicators Research, 92,* 69–79.

Stutzer, A. (2004). The role of income aspirations in individual happiness. *Journal of Economic Behavior & Organization, 54,* 89–109.

Stutzer, A., & Lalive, R. (2004). The role of social work norms in job searching and subjective well-being. *Journal of the European Economic Association, 2*(4), 696–719.

Suls, J., & Wheeler, L. (Eds.). (2000). *Handbook of social comparison: Theory and research.* Kluwer Academic/Plenum Publishers.

van Praag, B., Frijters, P., & Ferrer-I-Carbonell, A. (2003). The anatomy of subjective well-being. *Journal of Economic Behavior & Organization, 51,* 29–49.

van Praag, B. M. S., & Ferrer-I-Carbonell, A. (2004). *Happiness quantified: A satisfaction calculus approach.* Oxford: Oxford University Press.

Veenhoven, R. (1984). *Conditions of happiness.* Kluwer Academic.

Veenhoven, R. (1987). Cultural bias in ratings of perceived life quality. *Social Indicators Research, 18,* 329–334.

Veenhoven, R. (1996). Developments in satisfaction research. *Social Indicators Research, 37,* 1–45.

Warburton, D., & Sherwood, N. (Eds.). (1996). *Pleasure and quality of life.* Hoboken: Wiley.

Ward, G. (2019). *Happiness and voting behavior. World happiness report 2019.* Sustainable Development Network.

Watson, D., Clark, L., & Tellegen, A. (1988). Development and validation of brief measures of positive and negative affect: The PANAS scales. *Journal of Personality and Social Psychology, 54,* 1063–1070.

Williams, A., Davies, H., & Chadury, Y. (2000). Simple pain rating scales hide complex idiosyncratic meaning. *Pain, 85,* 457–463.

Wilson, D., Williams, M., & Butler, D. (2009). Language and the pain experience. *Physiotherapy Research International, 14*(1), 56–65.

Zapf, W., & Glatzer, W. (1987). German social report: Living conditions and subjective well-being, (1978–1984). *Social Indicators Research, 19,* 1–17.

Chapter 4
The Well-Being Situation in Latin America

Abstract Latin Americans report high life satisfaction levels; as a region Latin America has the highest mean life satisfaction in the world. The affective situation of Latin Americans is also outstandingly high. The many political and socio-economic problems reflect on average life evaluation levels. Cultural factors associated to family satisfaction and satisfaction in relational domains play an important role in explaining high life satisfaction in Latin America. Some intra-region differences exist and the average figures cannot be extended to the whole population or to all the countries in the region.

Keywords Latin America · High life satisfaction · Positive affect · Interpersonal relations · Domains-of-life satisfaction

4.1 Well-Being Overview

4.1.1 Well-Being Information

As it was extensively discussed in the previous chapter it is important to make a clear distinction between well-being and its drivers. There has been a lot of confusion on this regard, and the dominant traditions in the study of welfare have contributed to this confusion by expressing and defining well-being in terms of a vector of variables or as an index which is constructed on the basis of these variables. This book follows the perspective that well-being is neither a list of variables nor an index; well-being is a living experience people have. It has also been argued in the previous chapter that the best way to know about this experience of being well people have is by directly asking them about their satisfaction with life and with some aspects in life, as well as by asking people about their affective, evaluative, sensory and flow experiences. Hence, this chapter starts with a general portray of the well-being situation in Latin America on the basis of people's reports to well-being questions.

The study focuses on five sets of indicators of people's well-being:

First, life satisfaction, which can be considered as an overall assessment people make regarding how well their life is going on. The substrate of information for the life satisfaction assessment involves evaluative, affective and sensory processes

© Springer Nature Switzerland AG 2020

M. Rojas, *Well-Being in Latin America*, Human Well-Being Research and Policy Making, https://doi.org/10.1007/978-3-030-33498-7_4

(Rojas and Veenhoven 2013). Life satisfaction can also be understood as the result from satisfaction in many domains of life which are associated to the daily life of people.

Second, the evaluation of life, which emphasizes cognitive aspects linked to the attainment of own aspirations and goals people have. Rojas and Veenhoven (2013) argue that this information has its substratum in the social environment because the aspirations and goals in life are contingent on the society where people live. Low life evaluation reflects a substantial gap between aspirations and achievements as well as between own standards and realizations.

Third, the affective experience; which reflects emotions and moods such as joy, anxiety, sadness, boredom, loneliness, depression, anger, enthusiasm, and love. The affective state has, in principle, its substratum in human nature and in the evolutionary factors that explain human emotions.

Fourth, the sensory experience associated to physical pain and pleasure.

Fifth, satisfaction in domains of life. People are able of reporting their satisfaction with specific aspects in their life, such as: their job satisfaction, their economic satisfaction, their satisfaction in their relationship with their partner, and so on.

4.1.2 Different Sources of Information

Worldwide surveys as well as representative surveys at the country level are now widely available. Worldwide surveys provide a comparative perspective which is useful to assess how the well-being of Latin Americans stands out in the world; unfortunately, worldwide surveys are designer with different purposes and they do not present an in-depth portray of the well-being situation in countries. Hence, this book complements the information from worldwide surveys with that coming from country-level and academic-run surveys which are useful to understand some well-being substrates as well as to study the relationship between well-being and some of its drivers. Most of the well-being information used in this book comes from the following surveys:

The Gallup World Poll provides yearly information regarding some well-being variables since 2006; the poll is implemented in almost all countries in the world. All Latin American countries are included in the survey with the exception of Cuba. Unfortunately, the Gallup World Poll included the life satisfaction question only in few of its surveys. On the other hand, the Gallup World Poll provides plenty of information on life evaluation and affective states.

The World Value Survey has been applied in many countries in the world since 1981; six waves have been implemented, the most recent one from 2010 to 2014. The World Value Survey has information on life satisfaction, but it has no information regarding evaluative and affective states as well as no information regarding satisfaction in domains of life. In addition, the survey only incorporates twelve Latin American countries; hence, there is no information on life satisfaction for Bolivia, Cuba, Costa Rica, Honduras, Nicaragua, Panama and Paraguay in the World Value

Survey. Furthermore, in some countries the survey has been implemented only once or twice at most.

The Latinobarometer; this is a yearly survey which has been implemented in all Latin American countries since 1995. It is a representative survey at the country level and it contains information on life satisfaction for many of the years in which the survey was implemented.

Other surveys: There are many country-level surveys, but probably the major effort in the region has been carried out by Mexico's National Statistical Office (INEGI) which implemented the Self-Reported Well-Being Survey (BIARE) in 2012—as an experimental survey—and in 2014 as a large State-level representative survey. INEGI also applies a quarterly survey on well-being which is representative at the country level. There are also many academic surveys which have been implemented during the past decade by researchers from the Latin American region; this book will rely on the Understanding Happiness in Latin America survey to address relational issues.

The life satisfaction variable usually comes from a question phrased as: 'All things considered, how satisfied are you with your life as a whole these days?' The Gallup World Poll uses a 0–10 response scale, where 0 is dissatisfied and 10 is satisfied. A similar question is used by the World Value Survey; the response scale goes from 1 (completely dissatisfied) to 10 (completely satisfied). The Latinobarometer poses the following question: 'Generally speaking, would you say you are satisfied with your life?', the response scale is categorical: Not at all satisfied, Not very satisfied, Fairly satisfied, and Very satisfied.

The domains-of-life satisfaction variables are based on questions phrased in a similar way to the life satisfaction question, but in this case the question asks about satisfaction with specific aspects in a person's life rather than with life as a whole. It is common to ask about satisfaction with health situation, economic situation, job or occupation, community, country, and relation with partner, children, parents, friends, colleagues, and neighbors.

The life-evaluation variable relies on the well-known Best Possible Life question—also known as the Cantril-ladder question—it is phrased as: 'Please imagine a ladder with steps numbered from zero at the bottom to ten at the top. Suppose we say that the top of the ladder represents the best possible life for you, and the bottom of the ladder represents the worst possible life for you. On which step of the ladder would you say you personally feel you stand at this time, assuming that the higher the step the better you feel about your life, and the lower the step the worse you feel about it? Which step comes closest to the way you feel?' The response scale is based on an imaginary 11-point scale whereby 0 designates one's worst possible life and 10 denotes the best possible life the respondent can imagine for herself.

The affective situation usually relies on what are known as 'the day before questions'; the general phrasing of the question is: Did you experience the following feelings during a lot of the day yesterday? Different feelings are mentioned, which are usually classified as positive—such as enjoyment, love, smile or laugh, learned something, treated with respect—or negative—such as worry, sadness, boredom,

anger, stress, and depression. It is common for the response scale to be dichotomous: Yes or no. A physical pain question is usually added to the general battery of
questions.

4.2   Well-Being: Latin America and the World

Latin Americans report very high levels of well-being in comparison to people from
other regions of the world. Different sources of information depict what can be
considered as a very good situation. Life satisfaction is very high in Latin America
and it seems to be explained by an outstandingly high positive-affect situation and a
good evaluation of life.

4.2.1   High Life Satisfaction in Latin America

Life satisfaction is considered as the best proxy for people's well-being. Researchers
such as Argyle (2002) and Rojas and Veenhoven (2013) argue that life satisfaction
contains good information on people's evaluative, affective and sensorial experiences
of being well. The response to the life satisfaction question can be understood as an
overall synthesis people make on the basis of their experiences of being well as
well as of their values and purposes in life. Table 4.1 presents information on life
satisfaction for different regions of the world[1] and from different surveys.

The Gallup World Poll included the life-satisfaction question in its waves 2 and
3, corresponding to the years 2006–2008. The second column in Table 4.1 presents
the information for life satisfaction from the Gallup World Poll. It is observed that
average life satisfaction in Latin America is 7.07 when measured in a scale from
0 to 10; life satisfaction in Latin American is below that for the Western European
and Anglo-Saxon countries but much higher than that for other regions of the world.
Hence, on the basis of the Gallup World Poll's information Latin Americans have,
on average, the second highest life-satisfaction levels in the world.

The Gallup World Poll comprises 125 countries but its life-satisfaction information refers to a very short and not so recent period of time. The World Value Survey
constitutes an alternative source of information; it has the advantage of incorporating
the life-satisfaction question in all of its six waves and the disadvantage of missing
a larger number of countries in the world than the Gallup World Poll. In fact, the
World Value Survey comprises about 100 countries when taking into consideration
all waves. The third and fourth columns in Table 4.1 present the mean regional value

---

[1] Any regional classification of the world is arbitrary; in this case the classification follows cultural
and geographical criteria. The classification's purpose is not to define a compartmentalization of
the world or to contribute to the cultural literature; it is just to depict the situation of Latin American
countries in comparison to the rest of countries in the world.

Table 4.1 Life satisfaction in regions of the world. Simple country-level means. Different sources and periods

Region	Life satisfaction[a]	Life satisfaction[b]	Life satisfaction[c]
Latin America	7.07	7.60	7.77
Western Europe and Anglo-Saxon	7.54	7.46	7.34
Southeast Asia	6.07	6.85	7.01
Arab/Muslim	5.81	6.34	6.36
Sub-Saharan Africa	4.23	5.69	6.37
Caribbean	6.54	7.24	7.47
Central Asia	5.53	7.30	7.37
Eastern Europe	5.64	5.64	6.34
South Asia	5.49	5.98	6.24
World	5.96	6.52	6.84

Notes Simple country-level means by region; not weighted by countries' population
Regions of the world
Latin America: Argentina, Bolivia, Brazil, Chile, Colombia, Costa Rica, Cuba, Dominican Republic, Ecuador, El Salvador, Guatemala, Honduras, Mexico, Nicaragua, Panama, Paraguay, Peru, Puerto Rico, Uruguay, Venezuela
Arab/Muslim: Iran, Algeria, Bahrain, Egypt, Iraq, Jordan, Kuwait, Libya, Mauritania, Morocco, Oman, Qatar, Saudi Arabia, Syria, Tunisia, United Arab, Yemen, Somalia, Lebanon, Palestinian, Northern Cyprus
Caribbean: Belize, Guyana, Haiti, Jamaica, Suriname, Trinidad & Tobago
Central Asia: Afghanistan, Kazakhstan, Kyrgyzstan, Tajikistan, Turkmenistan, Uzbekistan
Eastern Europe: Turkey, Albania, Azerbaijan, Bosnia and Herzegovina, Kosovo, Armenia, Belarus, Bulgaria, Croatia, Czech Republic, Estonia, Georgia, Hungary, Latvia, Lithuania, Macedonia, Moldova, Montenegro, Romania, Russia, Serbia, Slovakia, Slovenia, Ukraine, Poland
South Asia: Bangladesh, Pakistan, India, Nepal, Sri Lanka, Bhutan
Southeast Asia: Indonesia, Malaysia, Cambodia, China, Hong Kong, Japan, Laos, Mongolia, Myanmar, Philippines, Singapore, South Korea, Taiwan, Thailand, Vietnam
Sub-Saharan Africa: Angola, Benin, Botswana, Burundi, Burkina Faso, Cameroon, Central Africa, Chad, Comoros, Congo-Kinshasa, Congo Brazzaville, Djibouti, Ethiopia, Gabon, Ghana, Guinea, Ivory Coast, Kenya, Lesotho, Liberia, Madagascar, Malawi, Mali, Mauritius, Mozambique, Namibia, Niger, Nigeria, Rwanda, Senegal, Sierra Leone, South Africa, South Sudan, Sudan, Swaziland, Tanzania, Togo, Uganda, Zambia, Zimbabwe, Mauritius
Western Europe and Anglo-Saxon: Australia, Austria, Belgium, Canada, Cyprus, Denmark, Finland, France, Germany, Greece, Iceland, Ireland, Italy, Luxembourg, Malta, Netherlands, New Zealand, Norway, Portugal, Spain, Sweden, Switzerland, United Kingdom, United States
Source [a]Gallup World Poll, waves 2 and 3 (2006–2008), scale 0–10. [b]World Value Survey, waves 1–6 (1981–2014), scale 1–10. [c]World Value Survey, wave 6 (2010–2014), scale 1–10

for life satisfaction on the basis of the World Value Survey information for the period 1981–2014 as well as for the most recent period (sixth wave) of 2010–2014. It is observed that Latin Americans report, on average, the highest life satisfaction level in the world. The average for the period 1981–2014 is 7.60 (in a scale from 1 to 10) in Latin America while it is 7.46 in the Western Europe and Anglo Saxon region. Figures that focus on the most recent wave (years 2010–2014) do also show that life satisfaction in Latin America is much higher than that in other regions of the world, including the Western European and Anglo-Saxon countries.

Figures from the Gallup World Poll and from the World Value Surveys are not directly comparable because they refer to different periods and because they comprise a different sample of countries; however, in general, it is safe to state that on average Latin Americans are highly satisfied with their lives in comparison with the situation of people in other regions of the world, even in those regions which are considered as highly developed.

It is important to state that high life satisfaction in Latin America does not necessarily imply that the region is a paradise and that Latin Americans have no problems and face no threats. In fact, there are many problems and threats in the region and some of them do depress Latin Americans' well-being; but not everything is problematic, in the region there are also some positive factors which contribute to high well-being and which have usually been neglected by the development literature. In addition, it is important to recognize that average levels do not adequately depict the situation of everybody in the region; there are particular population segments experiencing low well-being.

High life satisfaction in Latin America deserves further explanation; Why Latin Americans have, on average, such high well-being levels? Why is the region performing so well even when it is not considered as the most advanced on the basis of the situation as portrayed by commonly-used social and economic indicators? Why Latin Americans are so satisfied with their lives even when the region is the source of so many news and reports on income inequality, violence, poverty, and crime? These questions will be addressed in the following chapters; the next sections provide what can be considered as a first-level explanation which focuses on the essential experiences of being well.

4.2.2 *Essential Experiences of Being Well in Latin America and the Rest of the World*

There are different levels of explanation for people's satisfaction with life. The first level focuses on the essential experiences of being well people have; affective, evaluative and sensory experiences constitute this level of explanation (Rojas 2017a).

Table 4.2 presents the affective and evaluative situation in different regions of the world on the basis of information gathered by the Gallup World Poll from 2006 to

Table 4.2 Affective situation and life evaluation in regions of the world. Country-level means by region

Region	Positive affect	Negative affect	Life evaluation
Latin America	0.79	0.29	6.07
Western Europe and Anglo-Saxon	0.76	0.25	6.97
Southeast Asia	0.72	0.23	5.43
Arab/Muslim	0.67	0.32	5.34
Sub-Saharan Africa	0.68	0.27	4.29
Caribbean	0.72	0.28	5.75
Central Asia	0.66	0.20	5.15
Eastern Europe	0.61	0.27	5.25
South Asia	0.72	0.23	5.43
World	0.70	0.27	5.42

Note Country-level means by region; not weighted by countries' population
Positive affect: Smile or laugh yesterday, Learned something, Treated with respect, Experienced enjoyment, and Feel well-rested
Negative affect: Experienced worry, Sadness, Anger, Stress, and Depression
Regions of the world: see Table 4.1 note
Source Gallup World Poll, waves from 2006 to 2016

2016; the 11-years period is long enough as to consider the computed mean values as representing structural conditions rather than transient ones.

Positive affect is measured as a simple average of five 'day-before' questions inquiring on the experience of the following positive affect: Smile or laugh yesterday, Learned something, Treated with respect, Experienced enjoyment, and Feel well-rested. Yes (1) or no (0) answers are provided by respondents and a simple average is computed for each person and then along countries and across regions. Negative affect is computed on the basis of a similar exercise that uses the following affective variables: Experienced worry, Sadness, Anger, Stress, and Depression. Life evaluation is computed on the basis of people's respond to the so-called Cantril ladder question which asks the respondent to rate her life on a scale from 0 to 10, where 0 represents the worst possible life and 10 the best possible life.

It is observed in Table 4.2 that positive affect is very high in Latin America; as a matter of fact, Latin Americans experience—on average—the highest positive affect in the world; they are followed by people from the Western European region and from the Caribbean. Relatively low levels of positive affect are observed in Eastern Europe and in South and Southeast Asia. The 0.79 value for positive affect in Latin America basically means than in an ordinary day the average Latin American experiences a lot four out of the five positive emotions under consideration.

Latin Americans do also experience relatively high negative affect levels, only behind those in the Arab/Muslim region. Very low levels of negative affect are observed in Central Asia as well as in South and Southeast Asia. It can be stated that regarding the affective substrate of life satisfaction Latin Americans experience a more intense life while people in Central Asia and Eastern Europe experience a relatively smoother one.

Life evaluation is also relatively high in Latin America, with an average for the region of 6.1 which is only second to that in the Western Europe and Anglo-Saxon region (7.0). Life evaluation is very low in Sub-Saharan Africa, with an average value of 4.3. Life evaluation depends on the norms of evaluation people use to judge their life as good; hence, values and traditions do intervene in making this judgment. It has been shown that life evaluation is associated to some commonly used social and economic indicators; however, it would be a mistake to assume a close association between life evaluation and material conditions because this would depend on whether people hold materialistic values or not. In the end, people's evaluation of life depends on their access to those aspects in life that they consider of value.

It is important to state that the regional figures are not presented with the purpose of finding out what region ranks first in the world; it is not really about a competition to see who comes first but about learning from the best practices—as well as from the wrong ones—in order to contribute to knowledge on how to increase and sustain people's experience of being well.

4.3 Well-Being in Latin America

Latin America is a vast region both in territorial and in population terms; multiple nations coexist in the region and countries have experimented with different policies and development strategies during the past decades. Hence, even when common cultural elements across the region exist, some degree of heterogeneity is expected to show up.

4.3.1 Life Satisfaction

Table 4.3 presents the well-being situation in Latin American countries; it is observed that there is substantial dispersion in life satisfaction across them. Costa Ricans report an outstandingly high satisfaction of 8.48 in the 0–10 scale used by the Gallup World Poll, while Peruvians report an average life satisfaction of 5.98. The Costa Rican life satisfaction value is the highest for any country surveyed by the Gallup World Poll. Costa Rica, Mexico, Panama, Venezuela, and Brazil have life-satisfaction levels which are even greater than the average for the Western Europe and Anglo-Saxon region.

Life satisfaction levels are relatively low in the so-called Andean countries (Ecuador, Peru, Bolivia, and Chile); but even these low life-satisfaction countries in Latin America have levels that could be considered as above average in most regions of the world.

Table 4.3 Life satisfaction in Latin American countries, 2007

	Mean life satisfaction	Percentage unsatisfied[a]	Percentage highly satisfied[b]
Argentina	7.09	18.1	45.5
Bolivia	6.27	39.6	27.8
Brazil	7.53	16.4	56.6
Chile	6.45	34.0	31.8
Colombia	7.35	19.0	53.1
Costa Rica	8.48	7.1	79.9
Dominican Rep.	7.42	20.5	57.8
Ecuador	6.35	33.7	28.8
El Salvador	6.68	23.2	35.3
Honduras	7.04	26.0	48.3
Mexico	7.76	8.8	62.3
Nicaragua	7.07	27.1	50.5
Panama	7.76	15.4	61.6
Paraguay	6.77	31.9	40.2
Peru	5.98	44.4	19.4
Uruguay	6.72	27.2	41.3
Venezuela	7.59	11.3	55.3

[a]Unsatisfied: life satisfaction of 5 or lower
[b]Highly satisfied: life satisfaction of 8 or greater
Source Life satisfaction figures come from wave 2 (2007) of the Gallup World Poll

Average well-being is high in Latin America; however, mean values do not clearly portray the general situation of many people in the region. In fact, there are large patches of unsatisfied people in some Latin American countries. Table 4.3 presents the percentage of unsatisfied people (life satisfaction of 5 or lower) and the percentage of highly satisfied people (life satisfaction of 8 or greater); it is observed that about 45% of Peruvians are unsatisfied with their life as well as almost 40% of Bolivians. About one-third of the population of Chile, Ecuador and Paraguay are also unsatisfied with their life. On the other hand, almost 80% of Costa Ricans and more than 60% of Panamanians and Mexicans are highly satisfied with their life.

One important question that needs to be addressed is whether commonly-used deprivation indicators, such as income poverty and multidimensional poverty, appropriately inform policy makers about these unsatisfied population segments. A more general question is whether the widely used socio-economic indicators reflect the relevant drivers of people's well-being. These two important questions will be addressed in the following chapters.

Figures presented in Table 4.3 are relatively old; unfortunately, the Gallup Poll has not included the life satisfaction question in its recent surveys. A different source of information is the Latinobarometer, which has posed the life satisfaction question in many of its surveys. The response scale in the Latinobarometer is categorical, with only four categories: very satisfied, fairly satisfied, not very satisfied, and not at all satisfied. This information is used to construct Fig. 4.1 which presents the percentage of people in each Latin American country who report being very or fairly satisfied in the years 2005 and 2017.

Figure 4.1 provides a picture of the recent life-satisfaction situation as well as of its evolution between 2005 and 2017 in Latin American countries. Costa Rica, Colombia, Panama, and Dominican Republic have the highest percentages of satisfied people in the region in 2017; while Peru, Bolivia, Paraguay and Chile have the lowest percentages.

Substantial gains in life satisfaction between 2005 and 2017 are observed in the low-satisfied countries of Peru, Bolivia, Ecuador, Nicaragua and Honduras. These countries initiated with very low levels in 2005. Venezuela, which had the highest value in 2005, is the only country where loses in life satisfaction are substantial,

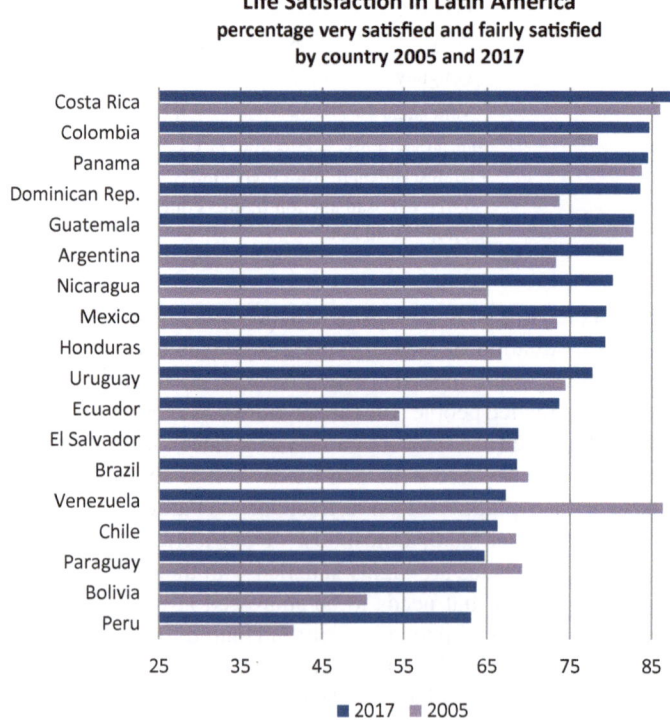

Fig. 4.1 Life satisfaction in Latin American countries in 2005 and 2017. Percentage of population who are very satisfied or fairly satisfied with their life. Latinobarometer 2005 and 2017

moving from 86 to 67% of people who report being very or fairly satisfied with life from 2005 to 2017. Minor loses in life satisfaction are also observed in Paraguay, Chile and Brazil. These findings are important because they show that substantial change may occur in life satisfaction over time.

4.3.2   Essential Experiences of Being Well. Life Evaluation

Table 4.4 presents the life evaluation, positive affect and negative affect situation in the Latin American countries on the basis of information from the Gallup World Polls from 2006 to 2016. Latin Americans' evaluation of life shows substantial dispersion across countries. The lowest values for life evaluation are found in Dominican

Table 4.4 Essential experiences of being well in Latin America. Mean values by country, 2006–2016

	Best possible life	Positive affect	Negative affect
Argentina	6.44	0.78	0.26
Bolivia	5.64	0.74	0.39
Brazil	6.28	0.74	0.29
Chile	6.44	0.77	0.29
Colombia	6.28	0.81	0.31
Costa Rica	7.15	0.83	0.28
Cuba	5.45	0.65	0.28
Dominican Rep.	4.93	0.75	0.33
Ecuador	5.61	0.81	0.32
El Salvador	5.83	0.82	0.31
Guatemala	6.17	0.81	0.29
Honduras	5.23	0.80	0.27
Mexico	6.92	0.78	0.25
Nicaragua	5.45	0.80	0.30
Panama	6.76	0.83	0.21
Paraguay	5.41	0.84	0.21
Peru	5.61	0.76	0.36
Uruguay	6.15	0.76	0.27
Venezuela	6.42	0.82	0.24

All other figures are computed as mean values on the basis of information from Gallup World Polls from 2006 to 2016
Life evaluation is measured in a 0–10 scale; where 0 correspond to 'the worst possible life' and 10 to 'the best possible life'. Positive and negative affect are measured in a 0–1 scale
Source Gallup World Polls 2006–2016

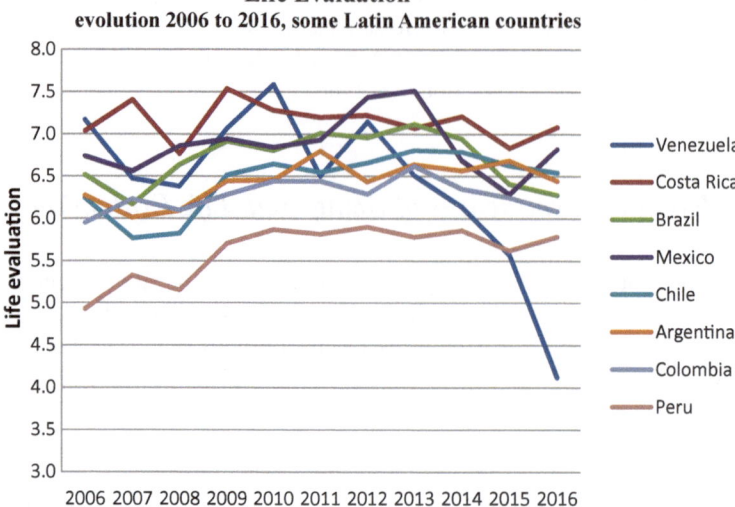

Fig. 4.2   Life-evaluation trends in some Latin American countries, 2006–2016. Gallup World Poll, 2006–2016 years

Republic, Honduras, Paraguay, Cuba and Nicaragua, while the highest values are found in Costa Rica, Mexico, Panama, Argentina and Chile. It has been argued that life evaluation—as measured by the Cantril's worst-to-best-possible-life ladder—is a cognitive-oriented variable which is highly sensitive to socio-economic conditions (Argyle 2002). Hence, it is not surprising for countries with good socio-economic indicators, such as Argentina and Chile, to have a relatively better position in the life-evaluation indicator than in the life-satisfaction one. Similarly, it is not surprising for countries with poor socio-economic indicators, such as Honduras, Paraguay and Nicaragua, to have a relatively worse position in the life-evaluation indicator.

Figure 4.2 shows the evolution of life evaluation since 2006. In most Latin American countries life evaluation shows a slight decline in 2008 followed by a recovery and then a slight decline in the recent years. It is important to remember that 2008 was a year of global economic crisis. A substantial downward trend in life evaluation is observed in Venezuela, where life evaluation moved from 7.58 in 2010 to 4.12 in 2016; this is a huge decline by all standards and it takes place in a country that has experienced severe political, economic and social turmoil during the past decade. Mexico also shows an important decline during the years 2013 and 2015, when economic and administrative reforms were implemented by a new government. Costa Rica shows a slight decline since 2010, and Brazil also shows an important decline in life evaluation since 2013 as a consequence of political chaos and economic problems in the country. On the other hand, a sustained gain in life evaluation is observed in Peru.

4.3.3 Essential Experiences of Being Well. Affective Experiences

As previously stated, positive affect is outstandingly high in Latin America; with the exception of Cuba, where positive affect is low, the other countries show levels that can be considered as high or even outstandingly high in comparison to the situation in the rest of the world. It is observed in Table 4.4 that Paraguay, Panama and Costa Rica have the highest average levels in the region, while Dominican Republic, Bolivia, Brazil and Colombia have the lowest levels.

Negative affect is high in the Andean countries of Bolivia, Peru and Ecuador as well as in Dominican Republic, while it is low in Paraguay, Panama, Venezuela and México. However, as it is going to be shown below, the mean value for Venezuela is not an appropriate indicator of its current situation.

Table 4.5 shows the top 15 countries in the world in terms of positive affect. It is observed that 10 out of the top 15 countries in the world are from Latin America; in fact, 8 out of the top 8 countries are Latin American. The high levels of positive affect, as well as the not-so-low levels of negative affect in Latin America deserve

Table 4.5 Top 15 countries in the world in positive affect. Mean values by country, 2006–2016

World rank	Country	Positive affect
1	Paraguay	0.842
2	Panama	0.833
3	Costa Rica	0.829
4	Venezuela	0.824
5	El Salvador	0.818
6	Guatemala	0.812
7	Colombia	0.810
8	Ecuador	0.809
9	Canada	0.804
10	Philippines	0.800
11	Iceland	0.799
12	Denmark	0.798
13	Honduras	0.797
14	Norway	0.797
15	Nicaragua	0.796

Note Positive affect measured as simple average of the following five 'day-before' dichotomous variables: Smile or laugh yesterday, Learn something, Treated with respect, Experienced enjoyment, and Feel well-rested

Average values computed on the basis of 10,750–12,200 observations per country, with the exception of Iceland (3131 observations) and Norway (6010 observations)

Source Gallup World Poll waves 2006–2016

further explanation; Chapter 8 presents data that shows that interpersonal relations do play an important role in explaining the affective state of Latin Americans.

Venezuelans used to enjoy high levels of positive affect and low levels of negative affect; however, the situation has reversed during the past decade. Figures 4.3 and 4.4 show recent trends in positive and negative affect in some Latin American countries. A strong negative trend is observed in Venezuela, where positive affect has declined from 0.87 in 2010 to 0.74 in 2016, while negative affect has increased from 0.13 to 0.42 in the same period. Negative affect has tripled in six years in Venezuela, reflecting the recent deterioration of social, economic and political conditions as well as the destruction of long-term interpersonal relations due to international migration, internal displacement, and high violence and crime rates. It is interesting to observe

Fig. 4.3 Positive-affect trends in some Latin American countries, 2006–2016. Gallup World Poll, 2006–2016 waves

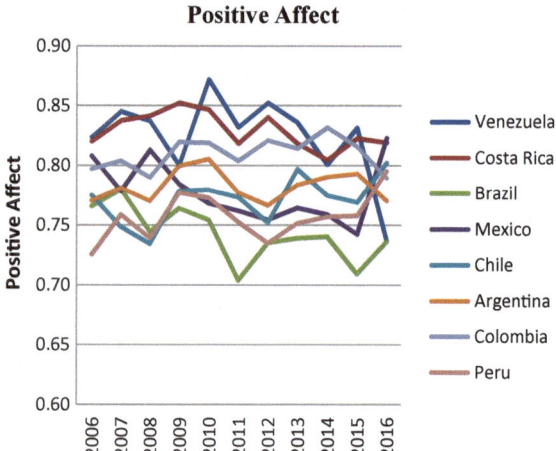

Fig. 4.4 Negative-affect trends in some Latin American countries, 2006–2016. Gallup World Poll, 2006–2016 waves

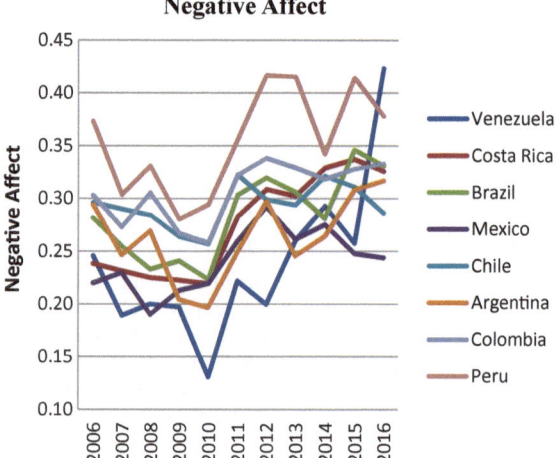

that the difficult situation in Venezuela has asymmetrically impacted negative and positive affect, indicating that their drivers are not necessarily the same.

4.3.4 Life Satisfaction, Life Evaluation and Affective State

It is noteworthy to state that life satisfaction is much higher than life evaluation in all Latin American countries and that this huge difference between a satisfactory life and a life that is considered as the best-possible one is a relevant feature in the Latin American region.

When evaluating their life, Latin Americans report a situation that is far from the best possible one; this is a report that appears to be consistent with some socio-economic indicators pointing towards the existence of social and economic problems in the region. However, Latin Americans are able to lead a highly satisfactory life even within this problematic socio-economic situation, which seems to be explained by the high values of positive affect in the region. The high positive affect allows Latin Americans to enjoy high levels of life satisfaction even when their socio-economic conditions are not so favorable. In other words, when assessing whether their life is good or not Latin Americans recognize many deficiencies in their socio-economic and political conditions; but, life is not fully comprised by these conditions. There is more to life than the socio-economic and political conditions and Latin Americans seem to enjoy a very good situation in those other conditions that also impact in their well-being, as it is reflected by their high positive affect. Chapter 8 will further address the other conditions that are relevant for the well-being of Latin Americans.

Figure 4.5 presents the correlation coefficients between life satisfaction and essential experiences of being well for Latin America as well as for the rest of countries in the World. It is observed that the correlation between life satisfaction and life evaluation is much smaller in Latin America; in other words, life evaluation—and the conditions associated to it—seem to be less important in determining life satisfaction in Latin America with respect to their importance in the rest of the world. The correlation between life satisfaction and positive affect is similar in Latin America with respect to that in the rest of the world; but it is important to remember that positive affect is very high in Latin America. In addition, it is interesting to observe that the correlation coefficient between life evaluation and positive affect is smaller in Latin America than in the rest of the world; this implies that in Latin America it is more likely to find people who experience high positive emotions even when their life-evaluation conditions are not good, and vice versa. Hence, positive affect and life evaluation do not go hand-by-hand in Latin America, suggesting that different drivers do intervene. It is also observed that negative affect has a larger correlation coefficient with life satisfaction in Latin America than in the rest of the world.

Hence, it seems that the high life satisfaction levels in Latin America emerge from: First, the abundance of positive affect and not from a larger importance of positive affect in explaining life satisfaction. Second, from the lower importance of life evaluation in explaining life satisfaction. Third, from a low correlation between

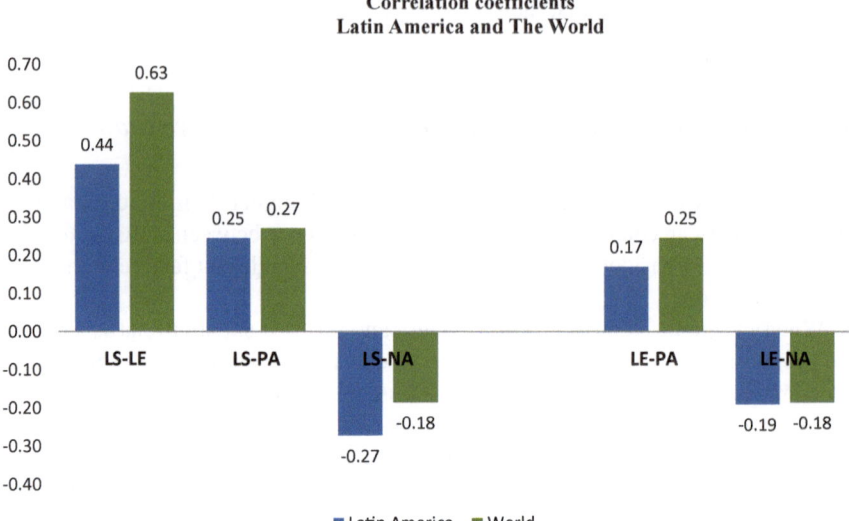

Fig. 4.5 Correlation coefficients for life satisfaction and essential experiences of being well; Latin Americans and the world. LS-LE (Life Satisfaction-Life Evaluation), LS-PA (Life Satisfaction-Positive Affect), LS-NA (Life Satisfaction-Negative Affect), LE-PA (Life Evaluation-Positive Affect), LE-NA (Life Evaluation-Negative Affect). *Source* Gallup World Polls 2006–2016; the life satisfaction correlations are computed on the basis of information from 2007

life-evaluation conditions and positive affect; this is, from the possibility of enjoying high positive affect even under not-so-good socio-economic conditions.

4.4 Satisfaction in Domains of Life

Domains of life provide a second way of understanding life satisfaction. It is argued that life satisfaction can be understood as a result of satisfaction in different areas of life; in other words, when people make an overall assessment of their life they take into consideration how well life is going on in different aspects of life. Why do Latin Americans experience such high levels of positive affect and are so highly satisfied with their lives even when socio-economic conditions are not good? The argument is that other aspects of life—beyond the economic one—are going relatively well for Latin Americans.

Not many surveys incorporate questions regarding satisfaction with different areas or domains of life. This section relies on an academic survey implemented in three Latin American countries (Colombia, Costa Rica, and Mexico) as well as to the white/Caucasian population in the United States within the research project 'Understanding High Well-Being in Latin America'. The survey is representative for the population of the three Latin American countries as well as for the United States population segment under consideration. The survey was implemented in 2018 and it has information regarding satisfaction in many domains of life.

Figure 4.6 presents the life satisfaction and satisfaction in domains of life situation for the Latin American and the United States' population under consideration. It is observed that the population of the three Latin American countries under consideration (Colombia, Costa Rica, and Mexico) has a mean life satisfaction which is much higher than that for the white population of the United States; this is not surprising because the three Latin American countries in the survey are well-known for their high life satisfaction levels. Latin Americans have very high satisfaction levels in their family domain as well as in their spiritual and occupational domains; their satisfaction is very low in the economic domain as is relatively low in their availability and using of free time. The low satisfaction in their economic domain reflects the economic difficulties that many Latin American households go through; however, this seems to be compensated by a very high family satisfaction.

It is interesting to observe that economic satisfaction is lower in the United States than in the Latin American countries; this takes place even when the purchasing power enjoyed by people in the United States is about seven times higher than that in Latin America. This issue of enjoying higher income but not higher economic

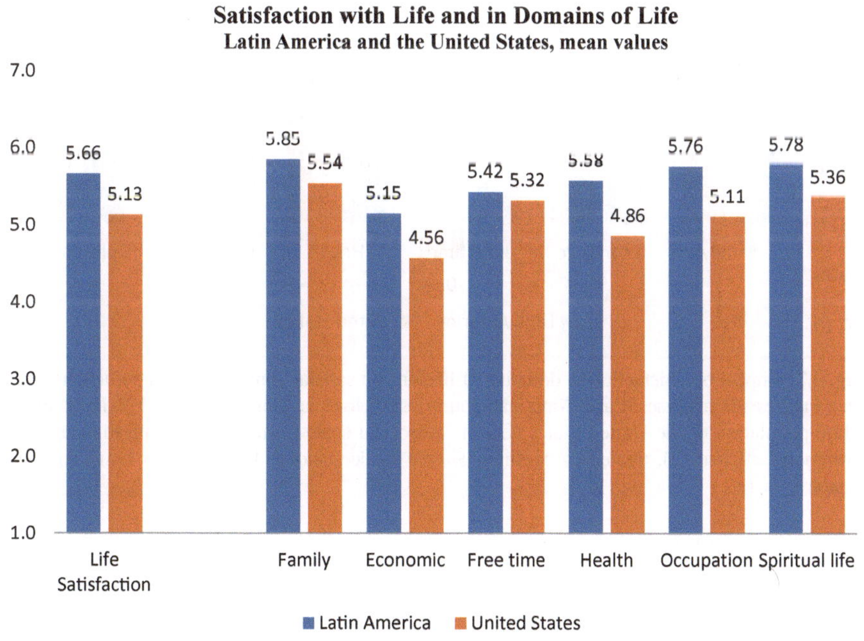

Satisfaction with Life and in Domains of Life
Latin America and the United States, mean values

Fig. 4.6 Satisfaction with life and in domains of life, mean values for some Latin American countries (Colombia, Costa Rica and Mexico) and for the white population of the United States (USA). Categorical scale from extremely unsatisfied (1) to extremely satisfied (7), treated as cardinal. *Source* Understanding Happiness in Latin America database, 2018

satisfaction will be discussed in Chap. 5; it shows that aspirations, social comparisons and endogenous evaluation norms play an important role in determining economic satisfaction.

Figure 4.7 further explores the importance of satisfaction in domains of life in explaining life satisfaction. It presents the estimated coefficients for the impact on life satisfaction of a raise of one unit in satisfaction in a specific domain of life. This information is useful to see which domains are more important in Latin America and in the United States.

It is observed in Fig. 4.7 that in Latin America the family domain is the most important one, followed by the health domain and then the economic one. In the United States it is the economic domain the most important one, followed by the family and the health domains. A huge difference in the importance of the economic domain is observed between Latin America and the United States.

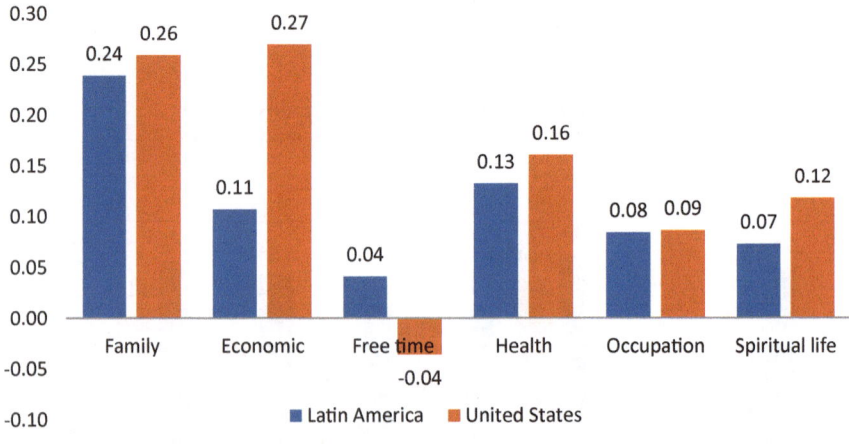

Fig. 4.7 Impact of satisfaction in domains of life on life satisfaction; estimated coefficients from linear regression analyses. Latin American countries: Colombia, Costa Rica and Mexico; and the white population of the United States (USA) categorical scale from extremely unsatisfied (1) to extremely satisfied (7), treated as cardinal. *Source* Understanding Happiness in Latin America database, 2018

4.5 Well-Being and Socio-demographic Groups

4.5.1 Gender

Figure 4.8 presents the life-satisfaction situation by gender in Latin American countries; in general, the gender gap in life satisfaction is very small; however, some gender differences are observed in Ecuador, Dominican Republic, Bolivia and Chile. In Ecuador the mean value for men's life satisfaction is almost 6% larger than that for women.

Figures 4.9 and 4.10 present the life satisfaction and experiences of being well situation by gender and for the Latin American region as a whole. It is observed that gender differences are small, with the exception of the experience of negative affect where women's value is 24% larger than men's value.

4.5.2 Age Groups

Figure 4.11 presents life-satisfaction figures by age groups for Latin American countries. Differences in life satisfaction by age are observed across Latin American countries. The elder are slightly more satisfied than adults and young people in Costa Rica and Brazil; their relative situation is also favorable in Nicaragua and Colombia. However, in other countries the life satisfaction of elder people is much smaller than that

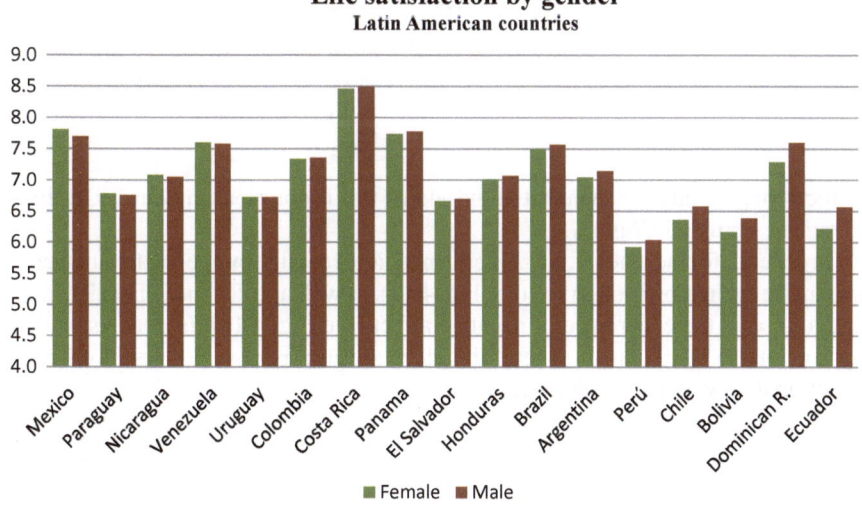

Fig. 4.8 Life satisfaction by gender and country. Life satisfaction: average of country means 2007. Gallup World Poll wave 2

Fig. 4.9 Life satisfaction and life evaluation in Latin America, by gender. Life satisfaction: average of country means 2007. Life evaluation: average of country means 2006–2016. Gallup World Poll 2006 to 2016

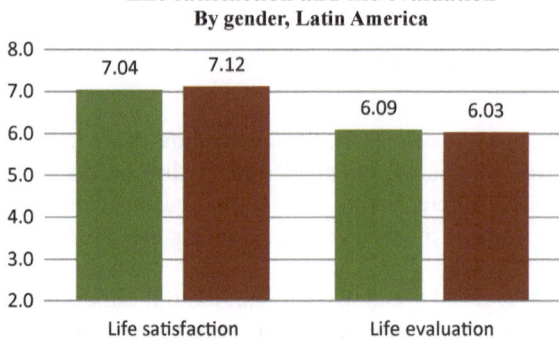

Fig. 4.10 Life satisfaction and life evaluation in Latin America, by gender. Average of country means 2006–2016. Gallup World Poll 2006 to 2016

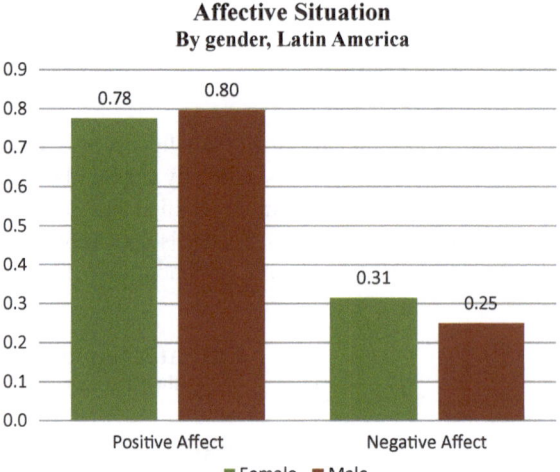

of the younger and even than that of the adults; this is notorious in Ecuador, Bolivia, Paraguay, Peru and Uruguay.

In general, for the whole Latin American region a decline by age in life satisfaction and in life evaluation is observed (see Fig. 4.12), as well as a decline in positive affect and a raise in the experience of negative affect (see Fig. 4.13). In conclusion, it is appropriate to state that in general the elder are in a relatively worse well-being situation than young and adult people.

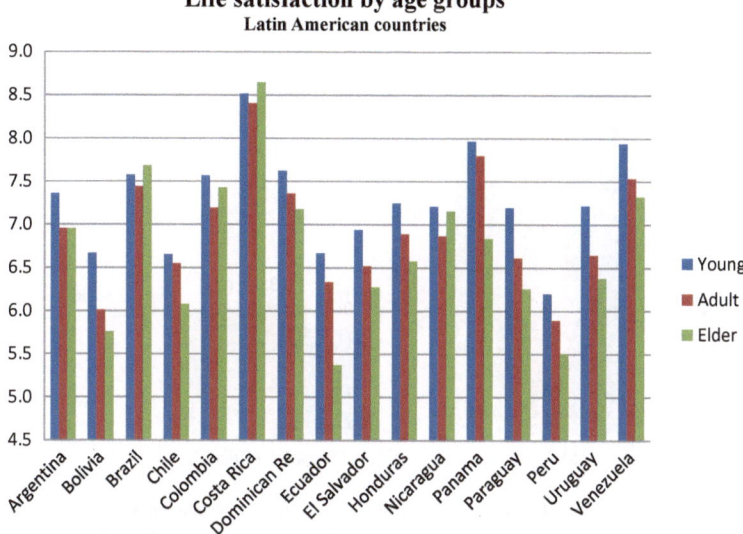

Fig. 4.11 Life satisfaction by age group and country, 2007, average values. Gallup World Poll wave 2. Young: 30 years old or less; adult: between 31 and 60 years old; elder: more than 60 years old

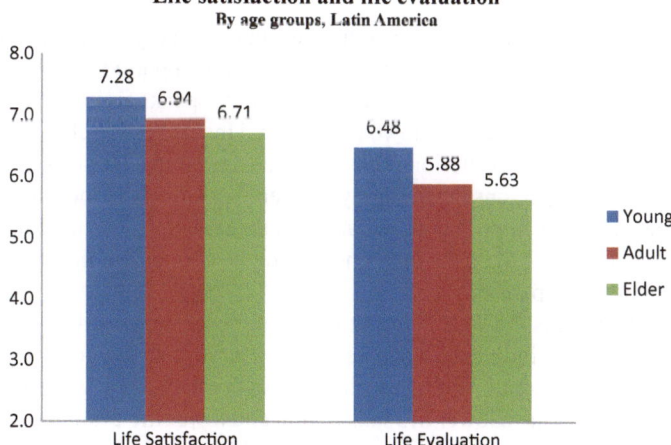

Fig. 4.12 Life satisfaction and life evaluation by age group and country, average values 2006–2016. Gallup World Poll 2006 to 2016. Young: 30 years old or less; adult: between 31 and 60 years old; elder: more than 60 years old

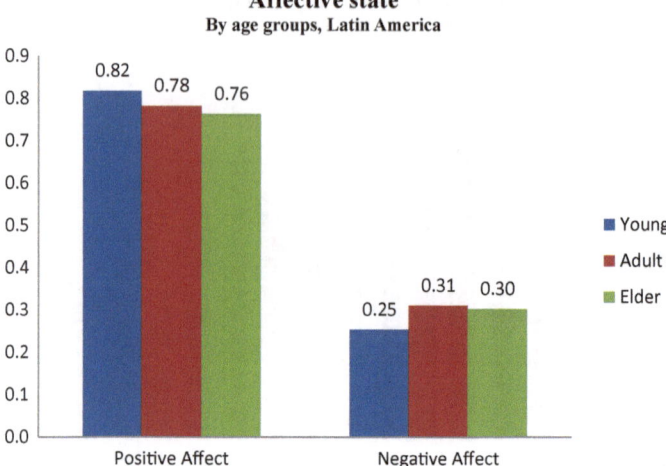

Fig. 4.13 Positive and negative affect by age group and country, average values 2006–2016. Gallup World Poll 2006 to 2016. Young: 30 years old or less; adult: between 31 and 60 years old; elder: more than 60 years old

4.5.3   *Indigenous Groups*

With few exceptions, there are no specific well-being surveys implemented to the indigenous populations in Latin America. Mexico's self-reported well-being survey (BIARE) asked in 2014 whether the interviewed person speaks an autochthonous language; this is a criterion usually followed by national institutions to classify people as indigenous (the alternative criterion is based on self-reported ethnicity) About 7% of the more than 39,000 persons in the survey answered positively to the autochthonous language question; it is important to remark than the question does not imply for the autochthonous language to be the only one spoken by the person; in fact, the survey was implemented in Spanish.

Figure 4.14 presents the well-being situation of the indigenous people in Mexico in comparison to non-indigenous people. It is observe that indigenous people do report lower life satisfaction and life evaluation, with the gap being significant. The indigenous people do have lower life satisfaction and lower life evaluation; however, their levels cannot be considered as very low. In addition, the positive and negative affect experienced by the indigenous groups are not different from that experienced by non-indigenous groups in Mexico. This is a very interesting finding considering that average household per capita income in indigenous households is about 50% of that in non-indigenous households (US$165 vs. US$325 per month).

One of the few studies that focuses on an indigenous population is the one by Rojas and Chávez (2019), which studies well-being in a couple of P'urhépecha communities in a rural area of Mexico. The study concentrates in the study of two indigenous communities which have followed different trajectories during the past decades; due

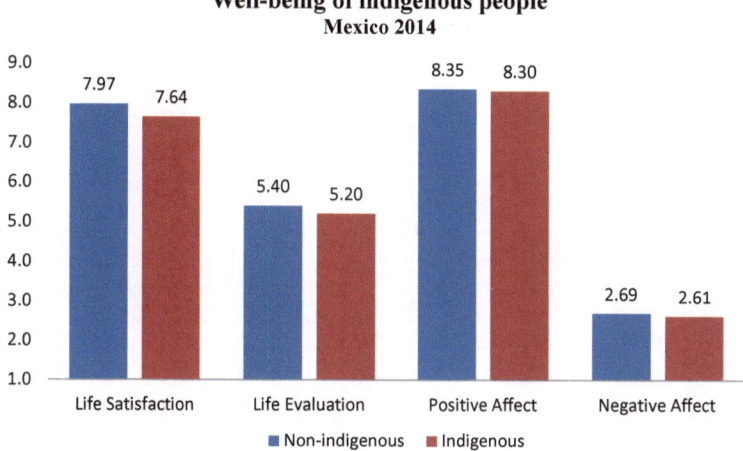

Fig. 4.14   Well-being of indigenous people, compared to non-indigenous people. Mexico 2014. Life satisfaction, positive affect and negative affect in a 0 to 10 scale; life evaluation in a 1 to 7 scale. *Source* BIARE 2014, INEGI

to the construction of a national road that goes through town one of the communities has been exposed to modernization and market-oriented practices, while the other community remains relatively isolated and has less contact to modernization practices and to the market. The study focuses on those who do still speak P'urhépecha language—the traditional ones—and those who do not—the modern ones. The study finds out that exposure to modernization practices is associated to a change in the importance of domains of life in explaining life satisfaction.

Modernization comes associated to the expansion of market-oriented practices, a greater division of labor, the expansion of regional trade, a different organization of working activities, and changes in aspirations. As expected, this social transformation is associated to a large increase in productivity and income; as a matter of fact, the mean monthly household income for those exposed to modernization is about US$250, while the same figure is US$170 for those not exposed. Modernization and market integration come associated to an increase in income, but the study also finds that the process also transforms the explanatory structure of life satisfaction. Those who are still traditional may have less income, but it is also true that the economic domain of life is less important in their life satisfaction. For the traditional group the important domains are health, family and spiritual life; while for the modern group the occupational and economic domains become more important (Fig. 4.15). Hence, low income is closely related to low life satisfaction for those exposed to modernization, but it is not so for those still living a traditional life (Yamamoto 2011; Yamamoto et al. 2008).

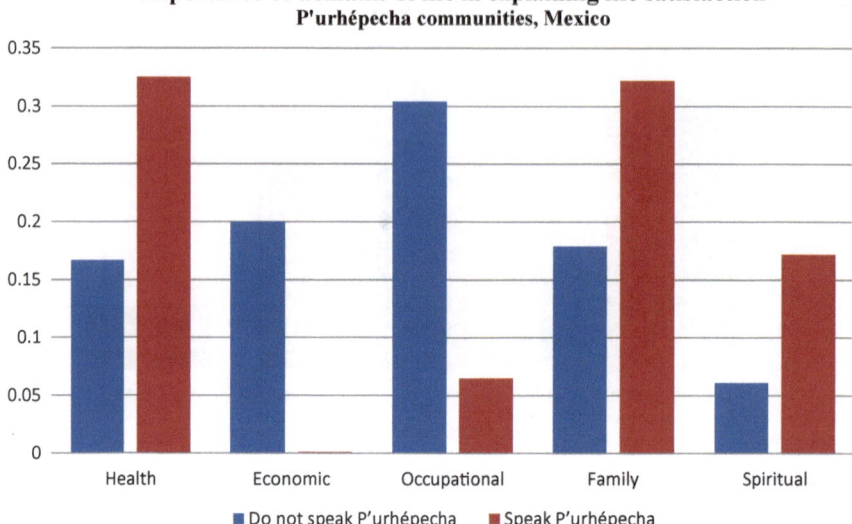

Fig. 4.15 Explanatory structure of life satisfaction, importance of domains of life. P'urhépecha communities, Mexico. *Source* Rojas and Chávez (2019)

4.6   Final Considerations

Well-being is high in Latin America. Life satisfaction is high, positive affect is outstandingly high and the evaluation of life is also good.

High well-being is not generalized across Latin American countries; some countries have very high well-being figures while others do not.

The family domain of life is very important in explaining life satisfaction in Latin America; high satisfaction in the family domain contributes to high life satisfaction in the region.

High well-being in Latin America is not directly associated to specific well-being policies implemented by governments in the region. Latin American governments have not directly promoted well-being; as a matter of fact, strength takes place in domains of life where governments have shown little interest.

There are low well-being populations across and within countries. Well-being differences by gender seem to be small, while there are substantial well-being differences by age in some countries.

Indigenous groups are clearly lagging behind in their socio-economic conditions; however, the well-being gap is not as large as it is depicted by their socio-economic conditions. Different values seem to play a role on this regard.

References

Argyle, M. (2002). *The psychology of happiness*. New York, NY, US: Routledge.

Rojas, M. (2017). The subjective object of well-being studies. In G. Brule & F. Maggino (Eds.), *Metrics of subjective well-being: Limits and improvements* (pp. 43–62). Berlin: Springer.

Rojas, M., & Chávez, P. (2019). Subjective well-being of the P'urhépecha people: Between tradition and modernity. In C. Fleming & M. Manning (Eds.), *Routledge handbook of indigenous wellbeing* (pp. 330–341). Abingdon: Routledge.

Rojas, M., & Veenhoven, R. (2013). Contentment and affect in the estimation of happiness. *Social Indicators Research, 110*(2), 415–431.

Yamamoto, J. (2011). Necesidades universales, su concreción cultural y el desarrollo en su contexto. Hacia una ciencia del desarrollo. In M. Rojas (Ed.), *La Medición del Progreso y del Bienestar. Propuestas desde América Latina* (pp. 93–102). México: Foro Consultivo Científico y Tecnológico.

Yamamoto, J., Feijoo, A. R., & Lazarte, A. (2008). Subjective wellbeing: An alternative approach. In J. Copestake (Ed.), *Wellbeing and development in Peru. Local and universal views confronted*. New York: Palgrave MacMillian.

Chapter 5
Income and Well-Being in Latin America

Abstract In general terms the Latin American region is a middle-income one. On average, it is not a region where starvation and economic calamities prevail, but in some countries large segments of the population may be in difficult economic situation. The income situation usually attracts the attention of policy makers because a close and strong relations between income and well-being is assumed; however, this chapter shows that the relationship between income and well-being is neither simple nor straightforward; it also shows that economic growth is not necessarily associated to greater well-being.

Keywords Latin America · Income · Well-being · Gross Domestic Product · Economic growth · Beyond GDP

5.1 A Mid-Income Region

Per capita income levels in Latin American countries are not low; however, there is wide dispersion in income levels across as well as within Latin American countries. It is widely known that high income inequality is a structural feature of Latin American societies.

Figure 5.1 presents Gross Domestic Product per capita (GDPpc) data for 2017 and 2000 in Latin American countries. It is observed that in 2017 GDPpc goes from as high as US$22,800 in Chile to US$4500 in Honduras. The Central American countries of Honduras, Nicaragua, El Salvador and Guatemala, as well as Bolivia, are placed at the bottom of the income ranking in Latin America, with GDPpc levels below US$10,000. Chile, Panama, Uruguay, Argentina, Mexico, Venezuela, and Costa Rica have GDPpc levels above US$15,000.

The World Bank classifies countries on the basis of their per-capita income. The high-income group in the world has a mean GDPpc of US$43,000, while the low-income group has a mean of US$2000. Hence, Latin American countries are far away from the high-income group, but they are also far from the low-income group. Even Honduras, the country with the lowest GDPpc in Latin America, has average income levels that are above the mean value of the low-income group in the world.

M. Rojas, *Well-Being in Latin America*, Human Well-Being Research and Policy Making, https://doi.org/10.1007/978-3-030-33498-7_5

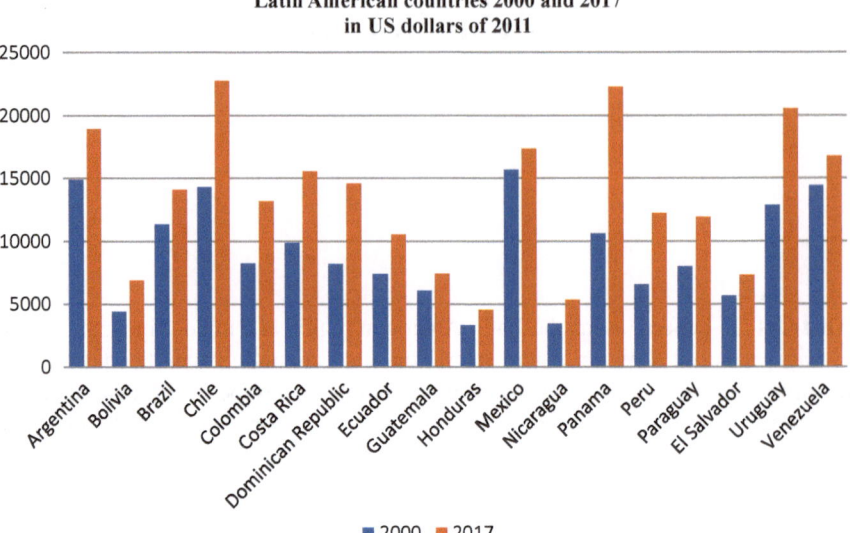

Fig. 5.1 Gross Domestic Product (GDP) per capita in Latin American countries, years 2000 and 2017 (2014 for Venezuela). GDP per capita in constant 2011 international dollars and adjusted by purchasing power parity (PPP). *Source* World Bank Indicators

Latin Americans enjoy income levels that, on average, are considered adequate; however, income inequality implies for per capita figures to be bad proxies of the purchasing-power situation of many Latin Americans.

It is also observed in Fig. 5.1 that GDPpc has increased during the past two decades in all Latin American countries. Economic growth has been substantial in Panama, Peru, Dominican Republic, Colombia, Uruguay and Chile, while minor increases are observed in Mexico, Venezuela, Guatemala and Brazil.

Economists—as well as policy makers—used to believe that income was directly and strongly related to people's experience of being well (Rojas 2019a). It was assumed that more income translated—almost automatically—into greater satisfaction with life, the experience of more positive emotions and of less negative ones. It was this assumption which made of economic growth a central objective in policy decisions; it was also this assumption which justified the worldwide effort to abate income poverty.

If well-being were closely associated to income levels then one would expect for people in Chile, Uruguay, Panama and Argentina to have a greater experiences of being well than people in countries like Honduras, Nicaragua, El Salvador, Guatemala and Bolivia. One would also expect for greater gains in well-being to take place in those countries that have experienced greater rates of economic growth. However, research has shown that the relationship between income and well-being is not straightforward (Rojas 2009).

5.2 Income and Well-Being: Research Findings

The assumption of a strong relationship between well-being and income went on for decades without any questioning; it seemed so evident that there was no interest in corroborating it (Rojas 2019a). Besides, economists were reluctant to work with people's reports; hence, they favored income as a good proxy for well-being. Hence, economists directed their effort to the creation of accurate measures of income and to the development of models of economic growth which could be used to guide policy.

It is not until de 1970s that the relationship between income and life satisfaction was empirically studied. The economist Richard Easterlin decided to use novel information on life-satisfaction reports from some countries to test the assumption of a strong and direct relationship between income and life satisfaction (Easterlin 1974). His finding triggered a vast research agenda on the nature of the relationship between income, economic growth and people's experience of being well. Easterlin's findings presented a puzzle: in a given moment in time those who have more income tend to report greater well-being than those who have lower income; however, increases of income over time are not associated to greater well-being. Hence, and contrary to what most economists and policy makers believed, the raising of people's income is not a powerful instrument to increase their satisfaction with life in the long run; in other words, economic growth does not increase the human lot.

This is not the place for an in-deep review of the main findings and new theories which emerged from research inspired by the Easterlin paradox (Rojas 2009, 2019b). In general, the main explanations to the Easterlin paradox point towards the importance of social comparisons, the endogeneity of aspirations to income, the existence of habituation-to-income processes, the heterogeneity in values people hold, and the negative correlation between income and other drivers of well-being.

5.2.1 Social Comparisons and the Status-Race Treadmill

It has been shown that people compare their standard of living—as well as some specific consumption goods—to that of their reference groups; thus, their experiences of being well do depend on their relative standing more than on their absolute situation (Montero and Rau 2016; Rojas 2019c, d). For example, a person's assessment of her life as good depends not so much on what she has but on what she has in comparison to what others have—in particular, what those persons she compares with have. In a similar way, the affective state is dependent on the relative position people have in society—at least in that segment of society they compare with (Rojas 2013).

The argument implies that income plays a status-marking role and that greater status is associated to greater well-being; hence, at one moment in time those who have more income tend to have a better status and this translates into greater well-being. However, generalized increases in income have little impact on people's well-being because their relative standing is not changing; everybody has more income but not a greater status and, in consequence, there is little impact on people's well-being. Economic growth gets trapped into a status-race treadmill: income increases for everybody but well-being does not. It could even be possible for some groups to see their income rise and their relative position fall if the income of those they compare with increases at a higher rate. It has been shown that in this case a person's well-being may decline even when her income increases (Graham and Pettinato 2002).

In consequence, having more income does not necessarily guarantee enjoying a more satisfactory life. Social comparisons promote a status race where people generate more income and have more assets but where their well-being is not increasing.

5.2.2   Increasing Aspirations

Life satisfaction does also depend on the aspirational gap; this is: on the difference between the income people have and the income they aspire to have (van Praag and Ferrer-I-Carbonell 2004; Stutzer 2004). In principle, the aspirational gap would be expected to shrink as income increases; however, there are two factors at play which may lead to a sustained—and even increasing—aspirational gap when income increases. First, aspirations do increase with income; the processes leading to greater income—such as migration and education—also intervene in the formation of people's aspirations. In addition, greater income induces behavioral changes—such as traveling abroad and becoming member of a social club—which end up modifying people's aspirations. Thus, aspirations do not remain constant as income raises, and it would be wrong to assume that the aspirational gap shrinks as income increases. Second, people are exposed to strong social trends that raise their aspirations and which are independent of what happens to their income. Globalization and advertising foster aspirations and tend to magnify the aspirational gap.

Hence, even if everybody's income increases as a consequence of economic growth this does not necessarily translate into greater well-being if aspirations are rising at a greater rate and the aspirational gap is not declining.

5.2.3   Consumption and Habituation

Greater income allows people to purchase more goods and services; however, the impact of these goods and services on well-being may be negligible if people opt for purchasing consumption bundles that are exposed to adaptation processes. It has been shown that the well-being impact of some expensive commodities—such as luxury houses or cars—is transient; thus, after a short period of time the well-being experiences obtained from these expensive commodities may not differ from those obtained from cheaper ones (DeLeire and Kalil 2010; Dumludag 2015; Okulicz-Kozaryn et al. 2015; Winkelmann 2012).

In addition, even if greater income allows the purchasing of more commodities this does not necessarily translate into more consumption. It is important to distinguish between consumption—the act of having well-being experiences by using commodities—and purchasing—the act of having the commodities. Linder (1971) argues that the act of consumption requires time and attention and that people may have more income but not more time to consume, so that they may have more commodities but no greater well-being.

5.2.4 Economic Growth May Weaken Other Well-Being Drivers

It would also be possible for the same process that leads to greater income to weaken other important drivers of well-being. For example, it has been argued that modernization implies social changes that destroy communitarian and kin networks which are important for people's well-being (Germani 1965; Sugden 2005). In addition, economic growth and the pressure to be competitive and productive may demand for a hurried pace of life, which is not compatible with the enjoyment of leisure activities and the nurturing of person-based interpersonal relations.

5.3 Income and Well-Being in Latin America

The Mexican Self-reported Well-being survey (BIARE) provides detailed information on people's well-being as well as information on their household income. It is a cross-section database; hence, the information is not so useful to study how a person's well-being changes as a consequence of changes in her household income, but it is it useful to compare the well-being of high and low income people.

5.3.1 Which Income Proxy Should Be Used?

Do high-income people tend to report greater well-being? Table 5.1 presents the correlation between life satisfaction and income when four different measures of income are used: Household income, household per capita income, and their respective logarithm values. The information is useful to address an important question: Which income measure is more appropriate to study the relationship between income and well-being?

Table 5.1 Correlation coefficient life satisfaction and income. Different income measures, Mexico

Income measure	Coefficient
Household income	0.083
Logarithm of household income	0.183
Household per capita income	0.064
Logarithm of household per capita income	0.168

Source BIARE survey, 2014

It is observed that:

First, there is a positive correlation between income and life satisfaction, with the greatest coefficient value attained in the case of the logarithm of household income. It is important to be very precise on the interpretation of correlation coefficients from cross-section data; the positive coefficient means that high-income people tend to report, on average, greater life satisfaction than low-income people. However, the positive coefficient does not necessarily imply for life satisfaction to increase with a person's income. Furthermore, the estimated coefficient is not large—even for the greatest value of 0.18. Such a low coefficient implies that it would be highly risky—and very inexact—to attempt predicting a person's life satisfaction on the basis of her income alone. In other words, there may be low-income people with high life satisfaction as well as high-income people with low life satisfaction.

Second, the using of household income provides a correlation coefficient which is a little bit higher than the using of household per capita income. This finding suggests that there are substantial size economies at the household level; this implies that when the number of household members doubles an increase in income of less than 100% is required to keep the life satisfaction of household members constant. This is an important finding from the well-being literature which questions the using of household per capita income figures to approximate the deprivation situation in household. In fact, deprivation measures—such as poverty rates—computed on the basis of per capita income figures may provide an inaccurate depiction of the well-being situation at the household level; and their inaccuracy rate is larger for larger households (Rojas 2006, 2007, 2014). In a similar way, the existence of size economies at the household level do imply for per capita GDP figures to provide an inaccurate portray of the situation in countries, with the inaccuracy rate being larger for countries with larger families.

Table 5.2 presents information on correlation coefficients between experiences of

Table 5.2 Correlation income and experiences of being well, Mexico

Experience of being well	Correlation coefficient
Live evaluation	0.197
Positive affect	0.073
Negative affect	−0.049

Note Income measured as the logarithm of household income
Source BIARE survey, 2014

being well and the logarithm of household income. There is a relatively high correlation between income and life evaluation, and a much smaller correlation between income and positive affect as well as between income and negative affect. These correlations are consistent with general findings in the literature: the affective state is weakly associated to socio-economic factors and it depends on other drivers that are not related to socio-economic conditions. The evaluation of life is more dependent of social and economic conditions. In other words, income and other socio-economic conditions have a stronger impact on how people evaluate their life than on how they live their emotional life.

5.3.2 The Importance of Relative Income in Latin America

Do Latin Americans care about their relative income situation? Is it possible for a status-race treadmill to exist in such a way that greater income does not necessarily translate into greater well-being? Are relative income and the status race generalized phenomena or do they apply only to high income groups?

Rojas (2019c) studies the importance of relative effects in the relationship between income and life satisfaction in Latin America. He works with the Gallup World Poll 2007 and finds out that an increase of 100% in income would raise life satisfaction in 0.40 (in a scale from 0 to 10). However, a large part of this impact of income on life satisfaction emerges from the greater status people get when having more income; if the increase in income would be generalized—everybody having twice as much income as before then life satisfaction would increase only in 0.17 rather than in 0.40. This means that economic growth, which implies generalized increases in income across the population, is expected to have a small impact on life satisfaction. Furthermore, Rojas also studies the relationship between income and life evaluation; he finds out that person-isolated increases in income are associated to an increase in life evaluation of 0.44; however, generalized increases in income would have a negligible impact on life evaluation. This finding suggests that income—and the commodities people can purchase with it—basically play a status-marker role in the evaluation of own life. Rojas also finds out that the role of income as status-marker is similar for high and low-income people; hence, relative income is not a high-income group's phenomenon but a generalized one.

In another study Rojas (2019d) uses information from Mexico's Self-Reported Well-Being Survey (BIARE) to study the impact of durable-goods ownership on life satisfaction. The author finds out that most durable goods play a status-marker role and that their impact on life satisfaction takes place basically through the status they provide rather than through the comfort they bring; hence, generalized increases in availability of durable goods are associated with little increase in life satisfaction.

Hence, even though greater income may lead to some increases in well-being; it is observed that there is a status race which leads to treadmill effects so that the impact of greater income is large when it comes associated with greater social status, but it is small when there is no status gain.

5.4   Gross Domestic Product and Life Satisfaction

Gross Domestic Product per capita (GDPpc) figures in Latin America do not seem to be closely associated to life-satisfaction figures. The country-level correlation between GDPpc and life satisfaction—measured as the percentage of people who are very or fairly satisfied with life—in Latin America is 0.12 in 2017, which can be considered as low. The lack of association between the two indicators is observed in Table 5.3, which presents the ranking of countries on the basis of each indicator. Chile ranks at the top when considering its GDPpc; however, the country is ranked in the bottom levels when considering the life satisfaction of Chileans. Costa Rica, Colombia, Dominican Republic, Nicaragua, Honduras and Guatemala rank relatively high on the basis of their mean life satisfaction, outperforming their ranking according to the GDPpc indicator. Chile, Uruguay, Venezuela, and Peru have relatively low life-satisfaction positions in comparison to their GDPpc ranking.

Table 5.3 Ranking of Latin American countries. GDPpc and life satisfaction, 2017

Country	GDPpc ranking	Life satisfaction ranking
Chile	1	15
Panama	2	3
Uruguay	3	10
Argentina	4	6
Mexico	5	8
Venezuela	6	14
Costa Rica	7	1
Dominican Republic	8	4
Brazil	9	13
Colombia	10	2
Peru	11	18
Paraguay	12	16
Ecuador	13	11
Guatemala	14	5
El Salvador	15	12
Bolivia	16	17
Nicaragua	17	7
Honduras	18	9

Note Life satisfaction refers to the percentage of people who report being very and fairly satisfied with their life
Source World Bank Indicators for GDPpc and Latinobarometer for life satisfaction information

It could be argued that GDPpc is not a good indicator of the purchasing power of most Latin Americans because of high income inequality; this is true, but inequality is high in all Latin American countries. The role of income inequality will be discussed in the following chapter.

5.5 Economic Growth and Well-Being

The conceptualization of development as economic growth has made of the later the main objective of public policies and of development strategies. Higher rates of growth are considered desirable because they contribute to increase people's income. However, economic growth is a process that demands social and economic transformations, such as the design and implementation of reforms, the pursue of greater competitiveness and productivity, the destruction and creation of new activities, the mobilization of people, the shift to new production activities, changes in the labor regime, transformation of institutions, and so on. Rapid social change accompanies these processes of rapid economic transformations; some sociologists have argued that these times of social transformation—in particular accelerated ones—are accompanied of greater uncertainty; things are not as they used to be and people do not know what is expected from them and what they can expect in the future (Durkheim 1997; Merton 1938; Orrù 1987). In addition, there may be changes in the pace of life and in the aspirations people have. All these changes are not necessarily good for people's well-being (Genov 1998; Hirsch 1976; Huschka and Mau 2005). Also, there may be substantial environmental costs which GDP does not account for. In fact, there may be environmental limitations to economic growth.

Table 5.4 presents the correlation between the annual rate of growth of GDPpc and the country-level mean values for the experiences of being well in Latin America. The well-being information comes from the Gallup World Poll and the rate of economic growth is computed on the basis of GDPpc in constant dollars and adjusting for purchasing power parity.

It is observed in Table 5.4 that economic growth correlates negatively with life evaluation and with positive affect. The correlation with life evaluation is −0.12 and

Table 5.4 Correlation economic growth and experiences of being well. Latin America 2006–2016

Experience of being well	Correlation coefficient
Live evaluation	−0.115
Positive affect	−0.059
Negative affect	−0.009

Note Correlation between annual rate of growth of GDP per capita and year-to-year change in well-being experience during the period 2006–2016 in Latin American countries
Source Gallup World Poll 2006–2016 and World Bank Indicators

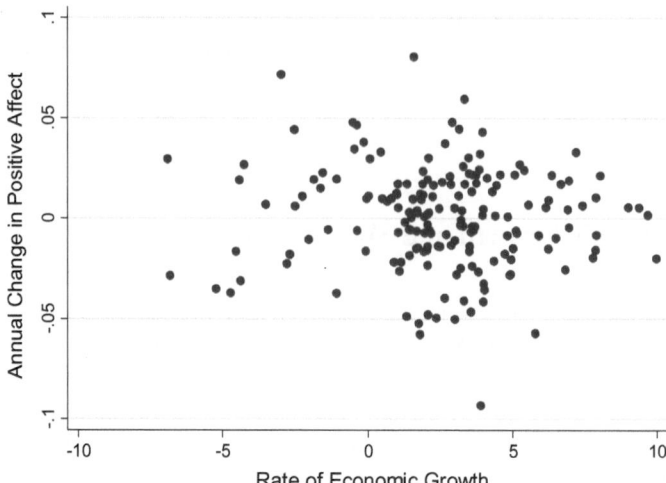

Fig. 5.2 Economic growth and change in positive affect. Latin American countries 2006–2016. *Source* Gallup World Poll and World Bank Indicators

the correlation with positive affect is −0.06; in addition, the correlation with negative affect is negligible. Hence, it seems that economic growth and the processes that generate it are not positively associated to well-being. Lora and Chaparro (2011) refer to this negative correlation between growth and well-being as the paradox of unhappy growth. This finding should worry economists and policy makers; in special because it has also been shown that attaining greater income is not a powerful instrument to increase people's well-being.

Figures 5.2, 5.3 and 5.4 present the dispersion of changes in experiences of being well across rates of economic growth in Latin American countries; it is observed that practically all cases are possible: High economic growth rates with increases in well-being, high economic growth rates with declines in well-being, negative growth rates with increases in well-being, and negative growth rates with declines in well-being. Further research is needed to identify and understand those cases where economic growth is pro-well-being as well as those cases where well-being increases even under situations of economic stagnation and recession. Important policy lessons could also be learned from those cases where growth is not associated to increases in well-being (Sarracino 2019).

5.6 General Policy Considerations

Income is a central variable in welfare economics; the idea that income is closely relation to people's well-being has justified the paradigm of development as economic growth. This chapter showed that the relationship between income and well-being

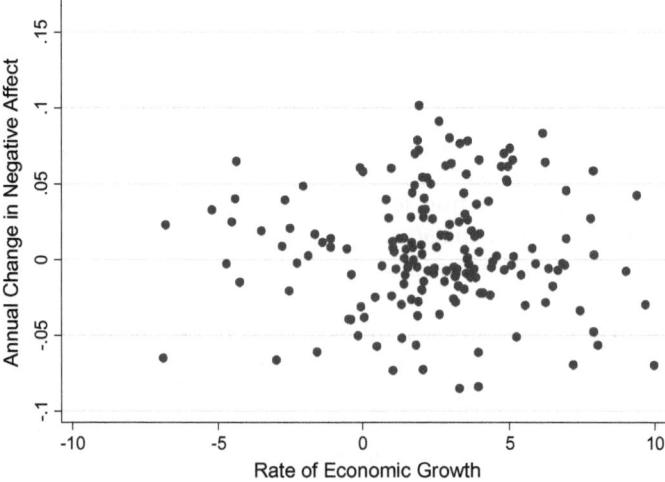

Fig. 5.3 Economic growth and change in negative affect. Latin American countries 2006–2016. *Source* Gallup World Poll and World Bank Indicators

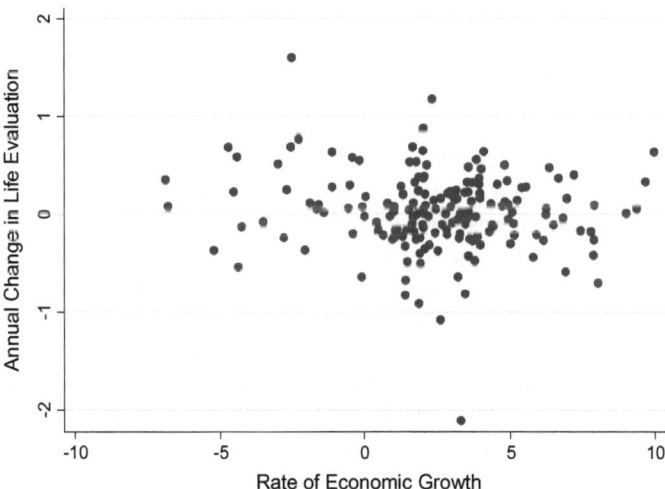

Fig. 5.4 Economic growth and change in life evaluation. Latin American countries 2006–2016. *Source* Gallup World Poll and World Bank Indicators

is neither simple nor straightforward; it also showed that economic growth is not necessarily associated to greater well-being.

Having more income does not necessarily translate into greater well-being. Social comparisons, increasing aspirations, and an inefficient using of additional money may imply for people to have greater income but not more well-being.

The focus on raising income may also lead to ignoring other sources of well-being. Policy makers would benefit from identifying and keeping track of the many drivers of well-being. Policies that aim at raising income could also have a negative impact on other drivers of well-being, so that countries may have more income but not more well-being.

It is important to recognize that different ways of promoting economic growth may have different well-being consequences. More research is needed to identify which ways may contribute to greater well-being. In any case, it is important to remember that economic growth is not a final end but a mere instrument to attain greater well-being. Not all processes leading to greater income are convenient from a well-being perspective; of course, environmental and sustainability considerations should also be taken into consideration.

It is also possible to think about non-material growth. In fact, there are many social paths where people and societies could grow and attain greater well-being and which are not related to increasing income. There may also be more well-being enhancing ways of using greater productivity and purchasing power.

Most Latin American countries already have mid per capita income levels. Societies should address the question of how much income is desirable and what kind of policies is convenient to attain it. It seems that the goal of attaining an ever increasing amount of income is not a good social objective because it does not ensure greater well-being. Should countries make of the attainment of high income levels a central aspiration? It seems convenient to expand the scope of intermediate goals in order to consider other instruments that may also contribute to greater well-being and which may have a lower cost to the planet.

The existence of a logarithmic relationship between income and well-being justifies the implementation of income redistribution policies. Additional income seems to make a larger well-being impact when channeled to low-income people rather than to high-income ones. This is common wisdom in economic theory which as always stressed the idea that there is a diminishing marginal utility of money; however, the argument is not so much stressed in policy making. The literature recommends distribution practices that target the mechanism intervening in the functional distribution of income, rather than distribution practices based on the simple idea of taking income from top deciles and giving it to the bottom ones.

Policy making should not be based on following a blind confidence on the role of income to increase people's well-being. Income is a potential instrument to increase well-being, but it is neither the only instrument nor the most efficient one; in any case, its importance needs to be corroborated rather than assumed.

References

DeLeire, T., & Kalil, A. (2010). Does consumption buy happiness? Evidence from the United States. *International Review of Economics, 57*(2), 163–176.

Dumludag, D. (2015). Consumption and life satisfaction at different levels of economic development. *International Review of Economics, 62*(2), 163–182.

Durkheim, E. (1997 [1893]). *The division of labor in society*. New York: Free Press.

Easterlin, R. (1974). Does economic growth improve the human lot? Some empirical evidence. In P. A. David & M. W. Reder (Eds.), *Nations and households in economic growth* (pp. 89–125). Academic Press.

Genov, N. (1998). Transformation and anomie: Problems of quality of life in Bulgaria. *Social Indicators Research, 43,* 197–209.

Germani, G. (1965). *Política y sociedad en una época de transición de la sociedad de masas*. Buenos Aires: Editorial Paidos.

Graham, C., & Pettinato, S. (2002). *Happiness and hardship: Opportunity and insecurity in new market economies*. Brookings.

Hirsch, F. (1976). *Social limits to growth*. Cambridge: Harvard University Press.

Huschka, D., & Mau, S. (2005). *Aspect of quality of life: Social anomie in South Africa*. Wissenschaftszentrum Berlin für Sozialforschung (WZB).

Linder, M. S. B. (1971). *The harried leisure class*. New York: Columbia University Press.

Lora, E., & Chaparro, J. C. (2011). *The conflictive relationship between satisfaction and income*. IDB Working paper No. 542.

Merton, R. K. (1938). Social structure and anomie. *American Psychological Review, 3,* 672–682.

Montero, R., & Rau, T, (2016). Relative income and job satisfaction in Chile. In M. Rojas (Ed.), *Handbook of happiness research in Latin America* (pp. 205–218). Berlin: Springer.

Okulicz-Kozaryn, A., Nash, T., & Tursi, N. O. (2015). Luxury car owners are not happier than frugal car owners. *International Review of Economics, 62*(2), 121–141.

Orrù, M. (1987). *Anomie: History and meanings*. Boston: Allen and Unwin.

Rojas, M. (2006). Communitarian versus individualistic arrangements in the family: What and whose income matters for happiness? In R. J. Estes (Ed.), *Advancing quality of life in a turbulent world* (pp. 153–167). Berlin: Springer.

Rojas, M. (2007). Estimating equivalence scales in Mexico: A subjective well-being approach. *Oxford Development Studies, 35*(3), 273–293.

Rojas, M. (2009). La Economía de la Felicidad: Hallazgos Relevantes sobre el Ingreso y el Bienestar. *El Trimestre Económico, LXXVI*(3), 303, 537–573.

Rojas, M. (2013). Estatus Económico y Situación Afectiva en América Latina. *Estudios Contemporâneos da Subjetividade (Contemporary Studies on Subjectivity), 3*(2), 202–218.

Rojas, M. (2014). Estimación de Escalas de Equivalencia en México: Un Enfoque de Bienestar Subjetivo. *Realidad, Datos y Espacio: Revista Internacional de Estadística y Geografía, 5*(3), 4–17.

Rojas, M. (2019a). The relevance of Richard Easterlin's groundbreaking work. A historical perspective. In M. Rojas (Ed.), *The economics of happiness: How the Easterlin Paradox transformed our understanding of wellbeing and progress*. Berlin: Springer (forthcoming).

Rojas, M. (Ed.). (2019b). *The economics of happiness: How the Easterlin Paradox transformed our understanding of wellbeing and progress*. Berlin: Springer.

Rojas, M. (2019c). Relative income and happiness in Latin America: Implications for inequality debates. In M. Rojas (Ed.), *The economics of happiness: How the Easterlin Paradox transformed our understanding of wellbeing and progress*. Berlin: Springer (forthcoming).

Rojas, M. (2019d). Affluence: More relative than absolute. In G. Brulé & C. Suter (Eds.), *Wealth(s) and subjective well-being* (pp. 147–165). Berlin: Springer.

Sarracino, F. (2019). When does economic growth improve well-being? In M. Rojas (Ed.), *The economics of happiness: How the Easterlin Paradox transformed our understanding of wellbeing and progress*. Berlin: Springer (forthcoming).

Stutzer, A. (2004). The role of income aspirations in individual happiness. *Journal of Economic Behavior & Organization, 54,* 89–109.

Sugden, R. (2005). Correspondence of sentiments: An explanation of the pleasure of social interaction. In L. Bruni & P. L. Porta (Eds.), *Economics and happiness: Framing the analysis* (pp. 91–115). Oxford: Oxford University Press.

van Praag, B. M. S., & Ferrer-I-Carbonell, A. (2004). *Happiness quantified: A satisfaction calculus approach.* Oxford: Oxford University Press.

Winkelmann, R. (2012). Conspicuous consumption and satisfaction. *Journal of Economic Psychology, 33,* 183–191.

Chapter 6
Income Inequality and Well-Being

Abstract Income is very unequally distributed in Latin America; in fact, the data shows that the region is the most unequal one in the world. There are different ways in which income inequality impacts on people's well-being. A gap in well-being is observed between the top and bottom income quintiles in most Latin American countries and this greater sense of unfairness in Latin America which reduces people's well-being. Other drivers of well-being do show a more egalitarian distribution across the Latin American population.

Keywords Well-being · Latin America · Income inequality · Unfairness · Income gap

6.1 High Income Inequality in Latin America

It is common to hear that the Latin American region is the most unequal in the world (Lustig 2012). When focusing on the distribution of income it is clear that the statement is correct. Table 6.1 presents the average Gini coefficient for the distribution of income across regions of the world; average values are computed on the basis of available information from 2000 to 2017. Income inequality is very high in Latin America; in fact, it is the only region in the world where the average Gini coefficient is above 0.50. Central Asia, Eastern Europe, and Western Europe and the Anglo-Saxon countries have mean Gini coefficients beneath 0.32.

There are huge income gaps in Latin America, with people in the top income decile enjoying a household per capita income which is as much as 36 times higher than that for those in the bottom income decile. Data presented in Fig. 6.1 shows that the gap is above 30 in Brazil, Panama, Colombia, Bolivia and Honduras. The gap is relatively small in El Salvador, Uruguay, Dominican Republic and Argentina.

Latin America may be the more unequal region in the world in terms of income; however, some progress in reducing income inequality has been made during the past decades (Gasparini and Lustig 2011; Puyana and Rojas 2019). Figure 6.2 shows the Gini coefficient for recent years—usually 2016 or 2017—and for early-2000 years. It is observed that the Gini coefficient is still very high in comparison to the rest of the world; however, it is important to recognize that some countries have made

© Springer Nature Switzerland AG 2020   71
M. Rojas, *Well-Being in Latin America*, Human Well-Being Research and Policy Making,
https://doi.org/10.1007/978-3-030-33498-7_6

Table 6.1 Gini coefficient in
the distribution of income, by
regions. Simple country-level
means, 2000–2017

Region	Gini coefficient
Latin America	0.507
Western Europe and Anglo-Saxon	0.316
Southeast Asia	0.381
Arab/Muslim	0.370
Sub-Saharan Africa	0.446
Caribbean	0.449
Central Asia	0.307
Eastern Europe	0.319
South Asia	0.355

Notes Simple country-level means by region; not weighted by
countries' population. Computed on the basis of available data
during the years 2000–2017
Regions of the world
See note to Table 4.1 for description of the regions
Source World Bank Indicators, 2000–2017

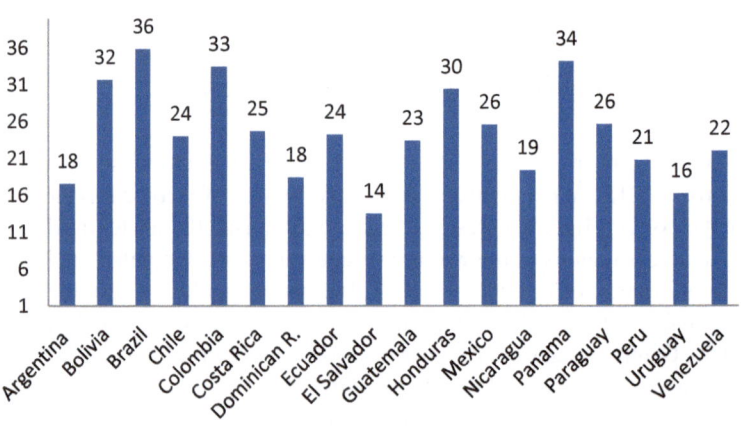

Income Gap
Decile 10 to Decile 1, Latin American countries

Fig. 6.1 Income gap, ratio between decile 10 and decile 1, Latin American Countries. Household
per capita income, recent data (2013–2016; except Venezuela—2006). *Source* CEDLAS

substantial progress in reducing income inequality. In particular, substantial declines
in the Gini coefficient are observed in Bolivia, El Salvador and Argentina, while the
decline is negligible in Venezuela and Costa Rica.

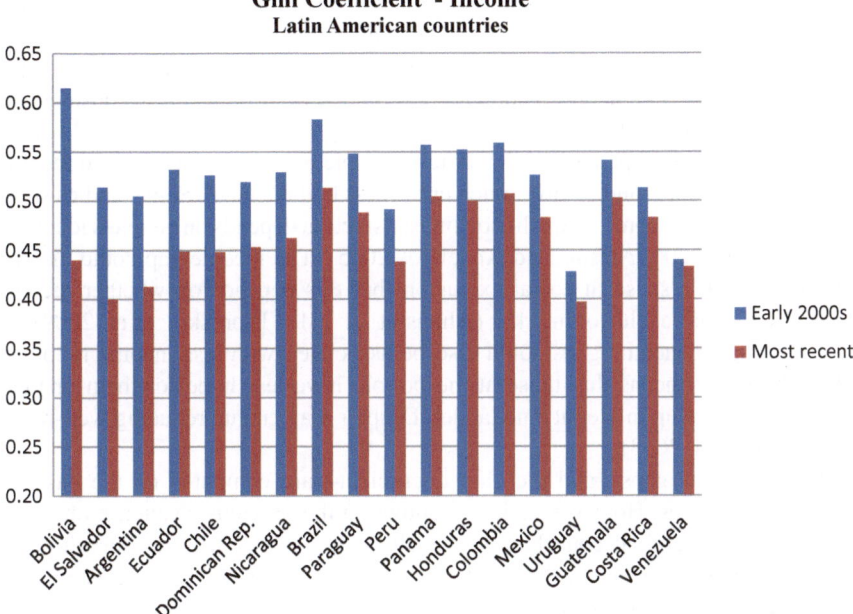

Fig. 6.2 Income distribution in Latin American countries: Gini coefficient. Computed by CED-LAS on the basis of household surveys. Distribution of household per capita income. Different methodologies are used in household surveys across countries and along years. Most recent figures correspond—in most cases—to 2017 and 2016

6.2 Income Inequality and Well-Being

From a well-being perspective income gaps and Gini coefficients are important due to many reasons:

First, the standard of living of the top deciles influences everybody's aspirations and could even determine the norms of evaluation used by the rest of the population, this is: the kind of life that people consider as the best possible one is influenced by the kind of life of those portrayed as the rich—and famous. Hence, a greater income gap may induce greater aspirations and could even raise the norms a person uses to evaluate her life. Raising norms and aspirations may end up reducing life evaluation and could even trigger negative affect in those who see their aspirational gap increasing. Of course, the relationship between the income gap and people's aspirations and norms of evaluation is not straightforward; people's values regarding the role of material success and the importance they give to income and consumption in the determination of social status mediate the relationship between the income gap and aspirations. In addition, social segmentation may reduce the possibilities for comparisons across bottom to top income deciles, while exposure to social networks and different media sources may induce cross-decile and even cross-country comparisons (Berg and Veenhoven 2010; Clark and D'Ambrosio 2015; Graham and Felton 2006; Kelley and Evans 2017; Oishi et al. 2011).

Second, income inequality is usually associated to concepts of fairness and social exclusion. The greater income inequality is the more likely for people to consider it as unfair, and the more unfair people think their society is the less satisfied with life they are. Of course, this depends on what criteria people use to consider a given income distribution as unfair and on how much unfairness bothers them. Some studies show that the impact of income inequality on life satisfaction depends on people's ideology (Alesina et al. 2004; Alesina and Angeletos 2005). The income gap could also be correlated with a sense of social exclusion; but this depends on whether income becomes a social-exclusion marker (Almås et al. 2010; Bjørnskov et al. 2009). In addition, higher income gaps could also be associated with less income mobility, which basically means that those at the bottom have less hope for them or their children to move up in the income ladder. Despair may end up reducing well-being (Bjørnskov et al. 2013).

Third, income gaps—and the Gini coefficient—are computed on the basis of raw income figures. However, as it was shown in the previous chapter, money has a diminishing marginal contribution to well-being—this is why the logarithm of income provides a better fit than that of raw income in explaining well-being. In consequence, income gaps and Gini coefficients computed on the basis of raw income could overstate the inequality in the distribution of well-being. In addition, it is important to remember that there is more to life than income and that a very high income inequality does not necessarily translates into high inequality in other drivers of well-being.

6.3   Income Inequality and Well-Being in Latin America

6.3.1   Well-Being by Income Quintiles

Table 6.2 presents information on the income gap as well as on the gap in life evaluation, positive affect, and negative affect across Latin American countries. The gap refers to the ratio of the situation of income quintile 5 to income quintile 1 and it is computed on the basis of information from the Gallup World Poll 2016. Because income is positively associated to well-being experiences in cross-section data then one expects people in the top income quintile (quintile 5) to enjoy higher well-being (greater life evaluation, more positive affect and less negative affect) than people in income quintile 1; however, it is useful to study how the well-being gap behaves across Latin American countries.

It is observed in Table 6.2 that:

First, the income gap between quintile 5 and quintile 1 is relatively high in Colombia, Chile, Argentina and Panama. The average income gap for Latin American countries is 29, while the gap in these countries is 42. On the other hand, the gap

Table 6.2 Income and well-being gaps in Latin America. Income quintile 5 to income quintile 1, 2016

Country	Income gap	Life evaluation gap	Positive affect gap	Negative affect gap
Argentina	37.9	1.11	1.20	0.59
Bolivia	22.4	1.25	1.16	0.71
Brazil	24.9	1.21	1.10	0.70
Chile	45.3	1.12	1.10	0.80
Colombia	47.8	1.37	1.08	0.63
Costa Rica	35.7	1.07	1.09	0.74
Dominican Rep.	21.8	1.39	1.11	0.71
Ecuador	18.8	1.17	1.16	0.74
El Salvador	22.5	1.05	1.03	0.84
Guatemala	26.3	1.04	1.09	0.75
Honduras	28.3	1.32	1.14	0.72
Mexico	20.8	1.11	1.19	0.66
Nicaragua	16.7	1.19	1.07	0.77
Panama	36.5	1.30	1.10	0.69
Paraguay	27.2	1.38	1.08	0.79
Peru	22.3	1.26	1.12	0.79
Uruguay	32.4	1.12	1.14	0.76
Venezuela	31.2	1.02	1.03	1.13
Country-mean Latin America	28.8	1.19	1.11	0.75

Income gap computed on the basis of household per capita income
Source Gallup World Poll 2016

is relatively low in Nicaragua, Ecuador, Mexico and Dominican Republic, with an average gap in these countries of 20.

Second, the income gap is very large in comparison to the gaps in well-being experiences. While the average income gap in Latin American countries is 29—the highest income quintile has 29 times the income of the lowest income quintile—the average life evaluation gap is only 1.19, the positive affect gap is 1.11 and the negative affect gap is 0.75. This is a very important feature which shows that focusing on gaps computed on the basis of raw-income figures tends to magnify the well-being disparities in the region. Income is not a good proxy for well-being and the income gap is not a good proxy for well-being disparities. Some of the reasons already mentioned are at play: Income has diminishing returns on people's well-being, and well-being depends on many other drivers beyond income which may be more equally distributed across the population.

Third, huge gaps in life evaluation are observed in Dominican Republic, Paraguay and Colombia. Colombia has a very large income gap that corresponds to this high life-evaluation gap between quintile 5 and quintile1; however, Dominican Republic and Paraguay have below average income gaps. Chile, which is a country with a large income gap, has a relatively small life-evaluation gap. On the other hand, very small life-evaluation gaps are observed in Venezuela, Guatemala, El Salvador and Costa Rica. It could be stated that in these countries money does not seem to 'buy' life evaluation and that top and bottom income quintiles may have similar assessments of how good their life is. Of course, there may be different explanations for this situation; for example: (a) The existence of a good and universal welfare system so that income disparities make no difference in the access to good education and health services. (b) It could be that there are different norms of evaluation within the country and that these norms are correlated to income; this could happen when nations with different values and standards of evaluation coexist in the same country and where segmentation across nations is strong. (c) There could be other drivers which are also correlated to income.

It is interesting to compare the cases of Costa Rica and Venezuela on this regard: In the case of Costa Rica the difference in life evaluation between income quintile 1 and income quintile 5 is just 7%; this happens because the bottom quintile has a very high life evaluation (6.9 in Costa Rica vs. 5.5 as an average in Latin American countries). In the case of Venezuela the difference in life evaluation between quintile 1 and quintile 5 is just 2%; this happens because the top quintile has a very low life evaluation (4.6 in Venezuela vs. 6.5 as an average in Latin American countries). Egalitarianism in life evaluation may take place as a consequence of leveling up or of leveling down processes.

Fourth, it is observed in Table 6.2 that the negative-affect gap is much larger than the life-evaluation and positive-affect gaps. It seems that the income gap has an asymmetric association with the affective state, showing up strongly in the negative affect; in other words, being at the bottom of the income distribution is associated with experiencing much more negative affect than being at the top.

The negative-affect gap is large in Argentina, Colombia and Mexico, where people in the highest income quintile experience, on average, about 60% of the negative affect experienced by people in the bottom quintile. The negative-affect gap is relatively small in Peru and El Salvador (where the top and bottom quintiles have levels above Latin America's average and where a 'leveling down' effect exists), and in Paraguay and Chile (where the top and bottom quintiles have levels below Latin America's average and there is a 'leveling up' effect).

The case of Venezuela is peculiar and even surprising, people in the top income quintile experience more negative affect than people in the bottom income quintile. It is the only country in Latin America with this peculiar behavior. Quintile 1 shows a negative-affect value of 0.38, which is very similar to the average for Latin America (0.39); hence, the peculiar feature emerges from the abnormal situation of people in the top quintile, where the negative-affect value is 0.43, which is very high in comparison to the average for the high-income quintile in Latin America (0.29). This is clearly a leveling-down situation which has gone to the extreme.

Fifth, the gap in positive-affect is relatively small in Latin America and it does not seem to be associated at all with the income gap. The positive-affect gap is high in Argentina, Mexico, Ecuador and Bolivia. Ecuador has a very large income gap, but the other countries have income gaps that are about average for Latin America. Very low positive affect gaps are observed in El Salvador, Venezuela, and Nicaragua. Once more, Venezuela reflects a leveling-down situation where the positive affect in quintile 1 is similar to the Latin American average for quintile 1, but where the positive affect of quintile 5 is much below the Latin American average for quintile 5. In general, it seems that the distribution of positive affect across the population is only very weakly associated to the distribution of income; which suggests that other drivers may be more relevant in explaining the distribution of positive affect.

6.3.2 The Atypical Venezuelan Case

The recent trends in Venezuela portrait a situation where well-being and well-being inequality are declining in what could be considered as a leveling-down process. People in the top and bottom income quintiles report substantial decline in life evaluation (Fig. 6.3), a reduction in the experience of positive affect (Fig. 6.4) and a huge increase in negative affect (Fig. 6.5). In addition, there is a reduction in the well-being gaps between the top and bottom income quintiles.

It is also interesting to see the behavior of the well-being indicators by income quintile in the year 2013; President Hugo Chavez died on March 2013 and in such a politically polarized society interesting differences in the well-being trends are observed for people in income quintile 1 and income quintile 5; this shows the importance than some political factors may have as drivers of well being for particular groups in society.

Fig. 6.3 Life evaluation in Venezuela, by income quintile 2009–2016. *Source* Gallup World Poll 2009–2016

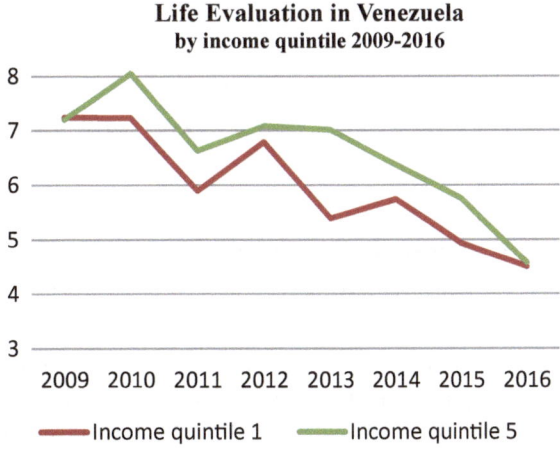

Fig. 6.4 Positive affect in Venezuela, by income quintile 2009–2016. *Source* Gallup World Poll 2009–2016

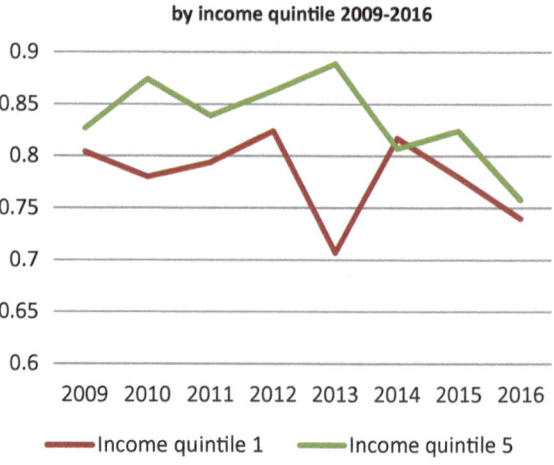

Fig. 6.5 Negative affect in Venezuela, by income quintile 2009–2016. *Source* Gallup World Poll 2009–2016

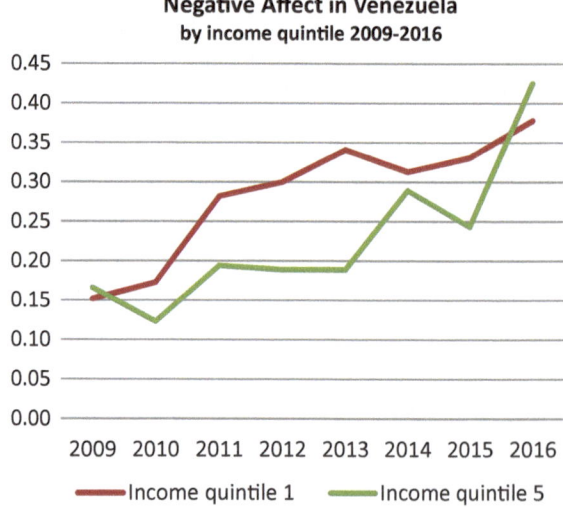

6.3.3   Sense of Unfairness in the Distribution of Income and Well-Being

Latin America is the more unequal region in the world; Latin Americans do also report high well-being levels. Does it mean that Latin Americans do not care about their income distribution? Data from the Latinobarometer 2016 allows exploring the opinion Latin Americans have regarding the fairness in their distribution of income. About 78% of the population in Latin America considers that the distribution of

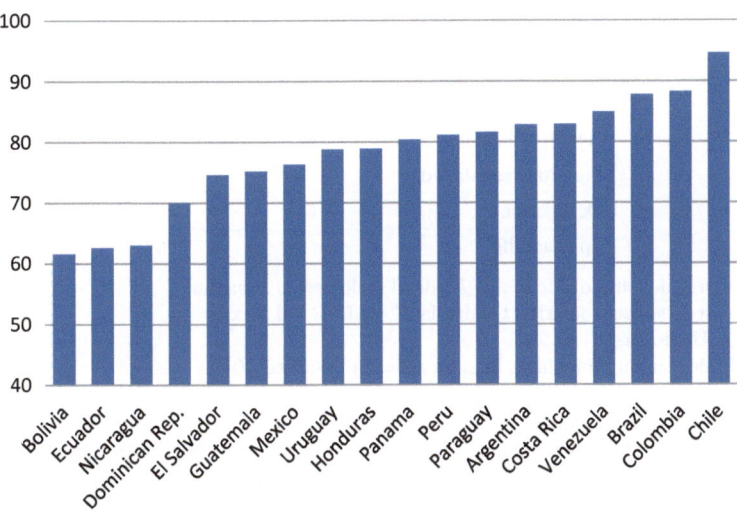

Fig. 6.6 Unfairness in the distribution of income; percentage who consider the distribution to be unfair or very unfair, Latin American countries 2016. *Source* Latinobarometer 2016

income is unfair or very unfair in their country; with values as high as 95% in Chile, and with the lowest value being about 62% in Bolivia and Ecuador (see Fig. 6.6).

There seems to be extensive recognition that the distribution of income is unfair. This sense of unfairness in the distribution of income is also associated to lower life satisfaction; 84% of those who believe the distribution of income is fair or very fair are satisfied with their lives (in the categories of very or fairly satisfied). This figure is 72% for those who believe the distribution of income is unfair or very unfair.

6.4 Egalitarianism in the Distribution of Other Well-Being Drivers

Income is unequally distributed in Latin America and most Latin Americans consider their country's distribution of income as unfair. There is also evidence that the greater the sense of unfairness the lower the life satisfaction. However, well-being is not as unequally distributed as income. Some possible explanations have already been advanced, such as the diminishing well-being returns from income and the existence of different values within a given society. Another potential explanation is for other drivers of well-being to be much more equally distributed than income. Table 6.3

Table 6.3 Distribution of well-being, income and satisfaction in domains of life, by income quintile, some Latin American countries, 2018

		Quintile 1	Quintile 5
Income	Household per capita income, per month	49.8	1013
Domains of life	Family satisfaction	5.75	5.88
	Economic satisfaction	4.89	5.41
	Health satisfaction	5.33	5.67
	Free-time satisfaction	5.26	5.49
	Occupation	5.56	5.85
	Spiritual life	5.61	5.82

Satisfaction in domains of life in a 1–7 ordinal scale treated as cardinal
Three Latin American countries: Colombia, Costa Rica and Mexico
Income in US dollars
Source Understanding Happiness in Latin America Database, 2018

presents figures on satisfaction in domains of life for people in income quintiles 1 and 5. It is observed that there is almost no difference in family satisfaction across quintiles. As a matter of fact, it can be stated that there is an almost egalitarian distribution of family satisfaction across the population; family satisfaction is a major driver of people's well-being in Latin America (see Chap. 8 for further study of this topic). It is also observed in Table 6.3 that there are no substantial gaps in satisfaction in other domains of life between quintile 1 and 5; the largest difference takes place in the economic domain, a result that is expected because economic satisfaction is associated to household income.

The Understanding Happiness in Latin America database contains information on well-being, income, and satisfaction in domains of life for three Latin American countries (Colombia, Costa Rica, and Mexico). Income is expressed in monetary terms and the Gini coefficient to measure its distribution can be computed without any problem. Well-being indicators and satisfaction in domains of life are measured in ordinal scales; however, just for the purpose of illustration these variables can be considered as cardinal and a Gini coefficient for their distribution could be computed. It is important to remark that the computation of these Gini coefficients has an illustration purpose and that it is beyond the scope of this book to address methodological issues in the estimation of Gini coefficients from ordinal variables. Table 6.4 presents the estimated Gini coefficients; on the basis of this simple exercise it is observed that the distribution of life satisfaction and well-being experiences as well as of satisfaction in domains of life is more egalitarian than the distribution of income. Hence, other drivers of well-being are not as unequally distributed as income is.

Table 6.4 Gini coefficient for well-being, income and satisfaction in domains of life. Some Latin American countries, 2018

		Gini coefficient
Well-being	Life satisfaction	0.082
	Life evaluation	0.130
	Positive affect	0.084
	Negative affect	0.149
Income	Household per capita income, per month	0.512
Domains of life	Family satisfaction	0.071
	Economic satisfaction	0.218
	Health satisfaction	0.234
	Free-time satisfaction	0.238
	Occupation	0.208
	Spiritual life	0.227

Life satisfaction and satisfaction in domains of life in a 1–7 ordinal scale treated as cardinal; Positive and Negative affect in a 1–3 ordinal scale treated as cardinal; Life evaluation in a 1–10 scale
Three Latin American countries: Colombia, Costa Rica and Mexico
Income in US dollars
Source Understanding Happiness in Latin America Database, 2018

6.5 General Policy Considerations

The distribution of income is very unequal in Latin America and this may have a negative impact on people's well-being through different processes such as social exclusion, sense of unfairness, and raising material aspirations for the bottom quintiles. Most people in Latin America believe that the distribution of income is unfair, and this has an impact on well-being. Income inequality seems to have a larger impact on negative affect and an impact on life evaluation; however, the impact on positive affect is negligible.

The distribution of well-being in Latin America is not as unequally distributed as income figures would suggest. There are many reasons explaining the more egalitarian distribution of well-being. First, the distribution of income is computed on the basis of raw income figures; however, income shows diminishing well-being returns. Hence, even if income were the only explanatory variable of well-being it would be necessary to approximate the distribution of well-being on the basis of an income transformation—such as the logarithm of income. Second, in many Latin American countries income is just one of the drivers of well-being and not necessarily the most important one; thus, a very unequal distribution of income does not necessarily translate into a very unequal distribution of well-being. Third, other important drivers of well-being in Latin America show a more egalitarian distribution; such is the case, for example, with the distribution of satisfaction in the family domain of life.

A more egalitarian distribution of income could contribute to level up the distribution of well-being; this is: to raise the well-being of the bottom income deciles. However, a focus on income alone would distract policy makers from other important drivers of well-being whose distribution should not be neglected.

References

Alesina, A., & Angeletos, G. M. (2005). Fairness and redistribution. *American Economic Review, 95*(4), 960–980.

Alesina, A., Di Tella, R., & MacCulloch, R. (2004). Inequality and happiness: Are Europeans and Americans different? *Journal of Public Economics, 88*(9–10), 2009–2042.

Almås, I., Cappelen, A. W., Sørensen, E. Ø., & Tungodden, B. (2010). Fairness and the development of inequality acceptance. *Science, 328*(5982), 1176–1178.

Berg, M., & Veenhoven, R. (2010). Income inequality and happiness in 119 nations: In search for an optimum that does not appear to exist. In *Happiness and social policy in Europe*. Edward Elgar Publishing.

Bjørnskov, C., Dreher, A., Fischer, J. A. V., & Schnellenbach, J. (2009). *On the relation between income inequality and happiness: Do fairness perceptions matter?* Working papers from chair for economic policy, 27, University of Hamburg.

Bjørnskov, C., Dreher, A., Fischer, J. A. V., Schnellenbach, J., & Gehring, K. (2013). Inequality and happiness: When perceived social mobility and economic reality do not match. *Journal of Economic Behavior & Organization, 91*, 75–92.

Clark, A. E., & D'Ambrosio, C. (2015). Attitudes to income inequality. In *Handbook of income distribution* (vol. 2, pp. 1147–1208). Amsterdam: Elsevier.

Gasparini, L., & Lustig, N. (2011). The rise and fall of income inequality in Latin America. In J. A. Ocampo & J. Ros (Eds.), *The Oxford handbook of Latin American economics*. Oxford: Oxford University Press.

Graham, C., & Felton, A. (2006). Inequality and happiness: Insights from Latin America. *The Journal of Economic Inequality, 4*(1), 107–122.

Kelley, J., & Evans, M. D. R. (2017). Societal inequality and individual subjective well-being: Results from 68 societies and over 200,000 individuals, 1981–2008. *Social Science Research, 62*, 1–23.

Lustig, N. (2012). Desigualdad y pobreza en América Latina. In M. Puchet, M. Rojas, R. Salazar, G. Valenti, & F. Valdés (Eds.), *América Latina en los Albores del Siglo XXI*. FLACSO-México.

Oishi, S., Kesebir, S., & Diener, E. (2011). Income inequality and happiness. *Psychological Science, 22*(9), 1095–1100.

Puyana, A., & Rojas, M. (Eds.). (2019). *Desigualdad y Deterioro Laboral: ¿Es Posible Romper el Círculo?* FLACSO-México.

Chapter 7
Income Poverty and Well-Being

Abstract High income inequality in Latin America translates into high poverty rates in many countries. Those in income poverty report lower well-being; however, the well-being impact of income poverty is not generalized across domains of life. Satisfaction in some important domains of life, such as the family and the affective ones, are not affected by people's material condition, and this implies for a not so strong association between income poverty and well-being deprivation. Thus, it is important for policy makers to expand their perspective in order to go beyond the limited income-poverty conception and incorporate other well-being considerations in poverty-abatement programs.

Keywords Latin America · Well-being · Poverty · Domains of life · Well-being deprivation

Poverty is a very old concept and its conception changes over time and across regions. In general terms, the concept makes reference to a situation where well-being is low or lacking at all; hence, poverty is a concept which is highly dependent on the well-being one.

During the past decades the concept of poverty acquired greater relevance as an indicator to assess social performance and policy success. The Millennium Development Goals and, more recently, the Sustainable Development Goals made of poverty reduction a central aim of international organizations and governments. In fact, governments and international organizations need to assess their success on the basis of the achievement of some goals which are considered valuable, and economic growth and the abatement of poverty have become the most frequently used standards. The failure or success of administrations is usually assessed on the rates of growth and on the reduction of poverty during the administration's period. It is common for the poverty-abatement objective to go hand in hand with the economic growth one; as a matter of fact, both goals are closely associated because they are conceptually based on the same postulate: the high importance that is attributed to income as a well-being driver. Hence it is not surprising at all that during the past decades poverty has been mostly understood as lack of income or as low income; some variations—such as multidimensional poverty—have being introduced, but they are still highly dependent on income.

M. Rojas, *Well-Being in Latin America*, Human Well-Being Research and Policy Making, https://doi.org/10.1007/978-3-030-33498-7_7

The setting of specific poverty-reduction goals by the Development Goals' initiatives made it necessary to define specific and universal measures on the basis of available information in order to keep track of the evolution of poverty rates and to declare the success or failure of the initiatives. Therefore, it became customary to conceptualize poverty on the basis of its measurement rather than to measure it on the basis of its conceptualization; for many policy-makers, politicians, economists and students poverty was associated to having a household per capita income per day beneath a given and externally-defined income threshold. Similarly, success in the abatement of poverty basically means that household income jumps over the income-poverty line.

This chapter studies how the income-based understanding of poverty relates with people's well-being. It was shown in Chap. 5 that the relationship between income and people's experience of being well is not straightforward; hence, it should not come as a surprise that an income-based conception of poverty is very limited to approximate well-being deprivation.

7.1 Income Poverty in Latin America

Latin America is, on average, a mid-income region, but the distribution of income is very unequal. Hence, on one hand, per capita income levels would imply a very small proportion of the population beneath the poverty line; on the other hand, high income inequality implies for large segments of the population to end up having low income and being classified as poor. The classification of people as poor on the basis of a definition that relies on household per capita income implies that the greater income inequality is—given a per capita income—and the lower the country's per capita income is—given an inequality coefficient—the larger poverty rate is. Hence, countries with a very unequal distribution of income and with low per capita income levels are expected to have larger rates of poverty.

Figure 7.1 provides poverty rates for Latin American countries on the basis of different poverty lines. If an 'extreme-poverty' line of US 1.9 dollars of daily household per capita income is used it is found that poverty rates are extremely low in Latin America, with the highest rates observed in Honduras (16%), Guatemala (9%) and Bolivia (6%). However, when a 'moderate-poverty' line of US 5.5 dollars is used it is found that there is an average increase of almost 20 percentage points in the rate of poverty in the region. With such a moderate-poverty line about half of the population in Honduras and Guatemala are classified as poor, and only Uruguay, Chile, Argentina and Costa Rica would have poverty rates beneath 10%. Of course, these figures are based on a universal income-poverty line that adjusts for the purchasing power parity of local currency; official poverty figures usually follow different criteria and may differ from this universal one.

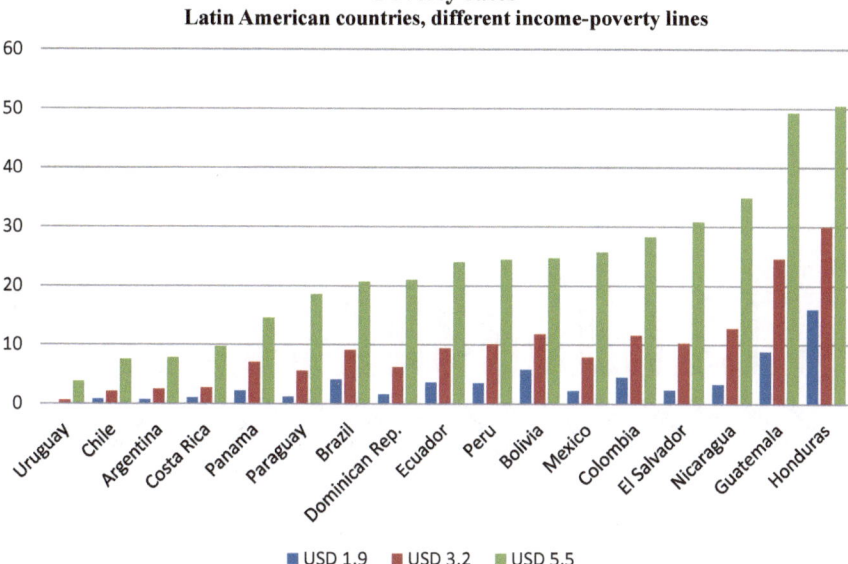

Fig. 7.1 Poverty rates in Latin American countries. Individual estimates of headcount ratio on the basis of three income-poverty lines at USD 1.9, USD 3.2, and USD 5.5 household per capita income per day. Lines defined in dollars of 2011 and adjusted by purchasing power parity. Most recent figures correspond to years 2015–2017, except for Guatemala (2014), Nicaragua (2014), and Panama (2014). Figures computed by CEDLAS on the basis of Household Surveys. Different methodologies are used in household surveys across countries and along years

Hence, it is safe to state that only a very small proportion of the Latin American population are facing severe material deprivation, but that in some countries important segments of the population are not in a situation of material comfort.

A positive trend in the reduction of poverty is also observed in Latin America. Figure 7.2 presents poverty rates in the early 2000s and in recent years (mostly 2016 or 2017); in all countries—with the exception of Guatemala—the percentage of people beneath the US$3.2 dollars of household per capita income per day has substantially decreased. Considerable declines are observed in Uruguay, Argentina, Chile and Costa Rica; with current poverty figures being 25% or less of previous figures. In all other countries, with the exception of Guatemala and Honduras, current poverty figures are 50% or less of previous ones.

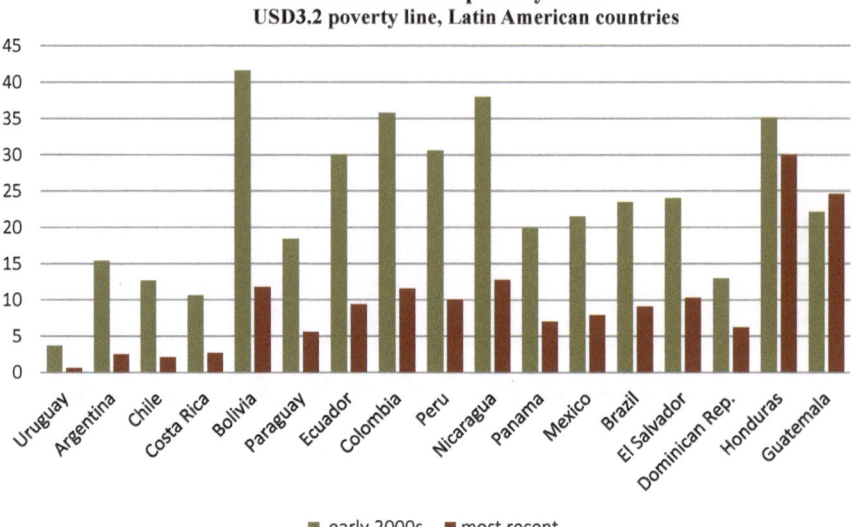

Fig. 7.2 Poverty rates in Latin American countries. Individual estimates of headcount ratio on the basis of an income-poverty line defined at USD 3.2 household per capita income per day. Lines defined in dollars of 2011 and adjusted by purchasing power parity. Most recent figures correspond to years 2015–2017 except for Guatemala (2014), Nicaragua (2014), and Panama (2014). Early figures correspond to years 2000–2001 except for Uruguay (2006). Figures computed by CEDLAS on the basis of Household Surveys. Different methodologies are used in household surveys across countries and along years

7.2   Poverty and Well-Being

7.2.1   Income Poverty and Well-Being

People's experiences of being well do depend on many factors and conditions; income is just one of the many variables that could be relevant. From a well-being perspective the exclusive focus on an income-based poverty conception is not justified; income is an important factor, but it is not the only one and it is not necessarily the most important one for everybody. Poverty studies have associated low income with deprivation and with low well-being; however, there are many reasons for a strong association between income poverty and well-being not to be expected (Rojas 2015a).

First, not everything of value can be purchased. Income allows for buying economic goods, but it has little impact on a person's access to non-economic goods. Some literature states that relational goods (the goods that are obtained through genuine and gratifying human relations, such as: love, emotional support, friendship, correspondence of sentiments, good relations with neighbors and colleagues, and so on) have a large impact on well-being (Bruni and Stanca 2005; Gui and Sugden 2005; Rojas 2012; Sugden 2005). In an empirical study based on a survey applied in central

Mexico, Rojas (2007a) shows that 'satisfaction with partner, children and family' is crucial for life satisfaction; similar results are obtained by other researchers in Latin America (Martínez and Castillo 2016; Mochón and de Juan Díaz 2016; Velásquez 2016). Because of their nature, relational goods cannot be traded nor purchased. The production of relational goods is time intensive because creating and sustaining genuine and gratifying relations takes time rather than money.

Second, spending more does not necessarily imply enjoying more. An increase in income may lead to little or no increase in well-being if it is not spent efficiently. Some research questions people's rationality as well as their ability to correctly foresee the well-being impact of their consumption decisions (Hsee and Hastie 2006; Scitovsky 1976; Thaler 1992, 2000; Tversky and Kahneman 1981, 1986). Rojas (2008b) found that most people do not use their purchasing power efficiently so that they end up getting less economic satisfaction than what is possible for their income. In addition, the well-being benefits from additional income do depend on how it is spent. It could be that satisfying some additional wants and desires has little impact on a person's well-being, even if income is used efficiently. Hence, it could happen that an increase in income does not have a strong impact on people's well-being because the satisfaction of some needs and wants is of little relevance in explaining people's well-being.

Third, there are some basic needs that cannot be satisfied with income. Psychologists argue that not all needs are material; some basic psychological needs—such as autonomy, competence and relatedness—can be considered as basic in the sense that those persons who are unable of satisfying them experience low well-being even if their basic material needs are being satisfied (Kasser 2002; Ryan and Sapp 2007). Psychologists argue that income makes little contribution to the satisfaction of psychological needs.

Fourth, income is not the only source of well-being. The domains-of-life literature states that a person's well-being depends on her satisfaction in many domains where she is performing as a human being (Cummins 1996; van Praag et al. 2003; Rojas 2006a, 2007a). Satisfaction in the domains of life depends on many factors beyond a person's income.

Sixth, there are many methodological issues in the measurement of income poverty that introduce noise to any potential relationship between poverty and well-being. For example: the definition of the poverty line requires some arbitrary decisions regarding the set of satisfactors under consideration; the estimation of the cost of purchasing these satisfactors also implies some arbitrary assumptions; household income needs to be converted into person-equivalent income and this requires further arbitrary assumptions; many assumptions need to be made regarding the handling of in-kind income, self-produced commodities, access to public services, and so on (Rojas 2006b, 2007b). It is also necessary to establish distinctions between transient and chronic poverty.

7.2.2   The Abatement of Income Poverty: Conditional Cash Transfer Programs

Focalized poverty-abatement programs acquired relevance in many Latin American countries during the 1980s and 1990s as a consequence of the implementation of pro-market reforms inspired by the so-called Washington Consensus (Rojas 2015b). The new narrative emphasized productivity, competitiveness, efficiency in the allocation of resources, adoption of international prices, openness, removal of market distortions and State intervention, and reduction of the size and scope of governments. The Consensus implied a separation of economic and social policy. Economic policies were designed to promote economic growth which required a market allocation of resources, with no government-induced distortions; in consequence, social policy should not be based on universal State-driven policies which could introduce distortions to the market system. The Washington Consensus found in conditional cash transfers a way of designing social policies which did not introduce distortions to the efficient allocation of resources and which, on the contrary, reinforced the pro-growth and pro-market policies. Focalized policies to abate poverty by increasing human capital emerged everywhere in Latin America; they implied new requirements: First, to identify those who would become the beneficiaries of specific social programs. Hence, the identification of beneficiaries became an important area of policy action; different methodologies and many indices were constructed to measure poverty and to 'identify the poor'. Unfortunately, this approach implied for poverty to end up being conceived in terms of its measurement, rather than being measured on the basis of its conception. Second, focalized programs were privileged in order to introduce no distortions to the market system. Thus, specific cash transfers to those identified as 'poor'—rather than universal policies benefiting everybody in society, but which could introduce market distortions—were widely implemented in Latin American countries. Third, cash transfers were given on a conditional basis in order to reinforce the pro-growth objective of pro-market reforms: the beneficiaries had to undertake actions to enhance their human capital. In particular, parents were required to undertake actions to increase their children's health and education. Thus, conditional cash transfer programs emerged almost everywhere in the Latin American region; in addition, classifying people as poor became a major occupation for many economists, and being poor or not depended on the classification criteria proposed by experts rather than on the experience of low well-being people had.

Conditional Cash Transfer (CCT) programs are based on the idea of influencing household behavior so that intra-household decisions lead to an increase in people's capacity to generate income. Within this approach education and health are considered key components of people's human capital and they are valued for their contribution to people's productivity. Thus, transfers are offered on the condition of families fostering the education and health of children; these actions are expected to break up the vicious cycle of income poverty. The vicious cycle of poverty states that children who grow up in low income families are more likely of having a lower capacity of generating income in the future; in consequence, income poverty tends to reproduce over time. CCT programs provide monetary transfers which, by themselves, contribute to increase household income; in addition, by conditioning the transfer to decisions that foster human-capital development, the programs also aspire to get people out of income poverty.

CCT programs must first establish an eligibility criteria; which defines the population that will receive the transfers from the program. Common criteria refer to persons with household (or household per capita) income beneath a given threshold, as well as persons living in communities where per capita income is low. CCT programs must also establish a behavioral conditionality to those persons who become beneficiaries of the program. Households are required to undertake specific actions, mostly in terms of their children attending school and regularly visiting health and nutritional centers.

The evaluation of CCT programs has also acquired great relevance (Rawlings and Rubio 2004). There are ex-post evaluations that compare the beneficiaries' performance with respect to control groups. Matching techniques are used to assess the programs' impact on income, school attendance, weight and height gain, incorporation into labor markets and so on. This poverty-abatement and social programs have no well-being inspiration; they are clearly inspired by the desire of raising income and contributing to economic growth. They have been designed under the assumption that raising income suffices to increase people's well-being; in addition, their evaluation is made in terms of income: the program is considered as successful if households are able of jumping over the externally-defined poverty line.

7.3 Poverty and Well-Being in Latin America

Poverty is basically defined in terms of low income; other definitions such as multidimensional poverty and asset poverty are also highly related to income. Because there is a relationship between income and well-being then a relationship between poverty and well-being is expected; however, because the relationship between income and well-being is not strong then it is also expected for poverty not to be strongly related to well-being.

7.3.1 Well-Being by Poverty Classification

Figure 7.3 presents the well-being situation for people classified in extreme, moderate, and non-poor situations on the basis of their household per capita income. The information comes from Mexico's BIARE survey, which gathers information on people's well-being. As expected, the non-poor are, on average, more satisfied with life and do also tend to evaluate their life in a much better way than the moderate and extreme poor. In a similar way, the non-poor enjoy a better affective situation, experiencing more positive affect and less negative affect than those in moderate

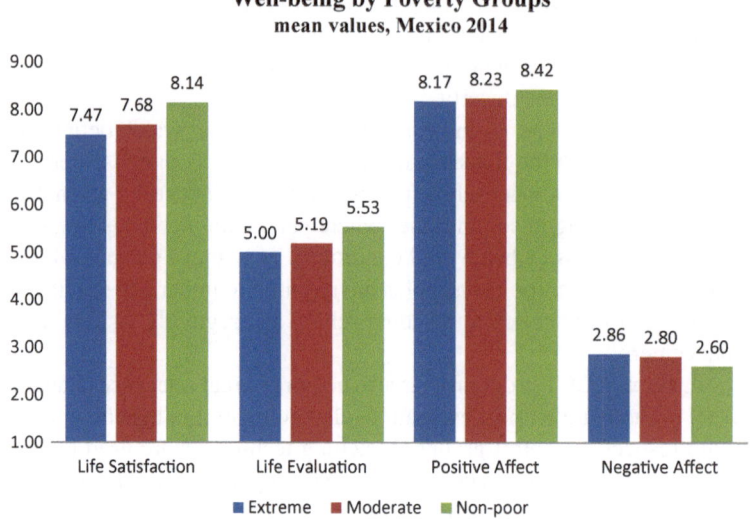

Fig. 7.3 Well-being by poverty groups. Extreme poverty: less than US$2 dollars of household income per capita per day. Moderate poverty: between US$2 and US$5 per day. Non-poor: greater than US$5 per day. Life satisfaction, positive affect and negative affect in a 0–10 scale; life evaluation in a 1–7 scale. *Source* BIARE 2014, INEGI, Mexico

and extreme poverty. However, it is observed that differences in the affective situation across poverty groups are relatively small in comparison to differences in life evaluation and in life satisfaction.

7.3.2   Domains-of-Life Satisfaction by Poverty Classification

Figure 7.4 provides a domains-of-life perspective by poverty category. It is observed that satisfaction with standard of living varies substantially along poverty groups, with the extreme poor reporting an average satisfaction of 7.21 and the non-poor of 8.01. The non-poor do also report being more satisfied with their social life, their occupation and their health. A negligible difference is observed in such an important domain as family life, where the extreme poor report a satisfaction of 8.89 and the non-poor of 8.96. Small differences between the extreme poor and the non-poor are observed in satisfaction with affective life, with free time and with the neighborhood. The poor report being more satisfied with the country than the non-poor.

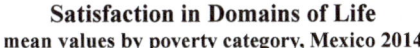

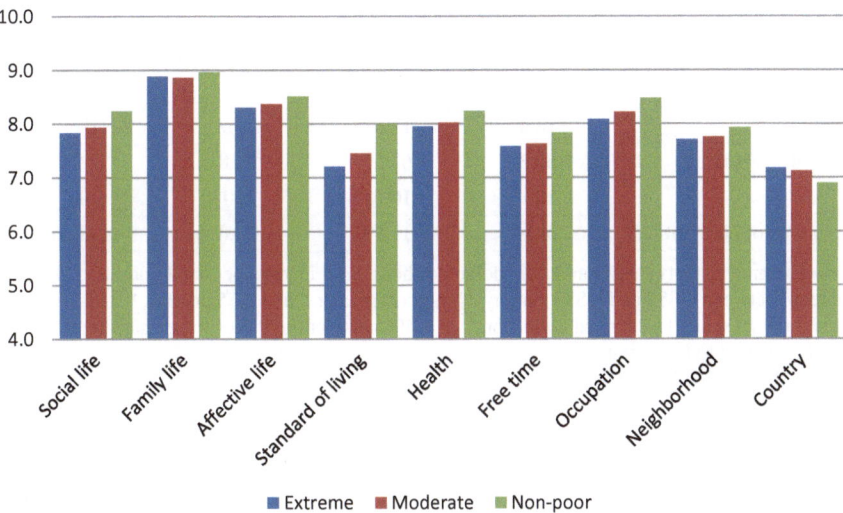

Fig. 7.4 Satisfaction in domains of life by poverty groups. Extreme poverty: less than US$2 dollars of household income per capita per day. Moderate poverty: between US$2 and US$5 per day. Non-poor: greater than US$5 per day. Satisfaction in domains of life in a 0–10 scale. *Source* BIARE 2014, INEGI, Mexico

7.3.3 Dissonances Between Poverty Classification and People's Well-Being

Even though those in poverty tend to report, on average, lower well-being than those classified as non-poor; it is possible for people classified as poor on an income-based measure of poverty not to experience low well-being. It may also happen that people who are classified as non-poor on the basis of their income report experiencing low well-being. These dissonances between the classification of people as poor on the basis of income-based measures and their reported experience of being well may raise some questions about the adequacy of the way poverty is understood and measured (Rojas 2008).

Table 7.1 presents the dissonances that are observed in the classification of people as poor on the basis of their income and on their reported life satisfaction. It is observed that the percentage of unsatisfied people decreases as one moves from extreme poverty to non-poor; similarly, the percentage of highly satisfied people increases as one moves in the same direction. However, of those who are classified as being in extreme poverty only 18% report being unsatisfied with life, while 63% report being highly satisfied with life. Figures for those classified as being in moderate poverty are more or less similar; 15% report being unsatisfied with life, while 67% report being highly satisfied. Hence, it is clear that a large proportion of those

Table 7.1 Life satisfaction and poverty classification. Dissonances and consonances in well-being and poverty. Percentage by poverty category, Mexico, 2014

Life satisfaction	Poverty category			Total
	Extreme	Moderate	Non-poor	
Unsatisfied	18.3	14.9	9.6	11.9
Satisfied	18.4	17.6	13.7	15.3
Highly satisfied	63.3	67.5	76.8	72.8
Total	100	100	100	100
Number of observations	3414	11,591	23,856	38,861

Note Extreme poverty: less than US$2 dollars of household income per capita per day. Moderate poverty: between US$2 and US$5 per day. Non-poor: greater than US$5 per day. Satisfaction with life in a 0–10 scale. Unsatisfied corresponds to a life satisfaction of 5 or lower; satisfied to 6 or 7; highly satisfied to 8 or greater
Source BIARE 2014, INEGI, Mexico

classified as poor on the basis of their income report high life satisfaction levels. In addition, almost 10% of those classified as non-poor (with a household per capita income of US$5 dollars or more per day) report being unsatisfied with their life.

Table 7.1 shows that it is possible to find a large percentage of poor people who experience high well-being (63%), as well as non-poor people who experience low well-being (10%); these figures reflect the existence of dissonances in the classification of people as poor and their well-being situation. Similarly, it is possible to find some consonances; non-poor people who experience high well-being (77%) as well as poor people who experience low well-being (18%).

Figure 7.5 focuses on the subsamples with high well-being (a life satisfaction of 8 or greater); it compares the life satisfaction and domains-of-life satisfaction of those classified as being in extreme poverty and those classified as being non-poor. The average household per capita income for those in extreme poverty is US$1.35 per day; while the same figure for the non-poor is US$15.80 per day. The huge difference in income shows up in the satisfaction with the standard of living, where the mean value for the non-poor is 8.46 and the mean value for the extreme-poor is 7.87. However, there is practically no difference in their satisfaction with family life (9.27 vs. 9.25) and in their satisfaction with the neighborhood (8.18 vs. 8.14), and there are small differences in affective life (8.93 vs. 8.85), health (8.63 vs. 8.46), and free time (8.18 vs. 8.05). Overall, the life satisfaction of the extreme poor is 8.72 while the average life satisfaction of the non-poor is 8.91. It is important to remark that we are focusing only on the high well-being sample. The main message is that for this group of people in extreme poverty low income affects their satisfaction with the standard of living, but has little impact in other important domains of life. They do also have very high satisfaction levels in the family domain of life, which is very important in explaining life satisfaction. Hence, there are people who are classified as poor and who high well-being; this is explained because those classified as poor get their life satisfaction from their situation in many domains of life, while they suffer in their

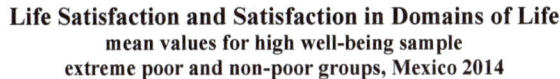

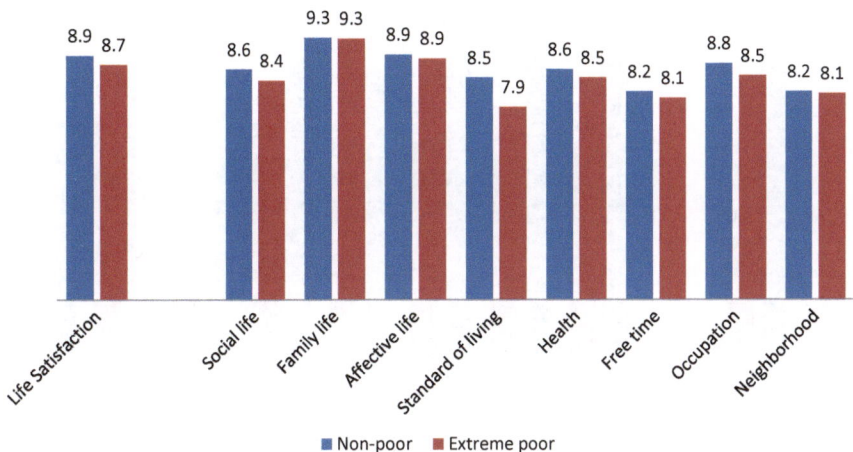

Fig. 7.5 Life satisfaction and satisfaction in domains of life, high well-being sample (life satisfaction of 8 or greater). Extreme poverty: less than US$2 dollars of household income per capita per day. Non-poor: household income per capita greater than US$5 per day. Satisfaction figures in a 0–10 scale. *Source* BIARE 2014, INEGI, Mexico

economic domain (their standard of living) this does not reflect in other domains of life which are important for life satisfaction.

Poverty-abatement programs aim to get people out of poverty; thus, it is important to see what the well-being situation of the non-poor is. Mean values do not provide a good perspective when there is high dispersion; in fact, there are non-poor people who are highly satisfied with life but there are also non-poor people who are miserable. Figure 7.6 shows the difference in life satisfaction and satisfaction in domains of life between these groups; the high well-being group has on average a household per capita income of US$15.8 per day, while the low well-being group has an average income of US$11.9 per day. There is clearly a difference in per capita income; though, income is far away from the poverty line in both cases.

By construction, the life satisfaction of the high well-being group is much higher than that of the low well-being group. However, it is surprising to observe a huge gap in satisfaction with the standard of living; which suggests that the association between income and satisfaction with the standard of living is mediated by other factors such as aspirations, social comparisons and materialistic values. In other words, having high income does not necessarily imply being highly satisfied with the standard of living. Figure 7.5 shows that there are people with low income— in extreme poverty—who are more satisfied with their standard of living than this rich but miserable group. In addition, it is also observed that there is an important gap in health satisfaction; this gap is very likely associated to differences in health

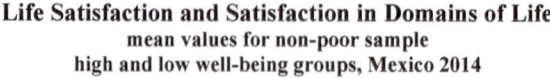

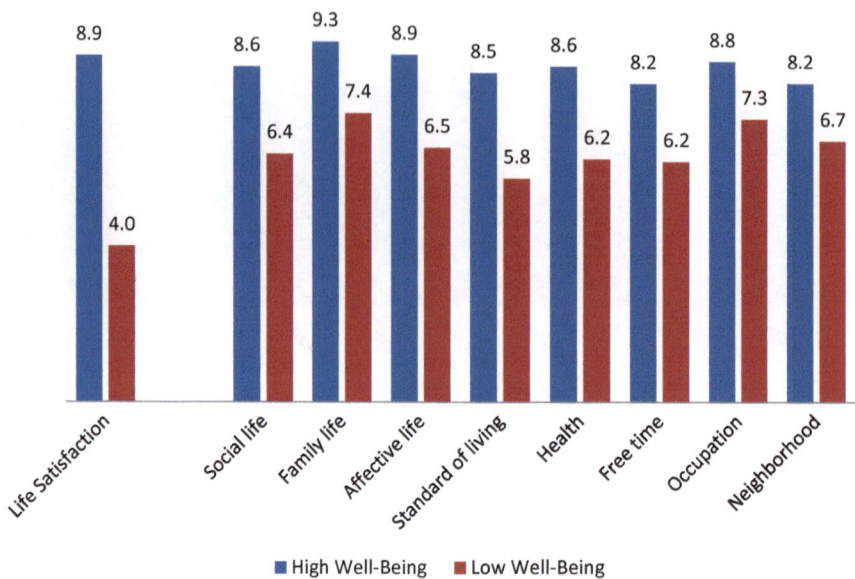

Fig. 7.6 Life satisfaction and satisfaction in domains of life, non-poor sample (Non-poor: household income per capita greater than US$5 per day). High well-being: life satisfaction of 8 or greater. Low well-being: life satisfaction of 5 or lower. Satisfaction figures in a 0–10 scale. *Source* BIARE 2014, INEGI, Mexico

condition—35% of the low well-being group people report having bad health versus 18% in the high well-being group; 19% were hospitalized during the past 12 months in comparison to 9% for the high well-being group. Furthermore, there are also important differences in satisfaction with family life, social life and affective life; in comparison to the high well-being group, the low well-being group incorporates more women as head of household, the interviewed has lower education levels, and a larger proportion are separate and divorced and a smaller proportion are married. About 11% of those with low well-being experienced a divorce or sentimental break during the past 12 months in comparison to only 5% for those in the high well-being group; and about 14% in the low well-being group experienced physical aggression versus 6% in the high well-being group. These findings indicate that contextual and life-events factors do also intervene in people's well-being and that it would be a mistake to restrain the focus of attention to economic factors; it would provide and incomplete and erroneous perspective on people's well-being situation.

7.3.4   Paths in Getting People Out of Poverty

The previous analyses show that it is possible to be non-poor and enjoy high well-being levels, but it is also possible to be non-poor and have low well-being levels. Thus, two different paths out of poverty can me conceived: a way that leads to high income and high well-being and a way that leads to high income but people being miserable. Figure 7.7 presents these possible paths out of poverty and well-being deprivation.

Point D represents the situation of a person who is in income poverty and who is also in well-being deprivation; points B and D correspond to a non-poverty situation. The path from situation D (poor and miserable) to situation B (non-poor and high life satisfaction) is highly desirable, while the path from situation D (poor and miserable) to situation A (non-poor and miserable) is not desirable at all. Unfortunately, most poverty-abatement programs are designed to raise income while completely neglecting the well-being situation; these programs evaluate their success by focusing only in the horizontal axis (the income variable) and are unable to distinguish between situation B and A. Hence, these poverty-abatement programs could risk announcing success when in fact people are still miserable. This is why it is crucial for poverty-abatement programs to have a well-being perspective and to incorporate this perspective in their design and in their evaluation.

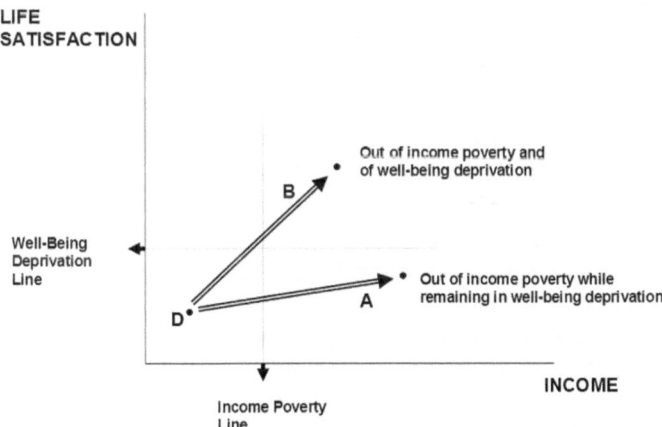

Fig. 7.7 Paths out of poverty

7.3.5 Further Problems with an Absolute-Income Conception of Poverty

The World Bank and the United Nations Development Programme have popularized a conception of poverty based on an absolute-income poverty line; this strategy is justified in terms of the availability of information and on the difficulty of justifying the using of different criteria across countries. However, the strategy assumes that those beneath the income-poverty line do suffer equally everywhere in the world. However, differences in socio-economic, cultural and institutional factors across countries may imply for those with low income to experience different well-being levels.

Figure 7.8 shows that low-income people in Costa Rica do experience high life-evaluation levels, which is a situation also observed—in a lesser degree—in Mexico, Uruguay and Chile. On the other hand, the low-income people in Dominican Republic and Paraguay do experience relatively low life-evaluation levels. The information presented in Fig. 7.8 shows that country-level contextual factors do also matter for the evaluative experiences of being well that those classified as poor have.

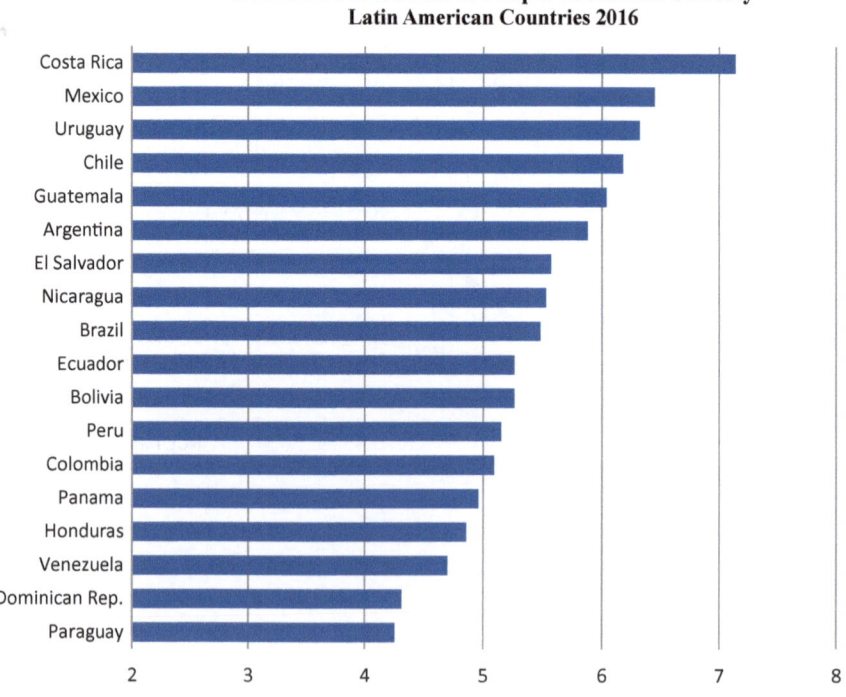

Fig. 7.8 Life evaluation of people classified as poor on the basis of a poverty line of US$2 of household per capita income per day. Latin American countries. Life evaluation in a 0–10 scale. *Source* Gallup World Poll 2016

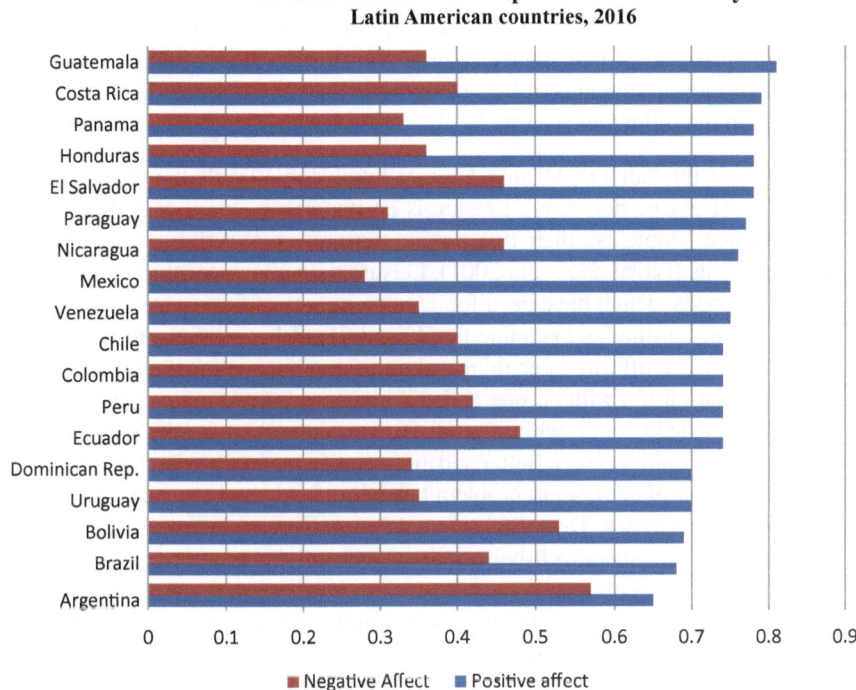

Fig. 7.9 Positive and negative affect of people classified as poor on the basis of a poverty line of US$2 of household per capita income per day. Latin American countries. Affective state in a 0–1 scale. *Source* Gallup World Poll 2016

Information in Fig. 7.9 complements the well-being situation of those classified as poor; it provides information on the affective situation. Those in poverty have relatively high positive affect in Guatemala, Costa Rica and Panama and very low positive affect in Argentina, Brazil and Bolivia. Negative affect is very low in Mexico, Paraguay and Dominican Republic and it is very high in Argentina, Bolivia and Ecuador. Hence, even though international organizations implement universal standards in the measurement—and conception of poverty—it is important to recognize that from a well-being perspective this universality does not sustain and that, in fact, important well-being differences across countries do exist for those classified as poor.

7.4 Well-Being Lessons for Poverty-Abatement Programs

Poverty-abatement programs have been designed to get people out of income poverty but not to get them into a high well-being situation. For poverty-abatement programs to be well-being enhancing it is desirable to go beyond an income-based perspective of poverty. Thus, it is important to recognize: First, that well-being deprivation is explained not only by low income but also by other relevant factors associated with satisfaction in many domains of life. Second, that raising well-being does not only require increasing income but also improving conditions associated to satisfaction in other relevant domains of life. Poverty-abatement programs should take into consideration the following issues:

– Recognizing the value of leisure: Even at low income levels the importance of leisure must not be neglected. Leisure is an important source of well-being, in special when people use their free time to nurture social activities and interpersonal relations (Lloyd and Auld 2001). Leisure time allows for the production of relational goods, which have been found to be important for people's well-being. Fostering long-lasting and genuine family and friendship relations requires time.
– Focusing on the nurturing of genuine and gratifying interpersonal relations. A satisfactory relationship with partner and children constitutes a main source of well-being for married people, while friends are very important for the well-being of single people (Rojas 2007a). Better and more gratifying family relations contribute to the reduction of adolescent problem behavior (Suldo and Huebner 2004). In a study with Korean data, Yang (2003) found that an increase in economic resources is associated with greater well-being only when family relations involve love, care, recognition and acceptance.
– Providing skills and knowledge for a satisfactory life. Conditional cash transfer programs have treated education and human capital as synonymous. Unfortunately, the understanding of education as human capital limits its potential and focuses only on its contribution to raise income. Education could make a greater contribution to well-being; but this requires a broader perspective on the role of education. Rojas (2018) has shown that a person's education is strongly related to her *family* (partner and children), *leisure* (personal development, use of leisure time) and *job* satisfaction. People with more education have more satisfactory family relations, work in more gratifying occupations, and pursue more stimulating hobbies and interests; they may also be more successful in preventing health-related problems. Education allows for more control over personal life and a better use of leisure time; it also allows women to socially integrate and to acquire more decision-making power within families and societies. Poverty-abatement programs should see in education a powerful instrument to increase people's well-being and not only a mean to raise their income.
– Creating communities. People's well-being also depends on the qualities of their communities. While some poverty-abatement programs have focused on providing housing solutions to poor families not much has been done on creating communities.
– Building consumption skills. An increase in income guarantees more spending but not necessarily more well-being. If beneficiaries of poverty-abatement programs lack consumption skills then it is possible for their additional purchasing power to be used in satisfying desires that contribute little to their well-being. Rojas (2008b) and Earl (2007) shows that there is considerable X-inefficiency in the use of income at all levels. Thus, well-being enhancing programs should focus not only

on raising income but also on providing the knowledge and skills, as well as the institutional arrangements, to enable people to spend it in a well-being enhancing manner.

– Avoiding materialistic values and ever-increasing material aspirations. Special attention must be placed on how poverty-abatement programs modify people's values, as well as in the kind of social context the beneficiaries will be placed in. There is little gain in well-being if people become more materialistic and base their life in the consumption of expensive and status-marking commodities. Ever increasing aspirations may induce people to work harder and to generate more income, but this is not a good path to increase people's well-being.

– Monitoring people's well-being. The evaluation of poverty-abatement programs should incorporate a well-being module. It would be very useful to know how life satisfaction, as well as satisfaction in many domains of life, is modified by these programs. Having appropriate information on experiences of being well would enable the design of better programs.

7.5 General Policy Considerations

This chapter has questioned the simplified view that associates well-being deprivation to a low-income situation. It is not that income is not important; it is that income is just an instrument to attain well-being and not a final end in itself. A social program is not successful just because people have more income, it is successful if people are more satisfied with life and enjoy more experiences of being well.

Getting people out of income poverty is fine, but would be no more than a statistics if it does not translate into greater well-being for the beneficiaries of social program. Social program beneficiaries should not be treated as simple gadgets that are moved from one situation to another or from one place to another; people's motivations and well-being expectations do intervene in their behavior and in how they welcome social programs. Social programs that aim at increasing people's well-being may count on the intrinsic motivation and high enthusiasm of their beneficiaries; this would be helpful in ensuring the success of the programs.

It is frequently stated that low-income countries with high income-poverty rates cannot afford to think about well-being; the argument claims that well-being is a kind of luxurious good that only high-income countries can aspire to. In accordance with this argument it is recommended for low-income countries to channel all their effort and resources in abating people's income poverty. This chapter has shown that this recommendation is erroneous; people in low-income countries would benefit a lot from poverty-abatement programs that do not only focus on rising people's income risk but also on increasing people's well-being. In fact, by neglecting the well-being perspective low-income countries end up wasting a lot of effort and resources in programs that do not impact on the experience of being well people have. The well-being perspective must be integrated into the design and evaluation of social programs in order to create policies and programs that have a higher impact on people's experience of being well and not only on their purchasing power.

A well-being perspective allows for considering alternative instruments to income which could be more effective in raising people's well-being as well as more ecologically friendly. These policy options could complement—and even substitute for—the goal of raising people's income and getting everybody out of income poverty. These alternative policies can also have a quicker effect on people's well-being and can be highly welcomed by those families in chronic income poverty.

The role of the surrounding context should not be neglected; social programs that raise income may have little well-being impact if the surrounding context promotes materialistic values and a status race based on higher consumption and ever-increasing aspirations.

References

Bruni, L., & Stanca, L. (2005). *Watching alone: Relational goods, television and happiness.* Working paper. Bocconi University.

Cummins, R. (1996). The domains of life satisfaction: An attempt to order chaos. *Social Indicators Research, 38,* 303–332.

Earl, P. (2007). Consumer X-inefficiency and the problem of market regulation. In R. Franz (Ed.), *Renaissance in behavioral economics, essays in memory of Harvey Leibenstein.* London: Routledge.

Gui, B., & Sugden, R. (Eds.). (2005). *Economics and social interaction.* Cambridge: Cambridge University Press.

Hsee, C., & Hastie, R. (2006). Decision and experience: Why don't we choose what makes us happy? *Trends in Cognitive Sciences, 10*(1), 31–37.

Kasser, T. (2002). *The high price of materialism.* Massachusetts: MIT Press.

Lloyd, K., & Auld, C. (2001). The role of leisure in determining quality of life: Issues of contents and measurement. *Social Indicators Research, 57,* 43–71.

Martínez, J., & Castillo, H. (2016). "Like the zompopito": Social relationships in happiness among rural and indigenous women in Nicaragua. In M. Rojas (Ed.), *Handbook of happiness research in Latin America* (pp. 113–127). Berlin: Springer.

Mochón, F., & de Juan Díaz, R. (2016). Happiness and social capital: Evidence from Latin American countries. In M. Rojas (Ed.), *Handbook of happiness research in Latin America* (pp. 143–161). Berlin: Springer.

Rawlings, L., & Rubio, G. (2004). Evaluating the impact of conditional cash transfer programs. *World Bank Research Observer, 20*(1), 29–55.

Rojas, M. (2006a). Life satisfaction and satisfaction in domains of life: Is it a simple relationship? *Journal of Happiness Studies, 7*(4), 467–497.

Rojas, M. (2006b). Communitarian versus individualistic arrangements in the family: What and whose income matters for happiness? In R. J. Estes (Ed.), *Advancing quality of life in a turbulent world* (pp. 153–167). Berlin: Springer.

Rojas, M. (2007a). The complexity of well-being: A life-satisfaction conception and a domains-of-life approach. In I. Gough & J. A. McGregor (Eds.), *Researching well-being in developing countries: From theory to research* (pp. 259–280). Cambridge: Cambridge University Press.

Rojas, M. (2007b). Estimating equivalence scales in Mexico: A subjective well-being approach. *Oxford Development Studies, 35*(3), 273–293.

Rojas, M. (2008). X-inefficiency in the use of income to attain economic satisfaction. *Journal of Socio-Economics*, 2278–2290.

Rojas, M. (2012). Happiness in Mexico: The importance of human relations. In A. Selin & G. Davey (Eds.), *Happiness across cultures: Views of happiness and quality of life in non-western cultures* (pp. 241–252). Berlin: Springer.

Rojas, M. (2015a). Poverty and people's well-being. In W. Glatzer, V. Moller, L. Camfield, & M. Rojas (Eds.), *Global handbook of quality of life* (pp. 317–350). Berlin: Springer.

Rojas, M. (2015b). Reformas Pro-Mercado y Bienestar Subjetivo. América Latina. In A. Puyana (coord.) *Paradojas de la Globalización y el Desarrollo Latinoamericano* (pp. 201–228). FLACSO-México.

Rojas, M. (2018). Educación, Capital Humano y Felicidad. In R. Millán & R. Castellanos (Eds.), *Bienestar Subjetivo en México*. UNAM.

Ryan, R., & Sapp, A. (2007). Basic psychological needs: A self-determination theory perspective on the promotion of wellness across development and cultures. In I. Gough & J. A. McGregor (Eds.), *Researching well-being in developing countries: From theory to research* (pp. 71–92). Cambridge: Cambridge University Press.

Scitovsky, T. (1976). *The joyless economy: An inquiry into human satisfaction and consumer dissatisfaction*. Oxford: Oxford University Press.

Sugden, R. (2005). Correspondence of sentiments: An explanation of the pleasure of social interaction. In L. Bruni & P. L. Porta (Eds.), *Economics and happiness: Framing the analysis* (pp. 91–115). Oxford: Oxford University Press.

Suldo, S., & Huebner, E. (2004). The role of life satisfaction in the relationship between authoritative parenting dimensions and adolescent problem behavior. *Social Indicators Research, 66*, 165–195.

Thaler, R. (1992). *Quasi-rational economics*. New York: Russell Sage Foundation.

Thaler, R. (2000). From homo economics to homo sapiens. *The Journal of Economic Perspectives, 14*(1), 133–141.

Tversky, A., & Kahneman, D. (1981). The framing of decisions and the psychology of choice. *Science, 211*, 453–458.

Tversky, A., & Kahneman, D. (1986). Rational choice and the framing of decisions. *Journal of Business, 59*(4), 251–278.

van Praag, B., Frijters, P., & Ferrer-i-Carbonell, A. (2003). The anatomy of subjective well-being. *Journal of Economic Behavior & Organization, 51*, 29–49.

Velásquez, L. (2016). The importance of relational goods for happiness: Evidence from Manizales, Colombia. In M. Rojas (Ed.), *Handbook of happiness research in Latin America* (pp. 91–112). Berlin: Springer.

Yang, O. (2003). Family structure and relation. *Social Indicators Research, 62*, 121–148.

Chapter 8
Relational Wealth: Quantity and Quality of Interpersonal Relations

Abstract The quantity and quality of interpersonal relations is an important driver of people's well-being. Latin Americans' high well-being levels can be explained by the abundance of close, warm and genuine interpersonal relations in all relational spheres of life. The quantity and quality of relations people have are independent of their economic condition; in other words; income does not buy good relations. Public policy should not assume that economic growth and higher income translates into better interpersonal relations; on the contrary, it is recommended for public policy to take into consideration the potential negative impact that some pro economic growth policies may have on the quantity and quality of interpersonal relations.

Keywords Relational wealth · Person-based interpersonal relations · Latin America · Well-being · Relational poverty

When little kids play at what they will do when growing up it is common to hear about occupations such as firemen, policewomen, doctors, nurses, and teachers. However, what most kids will be when growing up is spouses, parents, sons and daughters, friends, colleagues, and citizens. Interpersonal relations will occupy most of their time, and it is expected for these relations to be crucial for their well-being. Unfortunately, interpersonal relations are often neglected by well-being researchers; with the exception of social capital, which focuses on civic relations, there is little research on interpersonal relations as a major driver of people's satisfaction with life. This chapter focuses on interpersonal relations and shows that the quantity and quality of these relations constitutes a major driver of Latin Americans' well-being; as a matter of fact, the high well-being of Latin Americans is explained in great part by the abundance of high-quality relations in the region. The chapter shows that relational wealth is a major driver of well-being and that its importance may even be greater than material wealth. It also derives some important lessons for policy making.

M. Rojas, *Well-Being in Latin America*, Human Well-Being Research and Policy Making,
https://doi.org/10.1007/978-3-030-33498-7_8

8.1 Traditional Concerns in the Human Relations Literature

Research on human relations and well-being has concentrated on the role of trust in others and support from others. For example, the World Happiness Report incorporates the 'counting on someone' variable as a main determinant of people's evaluation of life, while the social-capital literature points towards the importance played by 'trusting others in society' (Bourdieu 2001; Fukuyama 1996; Helliwell and Putnam 2004; Lin 1999a, b).

8.1.1 Social Support

By world standards it can be stated that Latin Americans have a good social-support network. On average, 85% of Latin Americans report 'having someone to count on in times of trouble'; this figure is 81% for the whole world (Fig. 8.1). Figures for social support are above 90% in Venezuela, Panama, Argentina and Costa Rica, and are relatively low (beneath 80%) in El Salvador and Bolivia. The region with the highest average social support is Western Europe and the Anglo-Saxon countries, with 91%; while the region with the lowest value is South Asia, with 65%.

It is important to remark that social support is positively associated to well-being at the world level—as well as in the Latin American region. Having someone to count on is associated to greater life evaluation, more positive affect, and less negative affect (Helliwell et al. 2018). As a matter of fact, the estimated impact on life evaluation is more or less similar to that of an increase in 200% in household per capita income. Similarly, the estimated impact on positive affect (and in the reduction of negative affect) is more or less equivalent to that of an increase in 400% in household per capita income (Rojas 2018). Hence, Latin Americans have, in general, high levels of social support, which is an important driver of well-being.

8.1.2 Trust

Distrust in other people is a generalized phenomenon in Latin American countries. The Latinobarometer survey asks people to choose between two options: 'most people can be trusted' versus 'One can never be too careful when dealing with people'. Figure 8.2 presents the percentage of people who opt for the first option in each Latin American country. As observed, trust is very low everywhere in Latin America, with extremely low values in Brazil, Costa Rica, Honduras and Chile. Mexico, Argentina and Ecuador have the highest regional values regarding trust in others; however, it is important to remark that these values are low in comparison to other countries in the world. A very similar question applied in the United States—but with a different

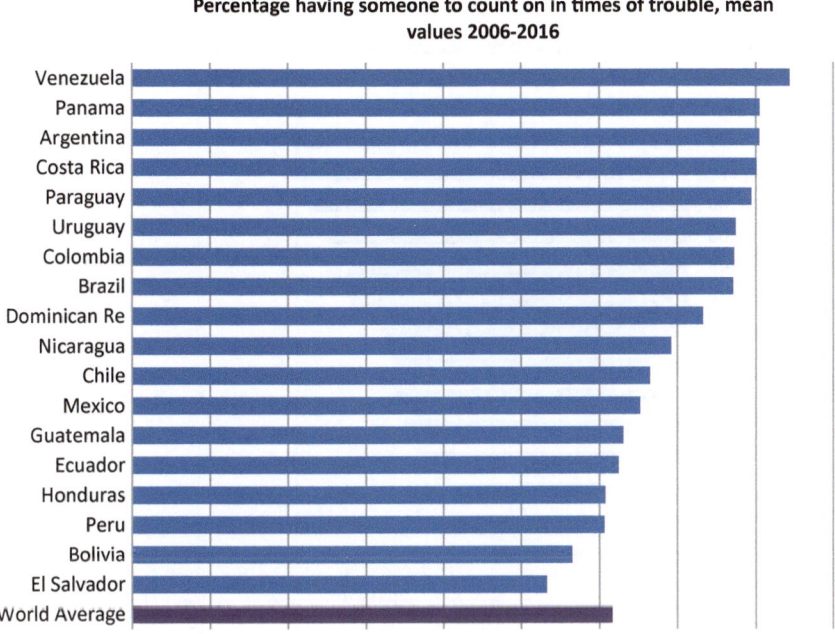

Fig. 8.1 Social support; percentage who report having someone to count on in times of trouble, Latin American countries and world average, mean values 2006–2016. Specific question: *"If you were in trouble, do you have relatives or friends you can count on to help you whenever you need them, or not?"*, binary response: Yes or No. *Source* Gallup World Poll 2006–2016

response scale—indicates that about 45% of people in the country state that they 'always' or 'usually' can trust someone else. A similar question—but also with a different response scale—is applied in some European countries, with more than 70% of people in Finland, Denmark and Norway being inclined to trust others (with a value of 6 or more in a 0–10 response scale). Figures in Europe are low in Portugal (22%) and Poland (23%).

The trust variable is positively associated to life satisfaction in Latin American countries, even after controlling for sociodemographic and economic variables. Hence, trust can be considered as a driver of well-being which, unfortunately, is scarce in Latin America.

Great attention has been placed on the Social Support and Trust variables; however, these variables are very limited in their capacity to portray the abundance and quality of interpersonal relations in societies. The social support variable ('counting on someone') approaches human relations as a source of emotional and material support; while the trust variable focuses on civic relations, this is: on relations that take place—mostly—with unknown people (fellow citizens at the community

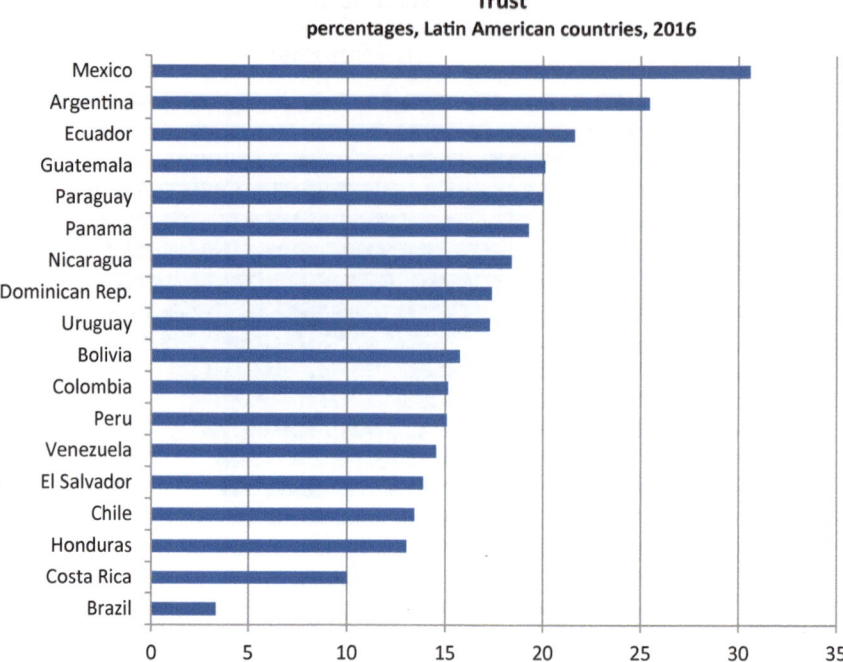

Fig. 8.2 Trust in Latin American countries. Percentage who respond that 'most people can be trusted' rather than the alternative option ('One can never be too careful when dealing with people'). *Source* Latinobarometer 2016

level). These two variables are important, but they neglect those human relations that are more frequent and more important to people: those which take place regularly between people who know each other on a personal level and on a long-run basis.

8.2   Relational Wealth in Latin America

8.2.1   On the Relational-Wealth Concept

People interact with fellow citizens on a regular basis and trusting each other may be important for well-being and for other reasons. However, the most frequent interpersonal relations take place with people who know and care about each other, generating relations that could be warm and close and which go much beyond the purpose of mutual support to become relations of mutual enjoyment.

This chapter emphasizes person-based interpersonal relations as a main driver of people's well-being. Person-based interpersonal relations make reference to relations where people take time to know each other and to nurture the relationship; they are interested in knowing more of each other and in becoming acquainted on the other person's situation. In person-based interpersonal relations those who are interacting know each other well; these relations call for a focus on persons and on their particular personal situation rather than for a focus on tasks to be performed and goals to be attained. Hence, these relations do not emerge out of an extrinsic motivation and they are not nurtured just to get some benefit; people approach the relationship as a source of joint enjoyment.

Person-based interpersonal relations are expected to be central to people's well-being not only because they are frequent but also because people genuinely care about the relationship and about the person they have in front, and this contributes to everybody's enjoyment of life. Person-based interpersonal relations involve enjoyment, nurturing, guidance, generativity, intergenerational contact, entertainment and recreation, and the mutual construction of identity within a long-run project of life. In some occasions they do also involve suffering and sense of failure, with the consequent reduction in life satisfaction. Positive emotions are expected to be highly sensitive to the joint enjoyment of life. Negative emotions are expected to be sensitive to the existence of relational problems in close circles. In a relational society people's sense of purpose in life does also depend on the quality of person-based interpersonal relations; thus, life evaluation is also expected to be sensitive to these relations.

Civic relations are based on following formal rules and norms, while function-based relations focus on the attainment of objectives. Civic and function-based relations are not expected to generate high positive and negative affect, and their contribution to life evaluation depends on how much people value the external goal they. In other words, politeness is not sufficient to contribute to the affective life of people and its contribution to life evaluation may be small.

Person-based interpersonal relations take place, mostly, within the nuclear family, with the extended family, with relatives, with friends, colleagues and neighbors. If person-based interpersonal relations are abundant and of high-quality then they may become an important driver for people's well-being; as a matter of fact, given their role in the generation of well-being it would be possible to conceive them as relational wealth, with is a concept that expands wealth beyond its commonly association material notion (Diwan 2000).

8.2.2 High-Quality Interpersonal Relations in the Latin American Nuclear Family

Figure 8.3 provides information on some variables associated to the quality of interpersonal relations in the nuclear family. It compares the situation in three Latin American countries (Colombia, Costa Rica, and Mexico) with that of the white/Caucasian population of the United States. The quality of the relations is assessed on the basis

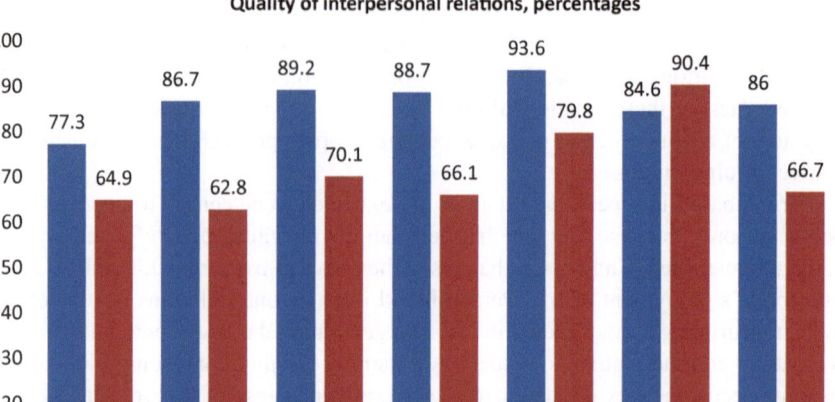

Fig. 8.3 Relational wealth in the nuclear family. Percentage with a high relational level attribute. Three Latin American countries (Colombia, Costa Rica and Mexico) and the white population of the United States. Seven relational variables: 1. Manifestations of affection with your partner. 2. Manifestations of affection with your children. 3. Everyone's decisions are respected in the family. 4. Taking into consideration the well-being of my family when making important decisions. 5. Being with the family gives the most meaning to my life. 6. Doing joint activities—such as reading or playing sports—with children. 7. Helping and supporting each other in the family. See Appendix for further details on measurement. *Source* Understanding High Happiness in Latin America survey, 2018

of manifestations of affection with partner and children, the respect to everyone's decisions in the family, the consideration of other family members when making important decisions, the meaning of life provided by the family, sharing time with children, and the provision of help and support in the family.

It is observed that in general the quality of interpersonal relations at the nuclear family level is much higher in Latin America than in the United States. A much larger proportion of Latin Americans show affection to their partner and children, respect and take into consideration their well-being when making important decisions, think of family relations as a major source of purpose in life, and are inclined to help and support each other in the family.

8.2.3 Abundance of High-Quality Relations in the Latin American Nuclear Family

It is not only that the quality of human relations is high in the nuclear families of Latin American; it is also that they are abundant. Abundance is a relative concept; it implies a comparison across countries or regions. Figure 8.4 presents information on frequency of interpersonal relations in the nuclear family; it contrasts the situation in Latin America with that for the white population in the United States. It is observed that people share positive emotions with close family more frequently in Latin America; they do also spend time with family and share time with partner and children as well as with adult children no longer living at home more often.

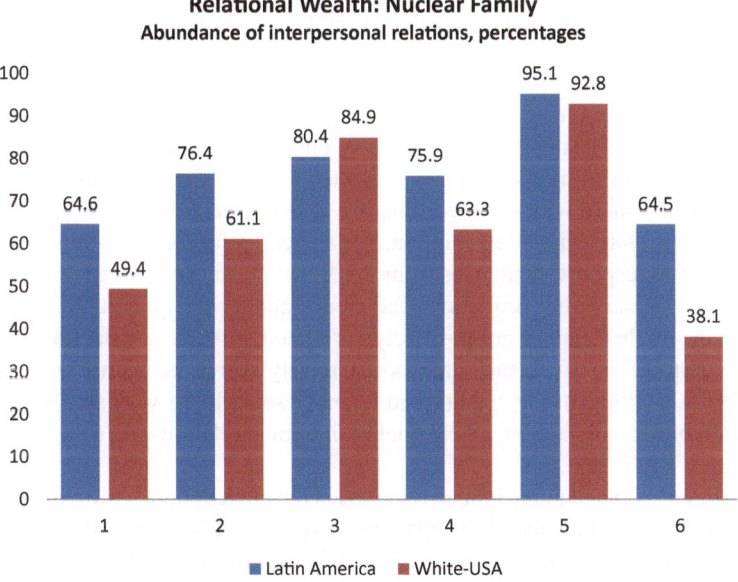

Fig. 8.4 Relational wealth in the nuclear family, quantity of interpersonal relations. Percentage with a high relational level attribute. Three Latin American countries (Colombia, Costa Rica and Mexico) and the white population of the United States. Six relational variables: 1. Sharing positive emotions with close family. 2. We in the family spend a lot of time doing things together. 3. Taking time to share with partner. 4. Taking time to share with children. 5. Sharing at least one meal a day with children. 6. Taking time to share with adult children. See Appendix for further details on measurement. *Source* Understanding High Happiness in Latin America survey, 2018

8.2.4 *Relational Wealth and Essential Experiences of Being Well*

Relational wealth is high in Latin American's nuclear families; there is high quantity (abundance) and quality of relations and this contributes to Latin Americans' life satisfaction.

Two relational variables were constructed to proxy the abundance and quality of relational wealth in Latin America's nuclear families:

Quality of relations in the nuclear family is constructed as a simple average of the following seven variables: Manifestations of affection with your partner, Manifestations of affection with your children, Everyone's decisions are respected in the family, Taking into consideration the well-being of my family when making important decisions, Being with the family gives the most meaning to my life, Doing joint activities—such as reading or playing sports—with children, and Helping and supporting each other in the family. See Appendix for the measurement of these variables. The response scale goes from 1 to 5.

Quantity of relations in the nuclear family is constructed as a simple average of the following six variables: Sharing positive emotions with close family, We in the family spend a lot of time doing things together, Taking time to share with partner, Taking time to share with children, Sharing at least one meal a day with children, Taking time to share with adult children. See Appendix for the measurement of these variables. The response scale goes from 1 to 7.

Table 8.1 presents the correlation coefficients; quality and quantity of human relations in the nuclear family are positively correlated with life satisfaction, life evaluation and positive affect; they are also negatively correlated with negative affect. Correlation coefficients for quality and quantity seem to be very similar, with the exception of life satisfaction, where quality of human relations has a stronger correlation.

Close, warm and genuine human relations in the nuclear family are associated to a very good affective balance; these relations increase the experience of positive affect and reduce the experience of negative affect. The outstanding affective situation of Latin Americans and their very high life satisfaction is in great part explained by the abundance of high quality interpersonal relations in the region. The abundance of close, warm and genuine human relations in the nuclear family are also associated

Table 8.1 Correlation relational wealth in the nuclear family and well-being, Latin America

Interpersonal relations in nuclear family	Life satisfaction	Life evaluation	Positive affect	Negative affect
Quantity of relations	0.219	0.271	0.296	−0.210
Quality of relations	0.280	0.252	0.297	−0.196

Three Latin American countries (Colombia, Costa Rica and Mexico)
Source Understanding High Happiness in Latin America survey, 2018

Table 8.2 Correlation relational wealth in the nuclear family and income and education, Latin America

Interpersonal relations in nuclear family	Education level	Income
Quantity of relations	0.112	−0.009
Quality of relations	0.197	0.010

Income corresponds to the logarithm of household per capita income
Three Latin American countries (Colombia, Costa Rica and Mexico)
Source Understanding High Happiness in Latin America survey, 2018

to a better evaluation of life; this indicates that the norms and purposes in life which Latin Americans use to evaluate their life incorporate their relational situation.

8.2.5   Relational Wealth Is not Correlated with Material Wealth

It seems that money cannot buy good relations in Latin America. The correlation between income and the quality and quantity of interpersonal relations in the nuclear family is practically zero (see Table 8.2), which indicates that relational wealth is not correlated with material wealth and that high and low income families in Latin America have the same probability of relational affluence.

A positive but not so high correlation between education and the quantity and quality of interpersonal relations is observed; however, it is important to remark that the educational system has placed greater attention in building skills and providing knowledge to increase material wealth than in skills and knowledge for relational wealth. Hence, the positive correlation between good relations and education may be a by-product rather than the direct consequence of an educational system that focuses on increasing people's well-being.

8.3   Relational Wealth Extends to Other Relational Spheres

Latin Americans' relational wealth is not circumscribed to the nuclear family; in fact, the extended family is also important for Latin Americans and it shows in frequent family gathering as well as in visits to and meetings with grandparents, siblings, cousins, aunts and uncles and the rest of the family. There also abundance and high quality of relations in other spheres such as friends, coworkers, and neighbors. Information not presented in this chapter shows that the quantity and quality of these relations is also correlated to people's well-being; they are positively correlated with life satisfaction, life evaluation and positive affect, and negatively correlated with negative affect.

8.3.1 Relational Wealth in the Extended Family

Figure 8.5 shows that there is a huge difference in relational wealth in the extended family between Latin Americans and the white population in the United States. For example, while 62% of Latin Americans report visiting their parents frequently or very frequently during their childhood this figure is only 42% in the United States. In all other extended-family relational variables the Latin American percentage practically doubles—or even triples—that of people in the United States.

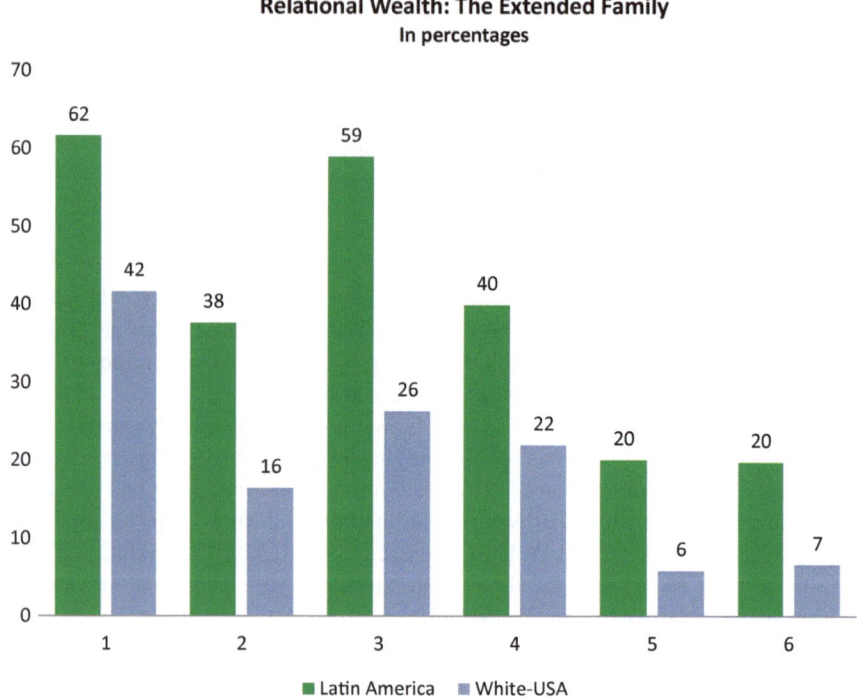

Fig. 8.5 Relational wealth in the extended family. Percentage with a high relational level attribute. Three Latin American countries (Colombia, Costa Rica and Mexico) and the white population of the United States. Six relational variables: 1 Visiting grandparents during childhood. 2 Extended family gatherings. 3 Manifestations of affect with siblings. 4 Meeting grandparents. 5 Meeting cousins. 6 Meeting aunts and uncles. See Appendix for further details on measurement. *Source* Understanding High Happiness in Latin America survey, 2018

8.3.2 Relational Wealth in Other Relations: Friends, Coworkers and Neighbors

High relational wealth extends to other relational spheres. Figure 8.6 shows abundance of high quality relations in the friendship, coworkers and neighbors spheres in Latin America.

In conclusion, the Latin American societies enjoy abundance of high quality interpersonal relations; this relational wealth contributes to explain the high well-being levels in the region.

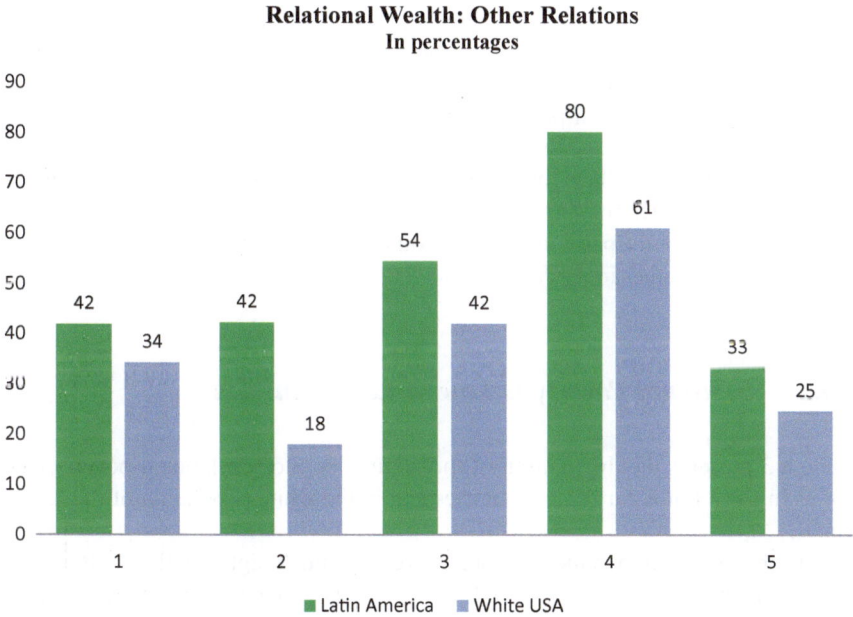

Relational Wealth: Other Relations
In percentages

Fig. 8.6 Relational wealth: Other relations. Percentage with high relational level. Three Latin American countries (Colombia, Costa Rica and Mexico) and the white population of the United States. Five relational variables: 1. Sharing positive emotions with friends. 2. Meeting with coworkers outside working place. 3. Talking with coworkers about interests, feelings and aspirations. 4. Helping and supporting each other in the working place. 5. Talking with neighbors about interests, feelings and aspirations. See Appendix for further details on measurement. *Source* Understanding High Happiness in Latin America survey, 2018

8.4   Relational Poverty and Well-Being in Latin America

8.4.1   Relational Poverty Concept

The concept of poverty has commonly make reference to a situation of deprivation in one or many of the drivers of well-being; given the importance that high-quality interpersonal relations have for people's well-being it makes sense to think about the concept of relational poverty. The following analyses do not deal with methodological issues in the construction of a relational-poverty measurement but aspire to motivate its research by showing its importance for people's well-being.

Information on quantity and quality of interpersonal relations in the nuclear family from the Understanding High Happiness in Latin America database was used to construct a single indicator for quality of relations, explore its distribution, and define a deprivation line. It is clear that any threshold level is arbitrary and that its purpose is merely to classify people in different groups on the basis of their relational situation; thus, a threshold was defined and three categories were generated: Extreme poverty, moderate poverty, and non-poor. The relational poor show less manifestations of affection to their partner and to their children, have a greater sense for their decisions not being respected in their family, take less into consideration the well-being of family members when making important decisions, attribute less meaning in life to being with their family, participate less in joint activities with their children, and help and support each other in the family less.

8.4.2   Relational Poverty Is Low in Latin America

Table 8.3 presents the distribution of the population along relational-poverty categories in three Latin American countries and in the white population of the United States.

It is observed that extreme relational poverty is much higher in the United States (41%) than in Latin America (18%). It is also observed that the percentage of people

Table 8.3 Relational poverty in Latin America and the United States. Percentage of the total population

Relational poverty category	Latin America	United States
Extreme poverty	18.1	41.0
Moderate poverty	30.8	28.1
Non-poor	51.1	31.0

Three Latin American countries (Colombia, Costa Rica and Mexico) and the white population of the United States
Source Constructed on the basis of information about quality of interpersonal relations in the nuclear family gathered by the Understanding High Happiness in Latin America survey, 2018

Table 8.4 Income and relational poverty. Cross-tabulation, in percentages, Latin America

Income poverty	Relational poverty			Total
	Extreme	Moderate	Non-poor	
Extreme	18.9	29.5	51.6	100
Moderate	18.9	29.6	51.6	100
Non-poor	17.7	31.4	50.8	100

Source Constructed on the basis of information gathered by the Understanding High Happiness in Latin America survey, 2018

who could be classified as non-poor is much higher in Latin America (51%) that in the United States (31%).

In consequence, relational poverty is a much larger phenomenon in the United States; but there are many relationally-poor families in Latin America and it is worth studying their well-being situation.

8.4.3   Relational Poverty Is not Correlated to Income Poverty

Are those in income poverty also relationally poor? Table 8.4 shows that there is no association between the relational-poverty classification and the income-poverty one; the distribution across relational poverty is practically the same for each classification of income poverty. This lack of association between the two poverty conceptions emerges from the previously studied fact that money—which is behind the income-poverty conception—does not buy abundance of high-quality interpersonal relations—which are behind the relational-poverty conception.

8.4.4   Relational Poverty and Well-Being in Latin America

From a well-being perspective the relational-poverty concept seems more relevant than the income-poverty one because it generates a clearer partition between those who are in well-being deprivation from those who are not. Table 8.5 presents the well-being situation of those in extreme relational poverty and those who are not in relational poverty; it also presents the situation for the income-poverty classification. It is observed that the gradient in life satisfaction, life evaluation, positive affect and negative affect between those classified as in extreme-poor and those classified as non-poor is much greater for the relational-poverty concept than for the income-poverty one.

The difference in life satisfaction between the non-poor and the extremely poor is of 0.69 (in a 1–7 scale) when a relational-poverty conception is used; however, this difference is only 0.18 when an income-poverty conception is used. A very

Table 8.5 Well-being in Latin America, by relational and income poverty classification mean values

	Relational poverty		Income poverty	
	Extreme poverty	Non poor	Extreme poverty	Non poor
Life satisfaction	5.16	5.85	5.53	5.71
Life evaluation	6.72	7.89	7.39	7.64
Positive affect	2.38	2.69	2.57	2.61
Negative affect	1.74	1.52	1.69	1.55

Life satisfaction in a 1 (extremely unsatisfied) to 7 (extremely satisfied) scale, Life evaluation in a 0 (worst possible life) to 10 (best possible life) scale, positive and negative affect in a 1 (not at all yesterday) to 3 (most of the time yesterday) scale
Source Understanding High Happiness in Latin America survey, 2018

large difference is also observed in life evaluation (1.17 for the relational-poverty conception and 0.25 for the income-poverty one, in a 0–10 scale) and in positive affect (0.31 for the relational-poverty conception and 0.04 for the income-poverty one, in a 1–3 scale).

It is interesting to see that the income-poverty conception is not capable of segmenting between those who are in positive-affect deprivation and those who are not. This is clearly a result from the fact that the relationship between income and positive affect is practically negligible. On the other hand, the quantity and quality of relations is strongly related to well-being; hence, the relational-poverty classification provides a better segmentation of those who are in well-being deprivation and those who are not.

It is also important to remark that any explanation of people's well-being needs to address the difficult issue of causation. The classifications of people as poor in this chapter are used not necessarily as an explanation of people's well-being but as criteria to segment the deprived ones from the non-deprived; this is very important for policy making in order to decide what population should receive more attention from policy makers.

8.4.5   A Closer Look at Poverty and the Affective State

The Understanding High Happiness in Latin America survey asked people about the frequency in experiencing some emotions the day before; the response scale included three categories: not at all during the day; a few times during the day, and most of the time during the day. The percentage of people experiencing the emotion 'most of the time during the day' was computed by poverty category (extreme poverty and non-poor) and by poverty conception (income poverty and relational poverty). The gradient for each emotion between those classified as non-poor and those in extreme poverty was computed. A small gradient indicates that there is no difference between the non-poor and those in extreme poverty. The exercise is useful to check which poverty conception generates larger gradients; this is: which poverty conception provides a better affective segmentation.

Figure 8.7 presents the gradients in positive affect between the non-poor and the extremely poor for the two conceptions of poverty: relational poverty and income poverty.

It is observed that the using of an income-poverty conception generates no gradient at all in the cases of experiencing enthusiasm, joy, and love or affection most of the time the day before, and the gradient is relatively small in the cases of tranquility and gratitude. Hence, from a positive affect perspective, the income conception of poverty errs in the classification of people as those classified in extreme poverty and as non-poor report more or less the same frequency in experience of positive emotions. On the other hand, the relational-poverty conception generates large gradients between those classified as non-poor and those classified as being in extreme poverty; for example, the percentage of those experiencing such an important emotion as love or affection most of the time the day before is 33 points greater for the relationally non-poor.

The same exercise was used to study gradients in negative emotions; Fig. 8.8 shows the computed gradients. It is observed that the relational-poverty conception generates larger gradients than the income-poverty conception in the experience of such important negative emotions as sadness, anger, anxiety and loneliness. The only exception happens with the experience of fear because high-income Latin Americans report relatively higher levels of this emotion.

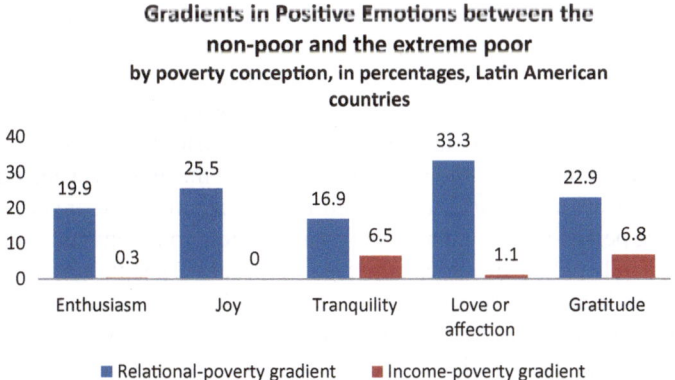

Fig. 8.7 Gradients in positive emotions, difference in percentage experiencing the emotion 'most of the day' yesterday between those classified as in extreme poverty and those classified as non-poor under two different conceptions of poverty. *Source* Understanding Happiness in Latin America survey, 2018

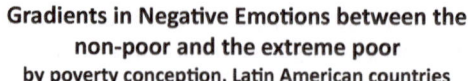

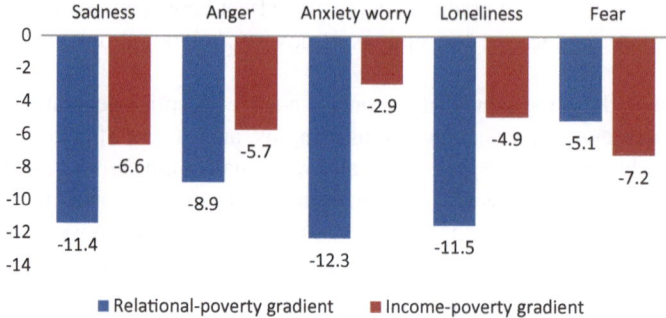

Fig. 8.8 Gradients in negative emotions, difference in percentage experiencing the emotion 'most of the day' yesterday between those classified as in extreme poverty and those classified as non-poor under two different conceptions of poverty. *Source* Understanding Happiness in Latin America survey, 2018

8.5   The Importance of Person-Based Interpersonal Relations

Close, warm and genuine interpersonal relations are central for people's well-being. This chapter has emphasized the importance of person-based interpersonal relations for people's well-being. It showed that the abundance of high-quality interpersonal relations in Latin America makes an important contribution to the high well-being levels in the region.

Unfortunately, the Social Capital literature has neglected this kind of relations in order to focus on civic and instrumental relations (Bjornskov 2003, 2008; Calvo et al. 2012; Rodríguez-Pose and von Berlepsch 2014) this implies a neglect of those relations which are more important for well-being. Civic relations are those that take place among people who share a general space (cities, communities, countries) but who are basically unknown to each other; in civic relations people are asked to follow norms and to adhere to some common practices in order to generate a functioning and comfortable coexistence. These norms contribute to generate civic relations that can be considered as polite and which, up to a certain degree, contribute to people's well-being. However, civic relations take place between people who do not know each other well and who are not even motivated of knowing each other. In consequence, good civic relations may aspire to politeness and respectfulness but not to warmness and personalized interaction; they are based on the implementation of generalized norms that do not take into consideration the specific circumstance of each person who is involved in the interaction. Hence, even though civic relations are important for a comfortable coexistence, they do not constitute the core of the relational wealth of societies. Social capital has also emphasized the importance of function-based relations; these are relations that take place out of an extrinsic motivation-such as exchanging or producing something. The social-capital concept emerged within the paradigm of progress as economic growth and its main goal is to study those relations that contribute to economic growth—by reducing transaction costs; function-based relations may be good to raise production, but their direct impact on people's well-being is not high because they are not warm, close and genuine; in other words, they are not person-based interpersonal relations.

The literature on family relations has stressed the supporting role of family bonds (Alesina and Giuliano 2010; Antonucci and Akiyama 1995; Antonucci et al. 2009; Nguyen et al. 2016; North et al. 2008). It has become common for surveys to aim at measuring this supporting role with questions about 'having someone to count on in times of trouble'. Within this perspective relatives and friends become a network of support and the family becomes an institution that emerges to face risks and in conditions where the market or the State fail in providing appropriate insurance and safety nets: the spouse, parents, and even children become an insurance of last resort.

Civic, function-based, and support relationships may be important for people's well-being, but they are missing many relevant aspects that take place in close, warm and genuine relations and which are highly relevant to people's well-being. It is in close and warm relations that people find a sense of identity and purpose in life; it is in these relations where joint enjoyment takes place and where positive emotions are mostly generated; it is in treating others as persons rather than as tools of production were a sense of value emerges. Not surprisingly, these close, warm and genuine person-based relations are strongly associated to positive affect, to evaluative experiences and, in the end, to life satisfaction.

In general the Latin American culture is a relational one; people dedicate a lot of time to be and enjoy with family, friends, coworkers and neighbors. People take their time to know each other and to take into consideration the particular situation the other person is in. This leads to a society of concrete persons rather than of shadows that accompany a person's journey in life. In this kind of society formal norms are considered as general guidelines which should not be applied without further consideration of each person's particular situation. A case by case consideration is expected and when the other person is well-known—as is the normal case for family, relatives and friends and coworkers—general formal norms may end up being completely ignored.

Modernization theory has also stressed the importance of civic—almost depersonalized—interpersonal relations based on the universal implementation of norms. Modernization theory has also associated the prevalence of close kin relationships with traditional—and somehow backward societies. Some modernization theorists have even interpreted the prevalence of close family relations as a reflection of market and State failure; this view emphasizes the supportive role of the family and proposes that the State—or the market, through private provision—are better options than the family to provide the social support. State and private organizations can provide care and insurance, they can also provide many other support services, but from a well-being perspective they are very bad substitutes to the family in what respects to generating identity, companionship, care and affection, nurturing and generativity, sense of purpose, and joint enjoyment (Baumeister and Leary 1995; Berscheid and Regan 2005; Gable et al. 2004; Grinde 2009).

The focus on the realm of relations—which comes accompanied with a relatively lower importance of the realm of objects—leads to a society that has a slower pace of life and which is not so much interested in transforming and producing as in the joint enjoying of life. The abundance of person-based interpersonal relations in Latin America is a major driver of well-being. This relational wealth seems to be more important than material wealth in contributing to people's well-being.

8.6 General Policy Considerations

Person-based interpersonal relations constitute an important driver of people's well-being. These relations take place between people who know and care about each other and where there is warmth and familiarity. They go far beyond mutual support in order to be relations of mutual enjoyment. They happen within the nuclear family, with the extended family, with friends, colleagues and neighbors. The abundance of person-based interpersonal relations in Latin America contributes to the explanation of high subjective well-being levels in the region and compensate for the well-being impact of many social, political and economic problems.

Person-based interpersonal relations are abundant in Latin America and relatively scarce in other parts of the world. However, research suggests that these relations are also very important for people's well-being everywhere; in addition, it seems that income cannot buy high quality person-based interpersonal relations and that it can neither compensate for them. Thus, it becomes important to keep track and promote these relations, even in high-income countries.

The notion of social capital has been stressed by the development literature. Civic, support and instrumental relations have a role to play; but they cannot compensate for person-based interpersonal relations. Politeness is not sufficient for fostering people's well-being.

Development strategies in Latin America need to take into consideration the importance of person-based interpersonal relations as well as of their relative abundance in the region. Development strategies focused on raising people's well-being should not neglect—and should even promote—these relations.

There is scattered information on quality and quantity of human relations. Some socio-demographic surveys contain useful information, and specific modules in social surveys may also provide information; however, these surveys are not designed from a well-being perspective and end up missing important questions to keep track of the deterioration or improvement of the relational wealth in countries. It becomes necessary to incorporate the measurement of relational wealth in systematically-run surveys.

It is possible to recognize a vast space for policy action aiming at strengthening person-based interpersonal relations and at deterring their deterioration, such as: education, public space, recreation, working shifts, social work and home visits, and so on. In fact, many countries have specific programs focused at strengthening family relations and the nurturing of children. It is not necessary to get into difficult philosophy-of-intervention discussions because public policy currently covers many aspects that are relevant to strengthen human relations. The main difference is that current policy is focused on fostering competitiveness and productivity in order to raise GDP; the well-being perspective provides a better framework to make of this policy a more effective instrument to attain greater well-being.

Current poverty-abatement programs are based on an income-conception of well-being and do completely neglect the importance of relational wealth; these programs are designed and evaluated on the basis of increasing income and they do not aim to increase—or at least sustain—the relational wealth which exists in Latin American households. Hence, these poverty abatement programs are prone to fail in increasing people's well-being even if they are successful in increasing their income.

Appendix

Interpersonal relations under consideration, criteria for high quality/quantity classification and percentage of high quality/quantity in Latin America and the United States

	Interpersonal relation	High-quality/quantity criterion	Percentage Latin America	Percentage United States
Nuclear family quantity	Sharing positive emotions with close family	Percentage always or very often	64.6	49.4
	We in the family spend a lot of time doing things together	% strongly agree or agree	76.4	61.1
	Frequency take time to share with partner	% at least several days a week	80.4	84.9
	Frequency take time to share with children	% at least several days a week	75.9	63.3
	Sharing at least one meal a day with children	% strongly agree of agree	95.1	92.8
	Frequency take time to share with adult children	% at least once a week	64.5	38.1

(continued)

(continued)

	Interpersonal relation	High-quality/quantity criterion	Percentage Latin America	Percentage United States
Nuclear family quality	Frequency of manifestations of affection with your partner	% frequent or very frequent	77.3	64.9
	Frequency of manifestations of affection with your children	% frequent or very frequent	86.7	62.8
	In our family everyone's decisions are respected	% strongly agree of agree	89.2	70.1
	I take into consideration the well-being of my family when taking important decisions	% strongly agree of agree	88.7	66.1
	Being with family is an activity that gives the most meaning to my life	% strongly agree of agree	93.6	79.8
	Reading or playing sports with children frequently	% strongly agree of agree	84.6	90.4
	We help and support each other in the family	% strongly agree of agree	86.0	66.7
Extended family	Visiting grandparents in childhood	% at least once a week	61.6	41.6
	Frequency of extended family gatherings	% at least once a month	37.6	16.4
	Manifestations of affect with siblings	% frequent or very frequent	58.9	26.3

(continued)

(continued)

	Interpersonal relation	High-quality/quantity criterion	Percentage Latin America	Percentage United States
	Frequency of meeting grandparents	% at least once a week	39.9	21.9
Rest of family	Frequency of meeting cousins	% at least once a week	20	5.8
	Frequency of meeting aunts/uncles	% at least once a week	19.7	6.6
Friends	Sharing positive emotions with friends	% Always or very often	41.8	34.2
	Friends you can talk about feelings and problems	Mean value	3.99	3.40
	Friends you can count in case of financial problems	Mean value	2.42	1.67
Coworkers	Meeting with coworkers outside working place	% at least once a week	42.2	17.9
	Talking with coworkers about interests, feelings and aspirations	% at least once a week	54.4	41.9
	In the working place we help and support each other	% agree or very much agree	80.1	61.0
Neighbors	Talking with neighbors about interests, feelings and aspirations	% at least once a week	33.2	24.6

Information for Latin America corresponds to surveys applied in Colombia, Costa Rica and Mexico. Information for the United States corresponds to survey applied to the white/Caucasian population
Source Understanding High Happiness in Latin America survey, 2018

References

Alesina, A., & Giuliano, P. (2010). The power of the family. *Journal of Economic Growth, 15,* 93–125.

Antonucci, T. C., & Akiyama, H. (1995). Convoys of social relations: Family and friendships within a life span context. In R. Blieszner & V. H. Bedford (Eds.), *Handbook of aging and the family* (pp. 355–371). Westport, CT: Greenwood Press.

Antonucci, T. C., Birditt, K. S., & Akiyama, H. (2009). Convoys of social relations: An interdisciplinary approach. In V. L. Bengtson, D. Gans, N. M. Putney, & M. Silverstein (Eds.), *Handbook of theories of aging* (pp. 247–260). New York: Springer.

Baumeister, R. F., & Leary, M. R. (1995). The need to belong: Desire for interpersonal attachment as a fundamental human motivation. *Psychological Bulletin, 117,* 497–529.

Berscheid, E., & Regan, P. (2005). *The psychology of interpersonal relationships.* Upper Saddle River, NJ: Pearson Prentice Hall.

Bjornskov, C. (2003). The happy few: Cross-country evidence on social capital and life satisfaction. *Kyklos, 56,* 3–16.

Bjornskov, C. (2008). Social capital and happiness in the United States. *Applied Research in Quality Life, 3*(1), 43–62.

Bourdieu, P. (2001). The forms of capital. In M. Granovetter & R. Swedberg (Eds.), *The sociology of economic life* (2nd ed., pp. 97–111). Oxford: Westview Press.

Calvo, R., Zheng, Y., Kumar, S., Olgiati, A., & Berkman, L. (2012). Well-being and social capital on planet earth: Cross-national evidence from 142 countries. *PLoS ONE, 7*(8), e42793.

Diwan, R. (2000). Relational wealth and the quality of life. *Journal of Socio-Economics, 29,* 305–340.

Fukuyama, F. (1996). *Trust: The social virtues and the creation of prosperity.* New York: Free Press.

Gable, S. L., Reis, H. T., Impett, E. A., & Asher, E. R. (2004). To whom do you turn when things go right? The intrapersonal and interpersonal benefits of sharing positive events. *Journal of Personality and Social Psychology, 87,* 228–245.

Grinde, B. (2009). An evolutionary perspective on the importance of community relations for quality of life. *The Scientific World Journal, 9,* 588–605.

Helliwell, J., Layard, R., & Sachs, J. (2018). *World happiness report 2018.* New York: Sustainable Development Solutions Network.

Helliwell, J. F., & Putnam, R. (2004). The social context of well-being. *Philosophical Transactions of the Royal Society London, 359,* 1435–1446.

Lin, N. (1999a). Social networks and status attainment. *American Review of Sociology, 25*(467), 487.

Lin, N. (1999b). Building a network theory of social capital. *Connections, 22*(1), 28–51.

Nguyen, A. W., Chatters, L. M., Taylor, R. J., & Mouzon, D. M. (2016). Social support from family and friends and subjective well-being of older African Americans. *Journal of Happiness Studies, 17,* 959–979.

North, R. J., Holahan, C. J., Moos, R. H., & Cronkite, R. C. (2008). Family support, family income, and happiness: A 10-year perspective. *Journal of Family Psychology, 22*(3), 475–483.

Rodríguez-Pose, A., & von Berlepsch, V. (2014). Social capital and individual happiness in Europe. *Journal of Happiness Studies, 15,* 357–386.

Rojas, M. (2018). Happiness in Latin America has social foundations. In J. Helliwell, R. Layard, & J. Sachs (Eds.), *World happiness report 2018.* New York: Sustainable Development Solutions Network.

Chapter 9
Education and Well-Being

Abstract Education has always had an important place in public policy. Unfortunately, during the past decades education policies have been inspired by the human-capital approach; this approach views the education sector as an instrument to provide skills and knowledge for people to be productive and competitive and to generate greater income. The educational sector is key in the promotion of skills and the provision of knowledge for well-being; however, by focusing too much in generating human capital the education sector risks reducing its potential impact on well-being.

Keywords Latin America · Well-being · Human capital · Skills and knowledge for life · Relative effects

The education sector is central to societies: it is large in terms of employment and it is frequently dominated by strong and powerful—although sometimes politically captured unions, a large percentage of public and private spending goes to the sector, vast segments of the population—in special little kids, children, adolescents and young adults—are directly involved with the sector, and their parents—which also constitute a vast segment of the population—are also indirectly involved. By any account this is an important sector in any country and without any doubt it must always be in the radar of policy makers and politicians.

Education, which can be considered as the general product of the sector, has always had a special place in the political discourse and in the set of indicators aiming at measuring progress. Unfortunately, the contribution that the sector could make to people's well-being has been weakened by the role that within the paradigm of progress as economic growth is expected from education; this role is: the provision of knowledge and the promotion of skills that generate a productive and highly competitive labor force.

The association between development and economic growth has called for an education that increases human capital and contributes to the rise of income. As it was stated by the Director of OECD Development Centre, Mr. Mario Pezzini: *"Education is a key element for economic and social development. An educated workforce increases the overall productivity of economic activities, allows shifting successfully towards high-growth sectors and facilitates technology absorption and innovation. Beyond strictly economic aspects, education is also critical for the effective functioning of democracy, enabling people to fully exert their rights and responsibilities as citizens*" (Daude 2011, preface). It is interesting to see that Mr. Pezzini emphasizes the human-capital role of education and that he ads the strengthening of democracy as a spinoff; within this approach education is basically an instrument for economic growth, and its contribution to better civic relations is also appreciated. In fact, the aim for education to contribute to the enhancement of a country's human capital is explicit in many public and private programs worldwide.

The well-being paradigm gives education a greater role. Within the development as well-being paradigm education is not only an instrument to raise income but, fundamentally, an opportunity to provide the knowledge and build the skills that people need to lead a satisfactory life. Human capital approaches education as an investment which necessarily implies some kind of sacrifice in the present; the well-being paradigm postulates that the educational system should not only contribute to the life satisfaction of people in the future but also to their life satisfaction in the present; little kids, adolescents and young adults should learn within a happy environment.

9.1   Education in Latin America

9.1.1   Good Literacy Rates

For decades, literacy rates were considered as the prime indicator on the education situation of the population; nowadays it is common to observe very high literacy rates almost everywhere in the world and, in fact, this is the situation with the young Latin American population.

Figure 9.1 shows that literacy rates for the young population—those between 15 and 25 years old—are above 90% in all Latin American countries; as a matter of fact, they are above 98% in all countries except for Honduras, Nicaragua and Guatemala. Literacy rates for the adult population—those in between 25 and 65 years old—are also above 90% in all countries but Honduras, El Salvador, Nicaragua and Guatemala. Figures for the elder population are beneath 80% in all countries with the exception of Argentina, Uruguay, Chile, Panama, Costa Rica and Colombia.

The information in Fig. 9.1 shows that during the past decades the attainment of the basic goal of people being able to read and write has become almost universal in Latin America. The comparison across age groups shows that many Latin American countries have made substantial progress in attaining this goal for the young generations.

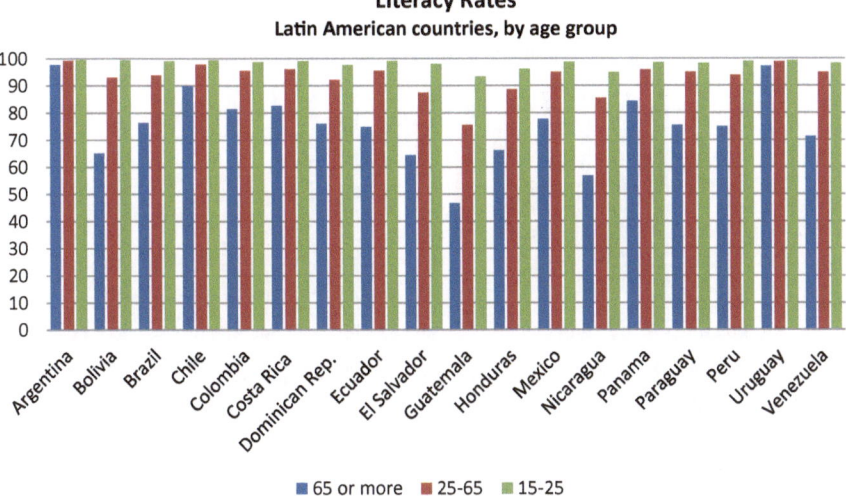

Fig. 9.1 Literacy rates in Latin American countries, by age groups. Most recent year available (2017 or 2016; except for Nicaragua—2014, Chile—2015 and Venezuela—2006). *Source* Socio-Economic Database for Latin America and the Caribbean (CEDLAS and World Bank)

9.1.2 Deficiencies in Enrollment Rates

The literacy rate is a very basic indicator which needs to be complemented with other indicators in order to have a good perspective on access to education. Figure 9.2 presents the net enrollment rates in Latin American countries by educational category. It is observed that the net enrollment rate in primary education is very high, going from 99.6% in Costa Rica to 81.1% in Guatemala; most countries have values above 97%, which means that almost all kids in primary-school age are attending primary school. An important drop in enrollment rates—of about 22 percentage points on average—is observed for secondary education; and a substantial drop is observed for tertiary education. Only about 27% of those in age of attending tertiary education are doing it in Latin American countries; this shows an important deficit regarding access to advanced knowledge in Latin America.

There are important challenges faced by the educational system when studying net enrollment rates in tertiary education by income quintile (see Fig. 9.3). In all Latin American countries there is a gap in net enrollment between the bottom and the top income quintiles; the gap is relatively small in Chile and Argentina, where the likelihood for young adults from the bottom income quintile of being at tertiary education is about 50% of that for young adults from the top income quintile. The gap is very large in Guatemala, where the likelihood for young adults from the bottom income quintile of being at tertiary education is only about 5% of that for young adults from the top income quintile. Big gaps are also observed in El Salvador and Panama.

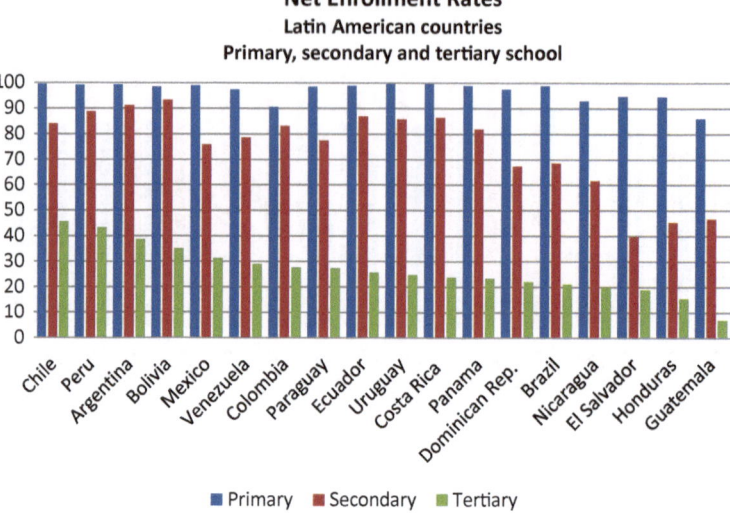

Fig. 9.2 Net enrollment rates in Latin American schools. Net enrollment defined as share of children in category school age attending their school category. Most recent year available (2017 or 2016; except for Nicaragua—2014, Chile—2015 and Venezuela—2006). *Source* Socio-Economic Database for Latin America and the Caribbean (CEDLAS and World Bank)

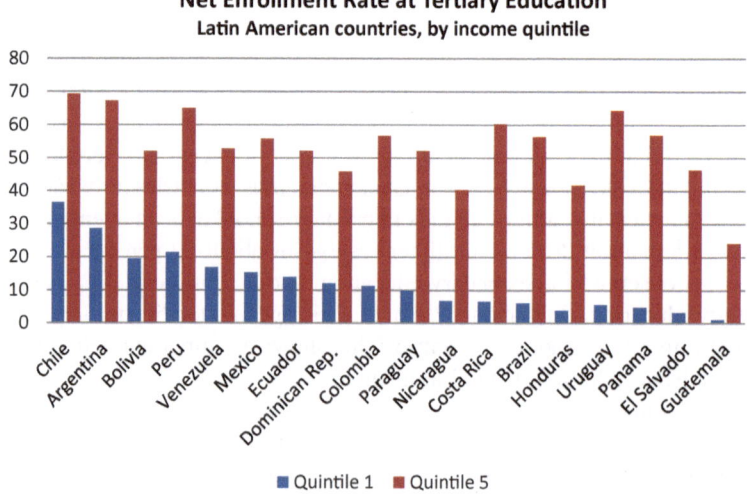

Fig. 9.3 Net enrollment rates in Latin American tertiary education, by equivalent-income quintile. Net enrollment defined as share of children in category X school age attending category X school. Most recent year available (2017 or 2016; except for Nicaragua—2014, Chile—2015 and Venezuela—2006). *Source* Socio-Economic Database for Latin America and the Caribbean (CEDLAS and World Bank)

Universal access to tertiary education is not a usual objective, and enrollment rates beneath 100% are expected; however, big differences by income quintile in access to tertiary education are considered unfair because it points to structural and beyond control conditions that influence the access to education of the young population; this situation also contributes to an inefficient allocation of talent in societies. For the bottom income quintiles the highest rates are observed in Chile (37%) and Argentina (29%), while the lowest rate is observed in Guatemala (1.3%). There is wide dispersion in enrolment rates—at any income quintile—across Latin American countries.

9.2 Human Capital Theory. Education as Investment

Human Capital theory approaches education as an input for economic growth; the role of education consists in raising the productivity of the labor force and in creating opportunities for people to get into the labor market. It is understood that education's major contribution is the increase of people's income. The paradigm of development as economic growth assumes that greater income translates directly, and almost automatically, into greater well-being.

Human Capital theory emerged at the beginning of the second half of the 20th century with the work of economists such as Mincer (1957, 1962), Schultz (1959, 1961, 1962, 1971) and Becker (1964) and it consolidated during the following decades. Basic capital concepts—such as physical, financial and natural capital—were not sufficient to explain income disparities across countries and over time, and new capital concepts were incorporated—such as human capital and social capital—into economic-growth models in order to explain these disparities.

Human Capital makes reference to the productive knowledge and skills the labor force has; education becomes the instrument to increase this capital. Hence, education is approached as a kind of investment, a term widely used in economics and which means that sacrifices are faced in the present in order to obtain monetary rewards in the future. Economic growth models assume that income is the main driver of well-being; thus, all sacrifices and benefits are monetized. The cost of education is measured by its monetary cost plus any forgone earnings due to the time invested in education, the benefits from education are approximated by the present value of the raise in income due to pursuing further education. Hence, like any other investment in the development as economic growth paradigm, it makes sense to pursue additional years of education when its benefits are greater that its costs. In consequence, the educational system must focus on providing the knowledge and promoting the skills that increase people's productivity and their long-run income flow; this implies for a more productive and competitive labor force. There are many studies of the impact of education on people's income (Becker 1994; Hanushek and Kimko 2000; Hanushek and Woessmann 2008, 2011; Jensen 2010; Moretti 2004; Teixeira 2005, 2010).

Governments and international organizations are highly involved in the promotion of an educational system that contributes to human capital and to economic growth.

For example, the Organization for Economic Cooperation and Development states: "*In the global knowledge economy, people's skills, learning, talents and attributes – their human capital - have become key to both their ability to earn a living and to wider economic growth. Education systems can do much to help people realise their potential, but when they fail it can lead to lifelong social and economic problems*" (OECD Insights—Human Capital—Chap. 2: The Value of People; Keeley 2007). The World Bank has launched its Human Capital Project with the following purpose: "*This effort is about building human capital in all countries*"; as part of the project the World Bank is constructing The Human Capital Index which aims to "*quantifies the contribution of health and education to the productivity of the next generation of workers. Countries can use it to assess how much income they are foregoing because of human capital gaps, and how much faster they can turn these losses into gains if they act now*".[1] In its Human Capital Project booklet, the World Bank states: "*By improving their skills, health, knowledge, and resilience—their human capital—people can be more productive, flexible, and innovative. Investments in human capital have become more and more important as the nature of work has evolved in response to rapid technological change. As highlighted in the 2019 World Development Report (WDR): The Changing Nature of Work, markets are increasingly demanding workers with higher levels of human capital, especially advanced cognitive and sociobehavioral skills. In Vietnam, for example, workers able to perform nonroutine analytical work earn nearly 25 percent more than those who cannot*". The United Nations Economic Commission for Europe has also produced its guidelines to measure human capital (UNECE 2016), as well as the World Bank (2018). Of course, the business sector has also adopted the human-capital perspective. The international organizations believe that a more productive labor force is associated to greater income and to greater profits and, in consequence, they are enthusiastic about an educational system that provides knowledge and promotes skills to increase the productivity of the future labor force. However, this seems to be an inefficient strategy to increase the well-being of present and future generations.

9.3   Education and Income in Latin America

9.3.1   The Contribution of Education to Income

Education is correlated with income in Latin America; people with higher education tend to earn more income. This is not really a surprise because the educational system has focused on providing the knowledge and fostering the skills for people to become more productive and to earn greater income. Figure 9.4 presents the income contribution of different educational levels in Latin American countries; the information refers to the male population. These figures are obtained on the basis of an

---

[1] http://www.worldbank.org/en/publication/human-capital.

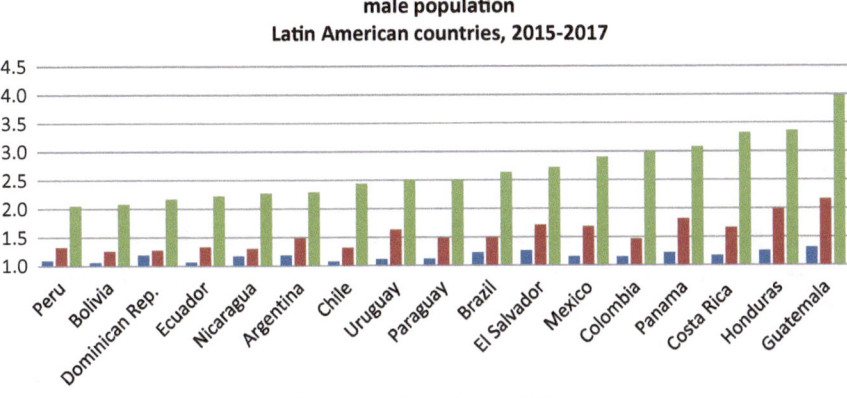

Fig. 9.4 Income ratios by education level, with respect to uneducated level, for male population, Latin American countries, recent years (2015–2017). *Source* Socio-Economic Database for Latin America and the Caribbean (CEDLAS and World Bank)

exercise known as the Mincerian equation, which estimates the marginal contribution to lifelong income from attaining an additional education level.

It is observed that the contribution of primary education is relatively small. The lowest values are observed in Bolivia and Ecuador (1.06), Chile (1.08) and Peru (1.09), while the highest values are observed in Guatemala (1.31), El Salvador (1.26) and Honduras (1.25). A value of 1.06—estimated in Bolivia and Chile—means that a male person with primary education is expected to earn during his lifetime about 6% more than a similar person with no education.

Secondary education makes almost no marginal contribution to income in Dominican Republic and Nicaragua, while its contribution is very large in Guatemala, Honduras, Panama and Mexico. The marginal contribution to income of moving from secondary to tertiary education is very large in Guatemala, Costa Rica and Colombia and it is relatively small in Peru, Argentina and Bolivia.

In all countries the biggest increase in income is obtained when moving from secondary to tertiary education. A male with tertiary education in Guatemala is expected to earn along his lifetime about 4 times more that an uneducated male. This figure is about three times in Honduras, Costa Rica, Panama, Mexico and Colombia, and it is more than two times in all Latin American countries.

Figure 9.5 presents the same information for the female population. Trends are very similar to those for the male population. Tertiary education makes the largest marginal contribution to income and primary education the smallest contribution. It is interesting to study the gender difference in the contribution of tertiary education to income by country; tertiary education contributes much less to the income of females than to the income of males in almost all Latin American countries, and the difference

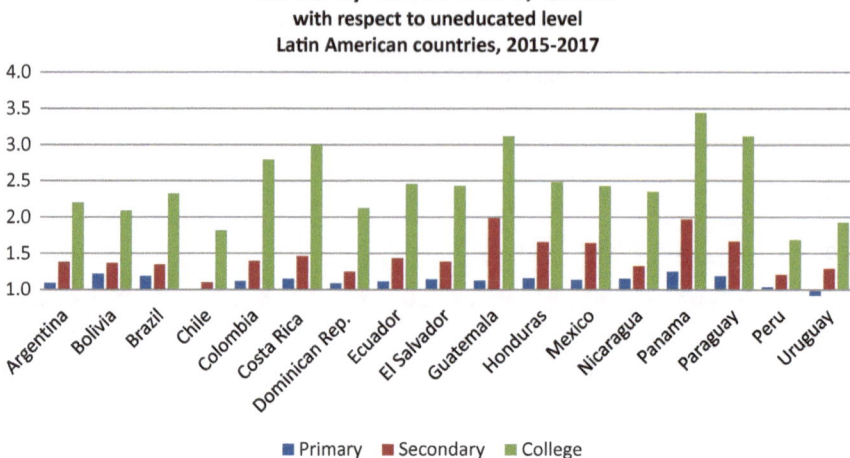

Fig. 9.5 Income ratios by education level, with respect to uneducated level, for female population, Latin American countries, recent years (2015–2017). *Source* Socio-Economic Database for Latin America and the Caribbean (CEDLAS and World Bank)

is very large in Honduras, Guatemala, Chile and Uruguay. Countries where tertiary education contributes more to the income of women than to the income of males are Nicaragua, Ecuador, Panama and Paraguay.

9.3.2   Relative Effects in the Relationship Between Education and Income

Cross-section studies show that highly educated people earn more income than uneducated ones; however, this finding does not necessarily imply for education to be a strong instrument in raising people's income. By moving from accomplishing secondary to accomplishing tertiary education people can aspire to attain greater income; however, what happens when everybody has more education? There are two effects in the relationship between education and income: First, following human capital theory, education could provide knowledge and promote skills that make people more productive and creative, which could lead to greater income; this is called the absolute effect of education on income, and it is independent of what happens to other people's education. Second, education plays a signaling role in the allocation of high-income jobs; those with the best education get the best jobs and the highest incomes. In this case, a relative effect takes place, so that the relationship between a person's education and her income do also depend on the education levels of everybody else's in society. A large relative effect may imply that universal increases in education levels across the population are accompanied of little increase in people's income.

In the case of a large absolute effect, an educational system designed to provide the knowledge and to develop the skills for people to be more productive and to earn greater income would lead to universal increases in income when enrollment rates and average education levels rise. However, in the case of a large relative effect, a universal increase in education levels will not be accompanied by universal increases in income, and education—even an education designed to provide the knowledge and promote the skills to be productive—will be a frail instrument in raising people's income.

During the past two decades there has been significant progress in education in Latin America. The attainment of primary education has become almost universal, and more people are now finishing secondary and even tertiary education than two decades ago. If the absolute effect dominates then more people having more education now than before should not influence the relationship between education and income; however, if the relative effect dominates then the larger the number of people with greater education levels the smaller the impact of attaining higher education levels on income.

Figure 9.6 presents the change in the marginal contribution of education to income over the past two decades for the male population in Latin American countries. With few exceptions, the change in the returns to education has been negative in most Latin American countries; college and secondary education are now associated to a smaller income gradient—with respect to uneducated people—than what it was two decades ago. Costa Rica constitutes a particular case where college and primary education are providing larger returns now than two decades ago; without doubt this shows that other factors associated to globalization trends and modifications in the job market which are beyond the education level of the person do also impact on the relationship between education and income.

Figure 9.6 shows that the income impact of having college education has strongly declined in most countries in the region. In other words, accomplishing college education in the present is not associated to the same relative income levels than it was in the past; this happens because more people have college education now than before. It shows that generalized increases in education levels in the region erode the capacity education has of yielding higher incomes. Thus, there are relative effects in the relationship between education and income, so that generalized increases in education do not translate into large increases in income.

Due to the existence of relative effects in the relationship between education and income the capacity of education to generate income is limited; in addition, as shown in previous chapters, the impact of income on well-being is weak. Hence, an educational system that focuses on providing the knowledge and in promoting the skills for people to be productive and competitive is not very effective in increasing people's income, and it is even less effective in raising people's well-being. Two treadmill effects could be at play: First, when enrollment rates increase people need more education to attain the same income; second, when there are generalized increases in income people need more income to attain the same economic satisfaction. Hence,

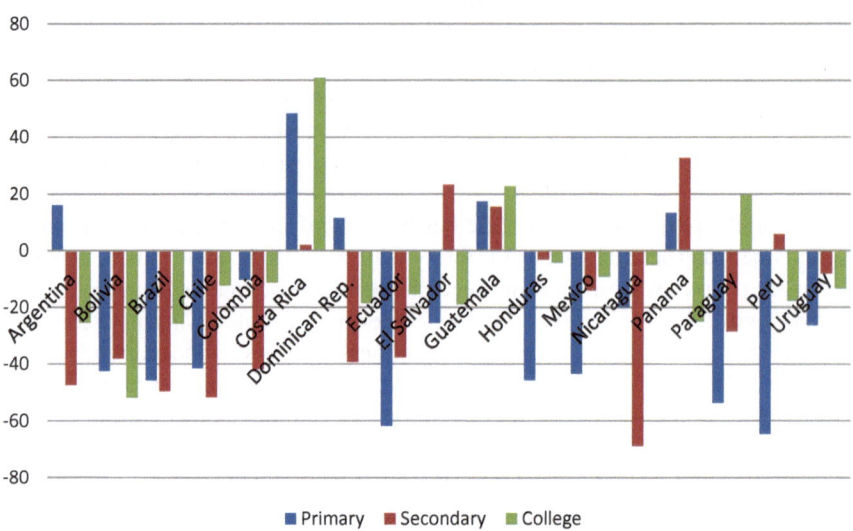

Fig. 9.6 Change in the marginal contribution of education level to income generation over the past two decades, for male population, Latin American countries, change between education contribution in the early 2000s and recent years (2015–2017). *Source* Socio-Economic Database for Latin America and the Caribbean (CEDLAS and World Bank)

the greater the number of people that pursue this path to well-being the less effective it becomes.

Of course, wages and income in general do depend on many other factors that could have changed during the past decades. Globalization, economic reforms, bargaining power of unions, and changing international conditions may impact the returns of education. There has also been some concern regarding the quality of education.

9.4 Education and Well-Being

The paradigm of development as economic growth assumes that income is the most important driver of people's well-being; it is within this paradigm that human-capital theory approaches education as an instrument to raise people's income and—in consequence—their well-being. However, as it was explained in previous sections, a strategy that focuses on promoting an educational system that provides knowledge and fosters skills aiming at raising people's productivity is not expected to be very effective in raising people's well-being in the long run due to the following reasons: First, as it was shown in previous chapters, income is not strongly related to people's well-being. Second, treadmill effects may imply for generalized increases in education levels to have a small impact on people's income. Third, education is understood as investment—which in economics is associated to the concept of sacrifice—rather than as enjoyment; hence, it is sacrifice rather than enjoyment which is at the core of educational programs inspired in human capital theory. Thus, the many years that little kids and young adults spend at schools and universities are not conceived to be happy years but years of sacrifice. Fourth, by focusing on promoting skills and providing knowledge to raise labor productivity the educational system is marginalizing—and even neglecting—the importance of that knowledge and those skills which could be useful for leading a satisfactory life. There is more to life than income and the educational system should focus on providing knowledge and promoting skills that do not only increase income but, fundamentally, to lead a satisfactory life.

In cross-section studies highly educated people are expected to report greater life satisfaction. This is not really a surprise: Education is positively associated to income in cross-section studies because more educated people tend to get the high-income jobs, and income is also positively associated to people's well-being because high-income people tend to have greater social status. However, it could also be that education—even in an unintended way—provides knowledge and fosters skills that contribute to leading a satisfactory life, even after accounting for its impact on income.

Doing empirical research on the relationship between education and well-being poses a major challenge: The educational system has been designed within a paradigm that emphasizes the knowledge and skills to be productive while neglecting the skills and knowledge to lead a satisfactory life. Hence, what empirical research on the relationship between education and well-being shows is not how education could contribute to well-being but how an education which has been designed to raise income ends up contributing—perhaps unintentionally—to people's well-being. To fully exploit the potential of the educational system to contribute to people's well-being it would be necessary to think about an educational system which explicitly aims at increasing people's well-being (Paoli 2011).

Are there well-being effects of education that go beyond its contribution to income? Rojas (2018) uses data from Mexico and shows that education has a positive association with people's well-being, even after controlling for income and socio-demographic variables. In fact, highly educated people report being more satisfied with life as well as more satisfied in such important domains of life as: health, economic situation, occupation and, in a smaller degree, family and friends. Figure 9.7 presents information on the gradient of education level (measured by the highest level accomplished) on people's satisfaction with life after controlling for the impact of education on income. Figure 9.7 also provides information on the impact of an increase in household per capita income on life satisfaction.

It is observed that education is positively associated to people's satisfaction with life even after controlling for income. This means that the current educational system may be contributing to people's well-being by providing skills and knowledge that are not only useful to be more productive but also to lead satisfactory lives. This is

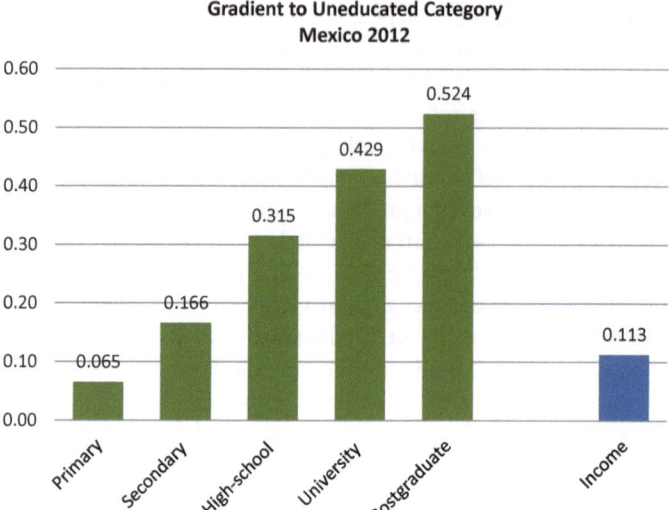

Fig. 9.7 Life satisfaction and education level, gradient with respect to uneducated category. Income refers to the logarithm of household per capita income. Life satisfaction in a 1–7 categorical response scale treated as cardinal in this quantitative exercise. Exercise controls by logarithm of household per capita income, gender, age, age squared, marital status, and municipality. *Source* ImaginaMéxico survey, Mexico, 2012

good news and it is something that shows that education has a greater value than that which human capital attributes to.

The estimated coefficient for the logarithm of household per capita income is about 0.11 (in a 1–7 life satisfaction scale). It is observed that every additional education level which is attained implies an increase in life satisfaction of about 0.10 points; this increase is as high as 0.15 in the case of moving from secondary to high school. Hence a person with postgraduate degree is expected to report a life satisfaction which is about 0.50 points above than that for a person with no education at all, after controlling by income and other socio-demographic variables. Furthermore, the impact of each educational level on life satisfaction is similar than that which corresponds to an increase of about 100% in income; this indicates that beyond its contribution to generate more purchasing power the current educational system is also contributing to people's well-being.

It is important to remark that the study uses data from Mexico which corresponds to people who were educated within a paradigm that emphasizes the provision of knowledge and to promotion of skills to generate income. Therefore, the estimated well-being contribution of education—beyond its contribution to income—takes place for an educational system that has not made of well-being its central aim. A greater impact of education on well-being would be expected if the system focuses on providing the knowledge and fostering the skills that contribute the most to people being satisfied with life.

The educational system could widen its scope and make of people's well-being its final aim. The capacity to generate income may be important, but the educational system should also take into consideration that the enjoyment of free time, the quality and frequency of interpersonal relations, the parenthood aptitudes, the prevention of health problems, and even the ability to spend carefully are important capacities that the system must also promote.

9.5 General Policy Considerations

Little kids in Latin America—and everywhere else in the world—are much more than future labor force: they are persons. Public policy should be concerned not only about these kids' capacity to generate income in the future but, fundamentally, about their present and future well-being.

The most important activity little kids will perform in the future is not about being productive workers but about being spouses and parents, sons and daughters, citizens and friends, neighbors and colleagues. They will also have to take decisions regarding their free time, their meals and exercise, their body and mental health, and their community and environment. These activities and decisions will be important for their well-being, and the educational system should focus on providing the knowledge and fostering the skills for them to take the appropriate decisions that contribute the most to their well-being.

The understanding of development as economic growth has induced governments and international organizations to overstress the importance of strengthening human capital, which ends up reducing human beings to the abstract figures of workers and producers and assuming that their well-being depends only on their purchasing capacity. This is a big mistake that makes of education an inefficient instrument to contribute to the well-being of human beings because income is not enough to ensure a person's well-being.

Human capital theory promotes an investment view of education; this is: education is conceived as an investment people make, with the associated sense of sacrifice it brings out. Hence, kids and adolescents are expected to make a sacrifice while studying rather than to enjoy their years of study. In fact, some people spend up to 20 years of their life in the educational system—which is about a quarter of their life. The well-being paradigm calls for approaching these years as a time of enjoyment rather than of sacrifice; learning and enjoying can go side by side.

Commonly used indicators of the educational situation focus on literacy rates and the accumulation of years of education; however, what really matters is for people to acquire the relevant knowledge and the appropriate skills to lead a satisfactory life.

It is important to remark that no significant relative effects are expected in the contribution of education to well-being; in other words: It is expected for generalized increases in education to imply generalized increases in well-being if the educational system focuses on providing the knowledge and fostering the skills that favor well-being.

Education for well-being is also important for the adult and retired population, even if this education will make no contribution to the generation of income. There is knowledge and skills that would benefit the well-being of elder people; education itself may provide the space for elder people to interact and share interests, activities and perspectives, which also contribute to their well-being.

It was shown that the educational system which currently predominates in Latin America and the world has an important impact on people's well-being. This educational system is based on the idea of providing the knowledge and promoting the skills to increase human capital. To fully grasp the potential of education for people's well-being it becomes necessary to move beyond the current philosophy behind the educational system in order to think about a system aiming at people's well-being rather than at their productivity. It would be necessary to get into the knowledge, skills and values which education promotes as well as on the appropriate pedagogies that transmit and allow people to grasp them.

References

Becker, G. (1964, 1993, 3rd ed.). *Human capital: A theoretical and empirical analysis, with special reference to education*. Chicago: University of Chicago Press.

Becker, G. (1994). *Human capital: A theoretical and empirical analysis, with special reference to education*. Chicago: The University of Chicago Press.

Daude, C. (2011). *Ascendance by descendants? On intergenerational education mobility in Latin America*. Working Paper No. 297. Paris: OECD Development Centre.

Hanushek, E., & Kimko, D. (2000). Schooling, labor force quality, and the growth of nations. *American Economic Review, 90*(5), 1184–1208.

Hanushek, E., & Woessmann, L. (2008). The role of cognitive skills in economic development. *Journal of Economic Literature, 46*(3), 607–668.

Hanushek, E. A., & Woessmann, L. (2011). The economics of international differences in educational achievement. In E. A. Hanushek, S. Machin, & L. Woessmann (Eds.), *Handbook of the economics of education* (pp. 89–199). Amsterdam: North Holland.

Jensen, R. (2010). The (perceived) returns to education and the demand for schooling. *Quarterly Journal of Economics, 125*(2), 515–548.

Keeley, B. (2007). *Human capital—The value of people* (Chap. 2, pp. 22–37). OECD Insights.

Mincer, J. (1957). *A study on personal income distribution* (Ph.D. dissertation). Columbia University, New York.

Mincer, J. (1962). On the job training: Costs, returns, and some implications. *Journal of Political Economy, 70*(5), 550–579.

Moretti, E. (2004). Workers' education, spillovers, and productivity: Evidence from plant-level production functions. *The American Economic Review, 94*(3), 656–669.

Paoli, A. (2011). La educación promotora del bienestar. In M. Rojas (coord.), *La Medición del Progreso y del Bienestar: Propuestas desde América Latina* (pp. 297–304). Mexico D.F.: Foro Consultivo Científico y Tecnológico.

Rojas, M. (2018). Educación, Capital Humano y Felicidad. In R. Millán & R. Castellanos (Eds.), *Bienestar Subjetivo en México*. Mexico: UNAM.

Schultz, T. W. (1959). Human wealth and economic growth. *Humanist, 2,* 109–117.

Schultz, T. W. (1961). Investment in human capital. *American Economic Review, 51,* 1–17.

Schultz, T. W. (Ed). (1962). Investment in human beings. *Journal of Political Economy, 70*(5, Part 2), 1–8.

Schultz, T. W. (1971). *Investment in human capital: The role of education and research.* New York: Free Press.

Teixeira, P. (2005). The human capital revolution in economics. *History of Economic Ideas, 13*(2), 129–148.

Teixeira, P. (2010). *Human capital—A reading guide* (pp. 152–159). Cheltenham: Elgar Companion on Chicago Economics; Edward Elgar.

UNECE. (2016). *Guide on measuring human capital.* Geneva: United Nations Economic Commission for Europe.

World Bank. (2018). The human capital project booklet.

Chapter 10
Crime, Violence and Well-Being

Abstract Latin Americans are exposed to high levels of violence associated to gangs, organized crime and even domestic violence. It is shown that victimization impacts negatively on the well-being of Latin Americans and that its impact is very large in the case of women. Exposure to victimization is concentrated in particular areas of the region; however, fear of crime is widely spread in many Latin American countries and it also impacts negatively on well-being. It is also shown that domestic violence has a very large impact the well-being of women.

Keywords Crime · Violence · Well-being · Latin America · Homicides

10.1 High Violence in Many Latin American Countries

Many Latin Americans are exposed to high levels of violence. Robs, kidnapping, extortion, cybercrime, homicides, guerrilla incursions and population displacements, paramilitary groups, are common language in some parts of the region. The term failed State is often used to characterize the situation in some cities and zones.

10.1.1 Homicide Rates

Many Latin American countries rank in the top 20 in terms of homicide rates. Table 10.1 shows that three Latin American countries top the ranking—according to recent data from 2015 or 2016: El Salvador, Honduras and Venezuela. Six other Latin American countries are also in the top 20: Brazil, Guatemala, Colombia, Mexico, Puerto Rico and Dominican Republic. It is important to remark that this list includes the three most populated countries in the region: Brazil, Mexico, and Colombia. It is also important to state that in some countries violence is concentrated in particular regions or cities, which implies that the average rate of homicides in a country does not really portray the situation faced by many citizens (Ajzenman and Jaitman 2016; Briceño-Leon et al. 2008). However, this also implies that violence rates are very high in some particular cities, with names such as Tijuana, Acapulco, Caracas,

© Springer Nature Switzerland AG 2020
M. Rojas, *Well-Being in Latin America*, Human Well-Being Research and Policy Making,
https://doi.org/10.1007/978-3-030-33498-7_10

Table 10.1 Most violent countries in the world. Homicides per 100,000 inhabitants

Country	Rate	Region
El Salvador	82.8	Latin America
Honduras	56.5	Latin America
Venezuela	56.3	Latin America
Jamaica	47.0	Caribbean
Lesotho	41.3	Sub-Saharan Africa
Belize	37.6	Caribbean
Saint Vincent and the Grenadines	36.5	Caribbean
South Africa	34.0	Sub-Saharan Africa
Trinidad and Tobago	30.9	Caribbean
Brazil	29.5	Latin America
Bahamas	28.4	Caribbean
Anguilla	27.7	Caribbean
Guatemala	27.3	Latin America
Colombia	25.5	Latin America
Central African Republic	19.76	Sub-Saharan Africa
Mexico	19.26	Latin America
Puerto Rico	18.51	Latin America
Guyana	18.37	Caribbean
Dominican Republic	15.18	Latin America
Democratic Republic of the Congo	13.55	Sub-Saharan Africa

Intentional homicide victims, counts and rates per 100,000 population
Most recent available information; in most cases it corresponds to 2015 or 2016
Source United Nations Office on Drugs and Crime (UNODC 2018)

Ciudad Juárez, Natal, Fortaleza, Belem, Culiacán, San Salvador, Tegucigalpa, and San Pedro Sula frequently being listed in the top 50 most violent cities in the world.

High violence is not generalized across all Latin American countries; Fig. 10.1 shows that recent homicide rates are relatively low in Chile, Cuba and Uruguay, and they are not far away from the global average (which is around 8.2 per 100,000 inhabitants) in Bolivia, Costa Rica, Nicaragua, Panama and Paraguay.

Figure 10.1 also shows that there have been important changes in homicide rates during the past two decades; for example, homicide rates are on the rise in El Salvador and Venezuela while they are declining in Colombia. There has also been an important increment in homicide rates in Brazil. Some countries present an inverted U-shaped behavior, with homicide rates rising during the first years of the 21st century and then declining; such is the case of Honduras, Dominican Republic, Ecuador and Nicaragua. In any case, high volatility along time in homicide rates is observed.

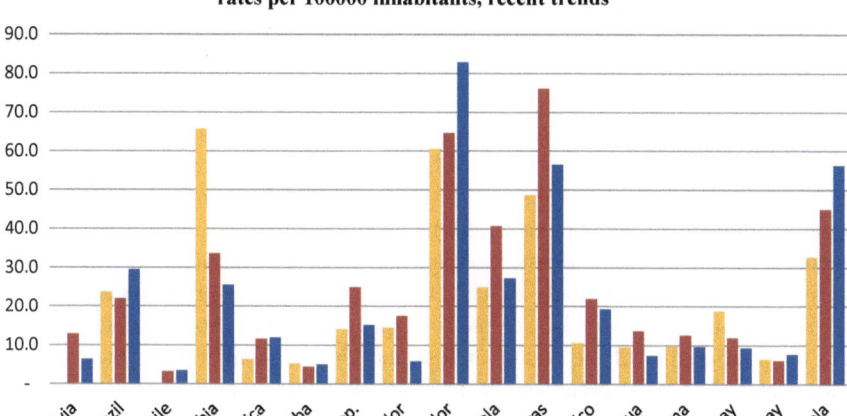

Fig. 10.1 Intentional homicide victims, counts and rates per 100,000 inhabitants. No data available for Argentina and Peru. Most recent available information; in most cases it corresponds to 2015 or 2016. *Source* United Nations Office on Drugs and Crime (UNODC 2014, 2018)

Of course, homicides constitute an extreme case of violence which illustrates a larger phenomenon in the region. Many Latin Americans are exposed to other kind of crimes which could be considered of lesser degree but which are more frequent, such as: serious assault, kidnapping, extortion, theft, robbery, and burglary. While homicides may be concentrated in specific geographical areas or in specific population groups (mostly young men) other kinds of crime impact on large segments of the population.

10.1.2 Many Causes of Violence

The high levels of violence in some Latin American countries cannot be explained by a single factor; however, this does not imply for all potential explanatory factors to be equally important (Dammert and Malone 2006; Díaz and Meller 2012; Imbusch et al. 2011; Naritomi and Soares 2010; Vilalta 2014).

Organized crime is a major problem in countries such as Mexico, El Salvador, Honduras, Brazil and Venezuela. It is a major economic activity which is run by well-organized groups who take advantage of a climate of impunity and corruption. The easiness to pay bribes and corrupt officers and judges reduces the penalties associated to illegal activities and substantially increases their rate of return. It is a highly profitable but illegal and harmful activity that attracts an important proportion of these countries' talent.

Of course, some socio-economic and demographic situations do also contribute to explain the high rates of crime in Latin America. The demographic structure of the population—with a larger percentage of the population in the 15–30 years old range—plays in favor of the prevalence of violent crimes. Income inequality and exposure to national and international high-income reference groups promote materialistic values and raise material aspirations which are not easily accessible to large segments of the population. Some people aspire to a sumptuous life which is not accessible given their education and surrounding conditions; the life style of many lawbreakers is commonly associated to the possession of luxurious cars, trips in private executive planes, and the display of expensive jewelry. Social marginalization and the poor-quality of the educational system do also contribute to incline many adolescents to join the organized crime. The deterioration of the social fabric, the increase in the rate of family disintegration or separation as well as on dysfunctional families, and the increasing rates of adolescent and single mothers point towards the weakening of nurturing schemes which traditionally used to promote values of integrity and respect to others, even under difficult economic conditions. Some Latin American countries have also being exposed to a phenomenon of migration of return which has been difficult to handle; gangs such as the MS-13 and M-18 have become prominently involved in crime activities in some Central American countries and are fully integrated with their counterparts in the United States. In addition, the closeness of the region to the largest drug market in the world is not helping at all (see Fig. 10.2).

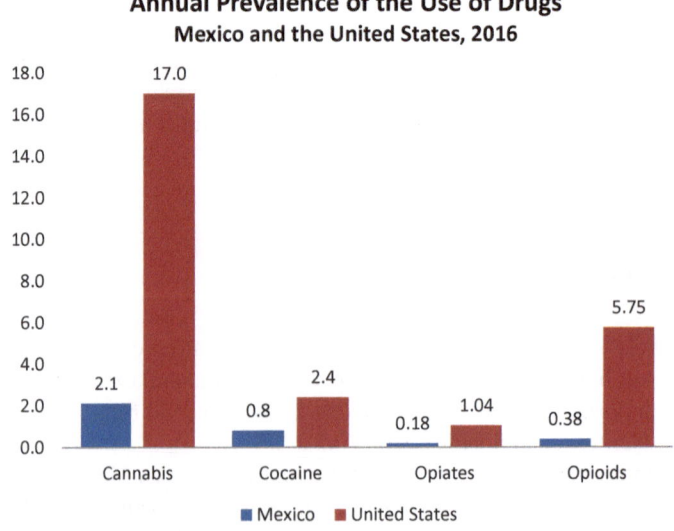

Fig. 10.2 Annual prevalence of the use of drugs in Mexico and the United States, 2016. It refers to the proportion of a population that uses a drug within the year. *Source* UNODC (2018)

Prevalence of the use of drugs is very high in the United States; in addition, it is a large market both in terms of population and purchasing power.

The strategy followed by the United States of battling drugs in their place of production rather than it their place of consumption aggravates the climate of violence and corruption in some Latin American countries. This strategy transfers the war on drugs to their place of production and to in-transit countries; the drug cartels get strengthened by the strategy either by selling a larger volume—if the strategy fails—or by selling at higher prices—if the strategy is successful. Latin American's efforts to reduce crime and violence would benefit from a decline in the demand for drugs in the United States; this strategy would require from the United States to focus on the internal socio-economic conditions which are fostering demand. It would also help if the United States could control the selling and trafficking of arms which cross southward the border. This is why some reports from the region and many Latin American presidents have called for reconsidering the current strategy followed by the so-called War on Drugs (OAS 2014; Organization of American States, Global Commission on Drug Policy 2016).

10.1.3 Economic Impact of Crime

There is abundant research on the economic impact of crime (Balmori de la Miyar 2016). Most researchers have studied the impact of crime on economic growth and there is general agreement that it reduces growth (Bel and Holst 2018; Cárdenas and Rozo 2008; Detotto and Otranto 2010; Pan et al. 2012). There is also research on how crime affects labor productivity (Cabral et al. 2016) and employment (Coronado and Saucedo 2018). Economists have placed particular interest on the impact of crime on foreign direct investments (Ashby and Ramos 2013; Cabral et al. 2019). Some researchers mention their interest in studying the welfare cost of crime and violence, but they end up focusing on foregone income, monetary cost of crime, and people's willingness to pay to avoid it (Jaitman 2015).

The interest in studying the relationship between crime and variables related to economic growth clearly shows the predominance of the development-as-economic-growth paradigm. This chapter will focus on how crime relates to people's experience of being well, which is an understudied area of research (Cohen 2008; Graham and Chaparro 2011; Hanslmaier 2013; Powdthavee 2005; Rojas 2017b; Staubli et al. 2014).

10.2   Crime and Well-Being

10.2.1   *Victimization in Latin America*

Rates of victimization are very high in Latin America; of course, there are many types of crime and their degree of violence as well as their expected impact on people's well-being varies across types. Figure 10.3 presents general victimization rates based on the simple question asked in the World Value Survey: 'Have you been the victim of a crime during the past year?' The response scale is dichotomous: No, Yes answer. It is observed that victimization rates in selected Latin American countries are much higher than those in the United States and Spain. About a quarter of the Peruvian population and one fifth of the Mexican population report being victims of crime during the previous twelve months. It is also observed that the gender gap is very large in Mexico and Chile, with men being more exposed to crime than women.

Victimization has a strong negative impact on people's well-being, in particular for women. Figure 10.4 presents the estimations from a quantitative exercise that studies the impact on life satisfaction of being a victim of crime; the exercise controls for other socio-demographic and economic variables. Women who were victims of crime report a life satisfaction which is 0.26 lower (in a scale of 0–10) than those who were not victims; the difference in the case of men is much smaller (0.06 lower). The available information does not allow for an explanation of this gender difference; it could be that men and women are exposed to different types of crime or that the repercussions of the same crime are sensitive to the gender of the victim.

Fig. 10.3 Percentage of people who report being victim of crime during the twelve months previous to the survey, by country and gender. *Source* World Values Survey wave 2011–2014

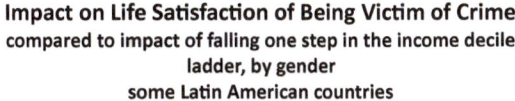

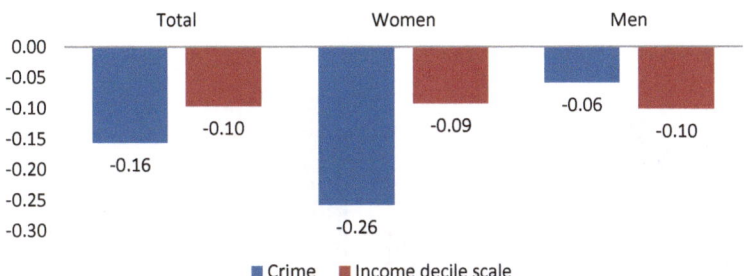

Fig. 10.4 Impact of being victim of crime—during the past 12 months—on life satisfaction. Compared to impact of falling one step in the income-decile ladder. By gender. Latin American countries: Argentina, Brazil, Chile, Colombia, Ecuador, Mexico, Peru, Uruguay. Life satisfaction measured in a 1–10 scale. Estimated coefficient from a regression that controls for: age, age squared, gender, education level, marital status, income position, and country. *Source* World Values Survey 2011–2014 wave

Figure 10.4 also presents information on the life satisfaction impact of falling one step in the income-decile ladder—as perceived by people; this information is useful to put into perspective the impact of crime victimization. It is observed that in the case of women victimization implies an impact similar to falling almost three steps in the income-decile ladder, while for men the impact is of about half a step.

10.2.2   Fear of Crime in Latin America

There are many types of crime and, as mentioned above, some of them may be concentrated in particular geographical regions and demographic groups; however, large segments of the Latin American population are indirectly exposed to the crime and violence phenomena and it reflects on their fear of crime. Figure 10.5 presents information on fear of crime for some Latin American countries; data for Spain and the United States are also presented to put into perspective the Latin American figures. It is observed that practically half of the population in Peru report that often or sometimes felt unsafe from crime in their own home; levels are also very high— around 40%—in the two most populous countries in the region: Brazil and Mexico. These figures in Latin America compare very high to those in the United States— 10% and in Spain—5%. It is also observed in Fig. 10.5 that women experience more fear of crime than men in practically all the countries.

Fear of crime reduces life satisfaction, and its impact is larger for women than for men. Figure 10.6 presents the estimates from a quantitative exercise that studies the

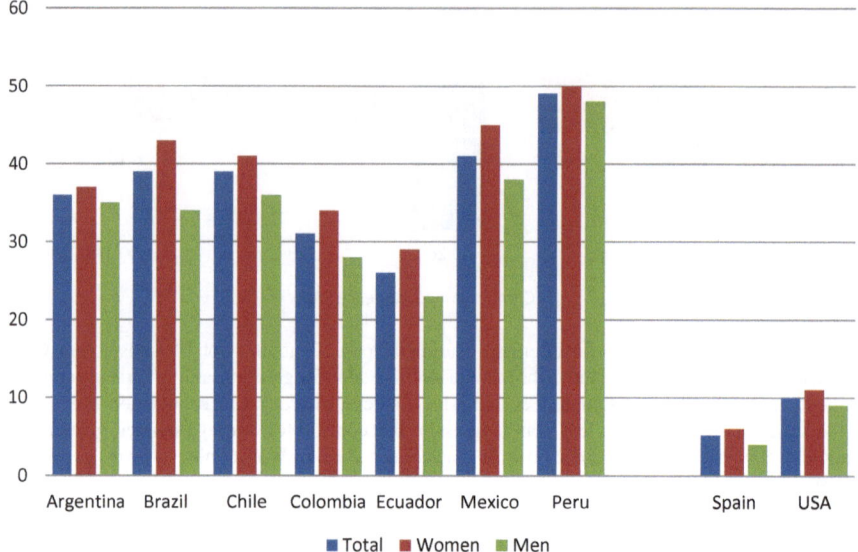

Fig. 10.5 Fear of crime by country and gender, percentage who often or sometimes felt unsafe from crime in their own home during the past 12 months. Other response options were rarely or never. Some Latin American countries, as well as Spain and the United States. *Source* World Value Survey (2011–2014)

impact of fear of crime on life satisfaction after taking in consideration other relevant socio-economic factors such as age, gender, education, marital status, reported income position, and country of residence. Those who respond that often or sometimes felt unsafe from crime in their own home during the past 12 months have a life satisfaction which is 0.23 lower (in a 1–10 scale) than those who respond that rarely or never felt unsafe. This impact is about three times larger than the impact of falling one step in the income-decile ladder; in other words: the impact of fear of crime is equivalent to a fall of three steps in the income-decile ladder. The impact of fear of crime on life satisfaction is relatively larger for women (decline in life satisfaction of 0.28) than for men (decline of 0.17).

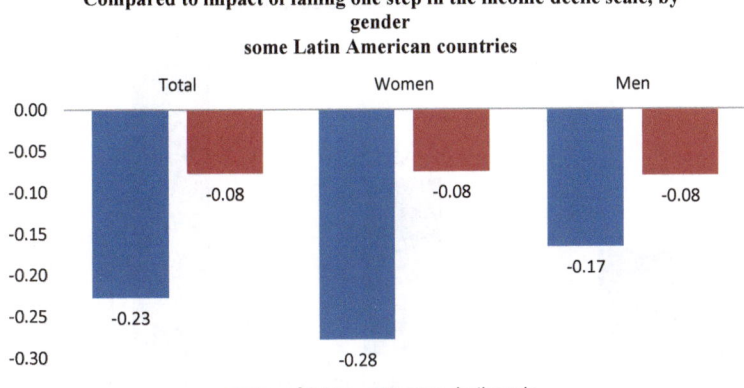

Fig. 10.6 Impact of fear of crime on life satisfaction. Fear of crime: often or sometimes rather than rarely, never during the past 12 months. Compared to falling one step in the income-decile scale. By gender. Latin American countries: Argentina, Brazil, Chile, Colombia, Ecuador, Mexico, Peru, and Uruguay. Life satisfaction measured in a 1–10 scale. Estimated coefficient from a regression that controls for: age, age squared, gender, education level, marital status, income position, and country. *Source* World Values Survey 2011–2014 wave

10.3 Aggression and Well-Being

The National Statistical Office of Mexico applied an experimental survey in 2012 to gather information on people's well-being as well as on people's living conditions. This survey asked three questions regarding physical aggression by type of the aggressor; the general question was: "During the past 12 months did you suffer physical aggression from?", and the types of aggressors were: 'somebody you live with', 'somebody you know', and 'somebody else'.

Figure 10.7 shows that about 5.3% of women and 2.7% of men—where victims of physical aggression by a person they live with. The trend is for men to be more exposed and for women to be less exposed to physical aggression as we move from the close relational circle (persons they live with) to other relational circles (persons they know, and someone else). Physical aggression in the close relational circle can be considered as domestic violence, while aggression by someone else (they do not know) may reflect exposure to rob with violence and other related crimes.

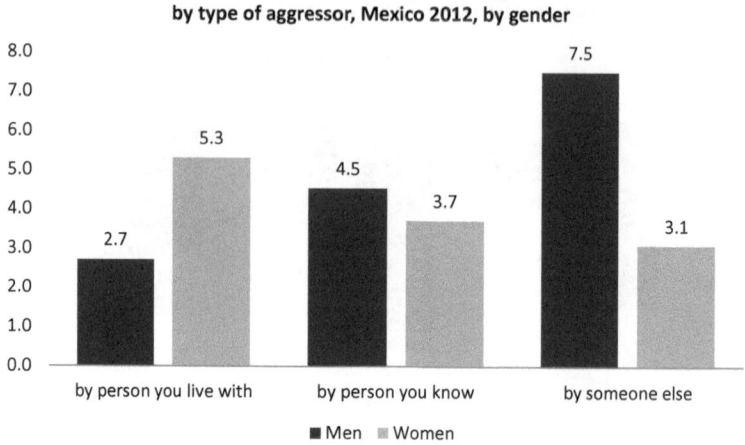

Fig. 10.7 Percentage victim of physical aggression by different types of aggressor, Mexico 2012, by gender. *Source* BIARE 2012, INEGI

Physical aggression has a large impact on people's well-being; its impact is very large in the case of women and when the aggression comes from someone in her close relational circles (a person she lives with or a person she knows). Figure 10.8 presents the estimates for the impact on life satisfaction of physical aggression on the basis of a quantitative exercise that controls for other socio-economic and demographic characteristics. It also presents the impact of a change of 100% in income in order to provide perspective on the magnitude of the impact of physical aggression.

Physical aggression by somebody a woman lives with reduces her life satisfaction in 1.13 (in a 0–10 scale); the decline is of 0.81 in the case of aggression from a person the woman knows and of 0.40 when it is from someone else (an unknown person). The much larger impact when the aggressor is someone in the woman's close relational circle may result from the recurrence of the aggression as well as from the greater emotional attachment that exists between the woman and the aggressor. It is interesting to see that the impact of physical aggression on the life satisfaction of men does not vary across different types of aggressors. In the case of an unknown aggressor it is observed that the life satisfaction impact is similar for men and women.

The impact on women's life satisfaction of physical aggression by someone they live with is very large (−1.13); it would require an increase of about 400–500% in income to compensate for such a decline in life satisfaction. This finding makes it clear that policy makers should put as much emphasis in reducing domestic aggression as they put in getting people out of income poverty. This information also shows the advantages of well-being data to guide policy makers in setting priorities and understanding the value that people attach to different policies.

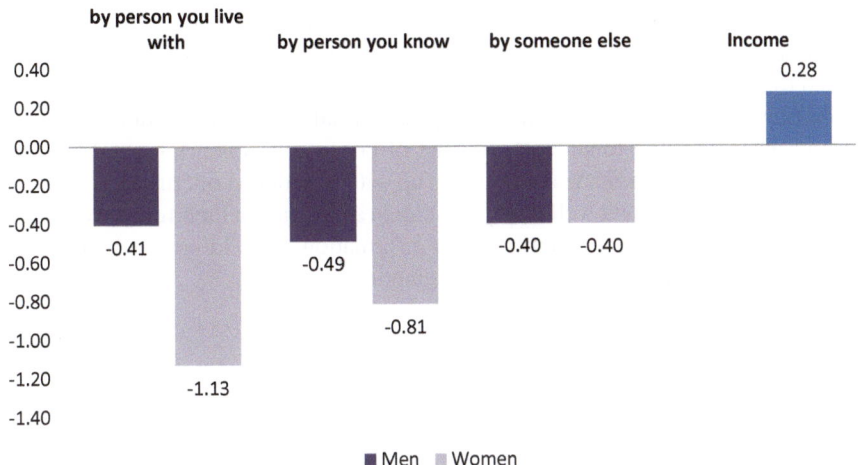

Fig. 10.8 Impact on life satisfaction of physical aggression; different types of aggressors. Life satisfaction in a 0–10 scale. Comparison with impact of a 100% increase in income. Quantitative exercise controls for gender, age, age squared, education level, marital status and logarithm of current expenditure (income). *Source* BIARE 2012, INEGI

10.4 General Policy Considerations

Crime and violence in Latin America have many causes, from the deterioration of the social fabric, the disintegration of family life, impunity and corruption in public spheres, and the geographic closeness to a very large drugs market.

The high rates of crime in Latin America impact negatively on people's well-being; those who have been victims of crime do report lower satisfaction with life. Even though violent crime may be concentrated in some geographical areas and some demographic groups, the fear of crime is a generalized phenomenon and it also impacts negatively on people's satisfaction with life.

The literature has emphasized the negative impact of high crime rates on economic growth and other economic variables; however, this approach misrepresents the impact of crime on people's well-being. The well-being approach shows that the reduction of crime rates should be a mayor goal of governments not only because it may foster economic growth but, fundamentally, because it increases people's well-being. The impact of victimization and of fear of crime is much larger for women than for men. This finding is important because it shows the value of following a subjective well-being approach which distinguishes between the driver (crime) and the experience people have (life satisfaction); it becomes possible to know how a similar driver may have different effects depending on other characteristics of the person.

It has also been shown that aggression substantially reduces well-being. The impact of domestic physical aggression on women's life satisfaction is so large that it would be almost impossible to compensate it with a rise of income. This finding makes it clear that some drivers may have a larger impact than others, which is very useful for policy makers in setting priorities and understanding the value that people attach to different policies.

Because subjective well-being surveys are usually applied to adult persons it has not been possible to study the impact of crime and violence on children and adolescents. One can assume that growing up within a context of crime and violence is not good for the present well-being of children as well as for their future well-being (UNICEF 2017). It is important to gather information on children and adolescent's life satisfaction in order to assess this assumption.

References

Ajzenman, N., & Jaitman, L. (2016). *Crime concentration and hot spot dynamics in Latin America*. Inter-American Bank Working Paper Series IDB-WP-699.

Ashby, N. J., & Ramos, M. (2013). Foreign direct investment and industry response to organized crime: The Mexican case. *European Journal of Political Economy, 30*(C), 80–91.

Balmori de la Miyar, J. R. (2016). The economic consequences of the Mexican drug war. *Peace Economics, Peace Science and Public Policy, 22*(3), 213–246.

Bel, G., & Holst, M. (2018). Assessing the effects of the Mexican drug war on economic growth: An empirical analysis: The Mexican drug war and economic growth. *Southern Economic Journal, 85*(1), 276–303.

Briceño-Leon, R., Villaveces, A., & Concha-Eastman, A. (2008). Understanding the uneven distribution of the incidence of homicide in Latin America. *International Journal of Epidemiology, 37*(4), 751–757.

Cabral, R., Mollick, A. V., & Saucedo, E. (2016). Violence in Mexico and its effects on labor productivity. *The Annals of Regional Science, 56*(2), 317–329.

Cabral, R., Mollick, A. V., & Saucedo, E. (2019). Foreign direct investment in Mexico, crime, and economic forces. *Contemporary Economic Policy, 37*(1), 68–85.

Cárdenas, M., & Rozo, S. (2008). *Does crime lower growth? Evidence from Colombia*. Working Paper No. 30. Washington, D.C.: The International Bank for Reconstruction and Development/The World Bank.

Cohen, M. A. (2008). The effect of crime on life satisfaction. *Journal of Legal Studies, 37*, 325–353.

Coronado, R., & Saucedo, E. (2018). Drug-related violence in Mexico and its effects on employment. *Empirical Economics*, 1–29.

Dammert, L., & Malone, M. F. (2006). Does it take a village? Policing strategies and fear of crime in Latin America. *Latin American Politics and Society, 48*, 27–51.

Detotto, C., & Otranto, E. (2010). Does crime affect economic growth? *Kyklos, 63*(3), 330–345.

Díaz, F. J., & Meller, P. (2012). *Violencia y cohesión social en América Latina*. Chile: CIEPLAN.

Global Commission on Drug Policy. (2016). *Advancing drug policy reform: A new approach to decriminalization*. 2016 Report.

Graham, C., & Chaparro, J. C. (2011). *Inseguridad, salud y bienestar. Una exploración inicial basada en encuestas sobre la felicidad en América Latina y el Caribe*. Washington, D.C.: Inter-American Development Bank.

Hanslmaier, M. (2013). Crime, fear and subjective well-being: How victimization and street crime affect fear and life satisfaction. *European Journal of Criminology, 10*(5), 515–533.

Imbusch, P., Misse, M., & Carrión, F. (2011). Violence research in Latin America and the Caribbean: A literature review. *International Journal of Conflict and Violence, 5*(1), 87–154.

Jaitman, L. (Ed.). (2015). *The welfare cost of crime and violence in Latin America and the Caribbean.* Washington D.C.: Inter-American Development Bank.

Naritomi, J., & Soares, R. R. (2010). Understanding high crime rates in Latin America: The role of social and policy factors. In R. Di Tella, S. Edwards, & E. Shargrodsky (Eds.), *The economics of crime: Lessons for and from Latin America.* Chicago: National Bureau of Economic Research and University of Chicago Press.

OAS. (2014). *The OAS drug report.* Washington, DC: The Organization of American States.

Pan, M., Widner, B., & Enomoto, C. E. (2012). Growth and crime in contiguous states of Mexico. *Review of Urban and Regional Development Studies, 24*(1–2), 51–64.

Powdthavee, N. (2005). Unhappiness and crime: Evidence from South Africa. *Economica, 72*(287), 531–547.

Rojas, M. (2017b). Crime and failure of community life in Mexico. In G. Tonón (Ed.), *Quality of life in communities of Latin American countries* (pp. 83–94). Berlin: Springer.

Staubli, S., Killias, M., & Frey, B. (2014). Happiness and victimization: An empirical study for Switzerland. *European Journal of Criminology, 11*(1), 57–72.

UNICEF. (2017). *A familiar face, violence in the lives of children and adolescents.* New York: United Nations Children's Fund.

UNODC. (2014). *Global study on homicide 2013.* Vienna: United Nations Office on Drugs and Crime.

UNODC. (2018). *World drug report 2018.* Vienna: United Nations Office on Drugs and Crime.

Vilalta, C. (2014). How did things get so bad so quickly? An assessment of the initial conditions of the war against organized crime in Mexico. *European Journal on Criminal Policy and Research, 20*(1), 137–161.

Chapter 11
Corruption and Weak Institutions

Abstract Corruption practices seem to be entrenched within the Latin American political system; they are the consequence of weak institutions and a casuistic implementation of the law. Latin American's perceptions of corruption in most State institutions reach very high levels; these perceptions are negatively associated to people's satisfaction with life. Latin Americans are also used to pay bribes to public officers and this seems to reduce well-being; however, some people may find that bribes facilitate the access to public services with a corresponding well-being increase.

Keywords Corruption · Bribes · Weak institutions · Latin America · Well-being

"To friends: justice and grace. To the enemies: the plain law". This phrase is attributed to one of the most prominent presidents Mexico has had: Benito Juárez. Casuistic law is entrenched into Latin American culture. It is a culture that places more attention to the persons than to the norms, and that is willing to take into consideration a person's particular situation and to put it above the cold application of rules and laws. Latin Americans recognize that laws are necessarily universal and that they may contribute to the functioning of society, but they also recognize that the cold application of the law ends up neglecting the specific circumstances in every person's life and that sometimes they are heartless. Latin Americans are used to the idea that *"by talking is how people understand each other"* and they expect others to listen to their particular situation and to react in accordance. Of course, this creates warm and person-based interpersonal relations that do also contribute—a lot—to people's well-being, but discretion in the application of the law also has some negative consequences.

The phrase attributed to President Benito Juárez reflects a common element that proliferates in Latin America: countries have modern laws, but their application is a matter of political discretion. Some people must face the heavy burden of the law while others are treated with mercy and benevolence, and this depends on the discretional disposition of the authorities. The centralization of power and its using to generate political clientele is associated to weak institutions which orbit around particular politicians rather than around general State policies. This implies for vertical societies where citizens cannot rely on the application of the law but need to align with the interests of those in positions of power (Granovetter 2007). Citizens need to convince, beg, create special bonds, show their loyalty, and even be willing

M. Rojas, *Well-Being in Latin America*, Human Well-Being Research and Policy Making,
https://doi.org/10.1007/978-3-030-33498-7_11

to return the favor they get from the political authorities who use their discretional power to build clientele and loyalties (Ionescu 2011; Keefer 2007; Licht et al. 2007). Of course, political authorities use the resources of the State to selectively allocate their courtesies. The consequences from this kind of application of the law are associated widespread of corruption practices. Hence, corruption is large in many Latin American countries and it reflects a larger phenomenon that has both positive and negative implications (Casas-Zamora and Carter 2017; Lavena 2013; O'Donnell 1999; Rotberg 2019; Rotondi and Stanca 2015; Transparency International 2017; Treisman 2000, 2007).

11.1 Corruption in Latin America

It is difficult to measure the levels of corruption in a society. The activity involves many practices and behaviors which are—in most cases—illegal; hence, information on this activity is opaque. Many types of agents may participate in these activities: businesspersons, politicians, bureaucrats, private-sector employees, citizens, international organizations, organized gangs, and so on. Different attempts on constructing an index of corruption exist; for example, the World Economic Forum constructs a Corruption Index based on three questions posed to business executives from 141 countries: How common is the diversion of public funds to companies or private groups? How do you rate the ethics of politicians? and How common is bribery by companies? According to this index five out of the ten more corrupt nations in the world are from Latin America: Venezuela, Bolivia, Brazil, Paraguay, and Dominican Republic. According to this index Mexico is the most corrupt country within the OECD group. By construction, this index provides a view from top business executives and reflects some—but not all—activities associated to corruption.

The World Bank constructs indicators on the quality of governance on the basis of information provided by institutes, think tanks, non-governmental organizations, international organizations, and private sector firms; with this information the World Bank constructed the Control of Corruption indicator which *"reflects perceptions of the extent to which public power is exercised for private gain, including both petty and grand forms of corruption, as well as "capture" of the state by elites and private interests."* Figure 11.1 shows the percentile in which Latin American countries are placed in the world ranking; it is observe that most Latin American countries are positioned in the bottom half of the world ranking. A good position is observed for Uruguay and Chile and, up to a certain degree, for Costa Rica and Cuba.

While most corruption indices rely on experts' information, the Latinobarometer survey relies on a representative sample of adults in the country to ask people about whether they think some types of officers are corrupt. The officers under consideration are: The President or Prime Minister and Officials in his/her office, Representatives in the Legislature (i.e. Members of the Parliament or Senators), Government officials, Local government councilors, Police, Tax Officials, Judges and Magistrates, and Business Executives. The response scale has the following options: All, Most, Some,

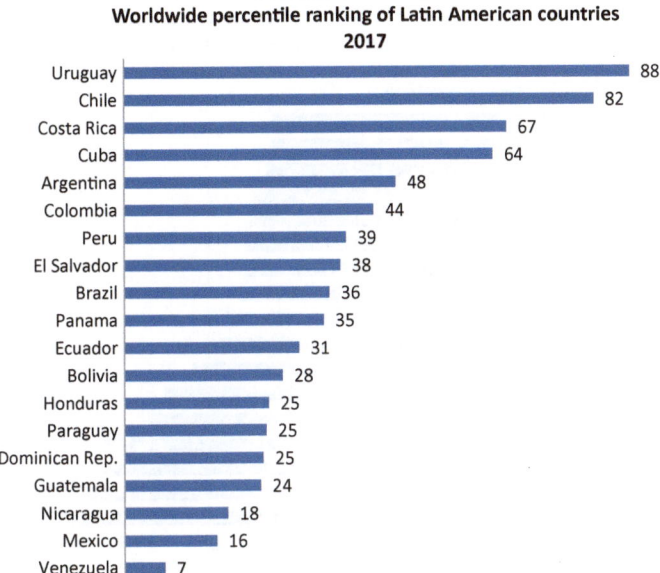

Fig. 11.1 Control of corruption reflects perceptions of the extent to which public power is exercised for private gain, including both petty and grand forms of corruption, as well as "capture" of the state by elites and private interests. Percentile rank in the worldwide classification. *Source* The Worldwide Governance Indicators (WGI)

None, and Don't Know. Figure 11.2 shows the country average for the percentage of respondents who think All or Most officers are corrupt; it is observed that more than 50% of the adult population in Mexico, Peru, Paraguay and Venezuela belief that All or Most of the officers mentioned above are corrupt. This figure on perception of corruption is low in Uruguay, and it is relatively low in Panama, Costa Rica and El Salvador.

Table 11.1 further explores the information on perception of corruption from the Latinobarometer; it shows the most corrupt institution in each country. About 73% of Venezuelans believe that All or Most of police officers are corrupt, this figure is 62% in Mexico. About 70% of Paraguayans believe that All or Most legislators are corrupt. In general the Police and the Legislature are the institutions with the greatest perception of corruption in Latin America, they are closely followed by the Local Government and The President/Prime Minister and his/her officers.

Uruguay has low levels of perception of corruption; however, it is interesting to see that Uruguayans perceive Religious Leaders as the most corrupt institution in their country, even above the levels for police, legislature and president's office.

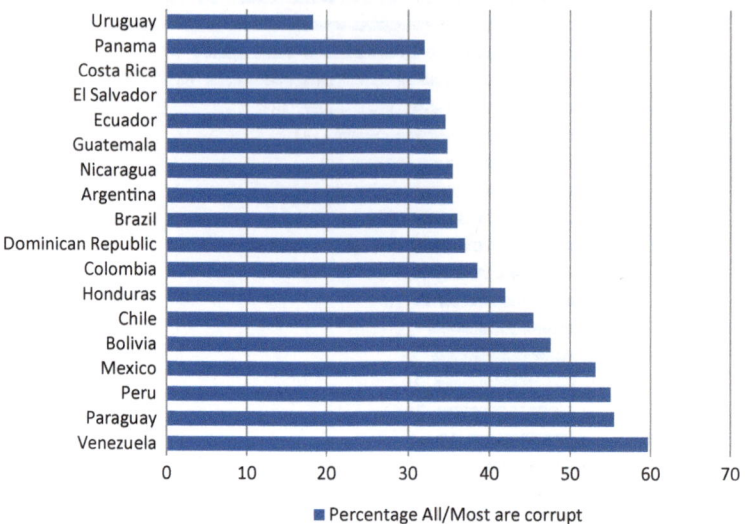

Perception of Corruption
Percentage who state that all or most of the officers are corrupt, Latin American countries, 2016

■ Percentage All/Most are corrupt

Fig. 11.2 Percentage who state that all or most of the officers are corrupt. Constructed as mean value for questions regarding the following officers: the (President)/(Prime Minister) and officials in his/her office, representatives in the legislature (i.e. Members of the parliament or senators), government officials, local government councillors, police, tax officials, judges and magistrates, business executives. *Source* Latinobarometer 2016

Table 11.1 Most corrupt institution. People's perception by country, in percentage, 2016

Country	Institution	Percentage all/most are corrupt
Argentina	Police	46.0
Bolivia	Police	61.6
Brazil	Legislature	57.2
Chile	Legislature	62.4
Colombia	Legislature	53.7
Costa Rica	President and officials	41.7
Dominican Rep.	Police	56.6
Ecuador	Legislature	42.7
El Salvador	President and officials	42.9
Guatemala	Police	51.6
Honduras	Police	54.0
Mexico	Local governors	63.8

(continued)

Table 11.1 (continued)

Country	Institution	Percentage all/most are corrupt
Nicaragua	Police	47.4
Panama	Legislature	42.9
Paraguay	Legislature	69.2
Peru	President and officials	65.3
Uruguay	Religious leaders	21.8
Venezuela	Police	73.4

Source Latinobarometer 2016

11.2 Perception of Corruption and Well-Being in Latin American

It is difficult to establish a causality relationship between perception of corruption and well-being. It could be that the perception of greater corruption reduces people's satisfaction with life, but it could also be that people who are less satisfied with life focus their attention on negative social aspects—such as corruption—and end up having a perception of greater corruption. Given the difficulties of establishing causality in studies that use cross-section data it seems better to talk about an association between perceptions of corruption and life satisfaction, with a possible causality going from the former to the later.

It happens that Latin Americans who have perceptions of greater corruption do also experience less life satisfaction. A quantitative analysis is run to study the difference in life satisfaction between a person who believes. None of the officers is corrupt and a person who believes All of the officers are corrupt; the exercise controls for other socio-demographic and economic variables with the purpose of isolating the role of perception of corruption. Figure 11.3 presents this difference for the Latin American population. Those who have a perception associated to the highest level of corruption report a life satisfaction which is, on average, 0.26 points lower (in a scale of 1–4) with respect to those who have a perception associated to the lowest level of corruption in the country. The associated loss in life satisfaction is observed across gender and along age groups. For comparison purposes Fig. 11.3 also presents the magnitude of the impact of being separated or divorced rather than married; this impact is about 50% of that associated to corruption perception.

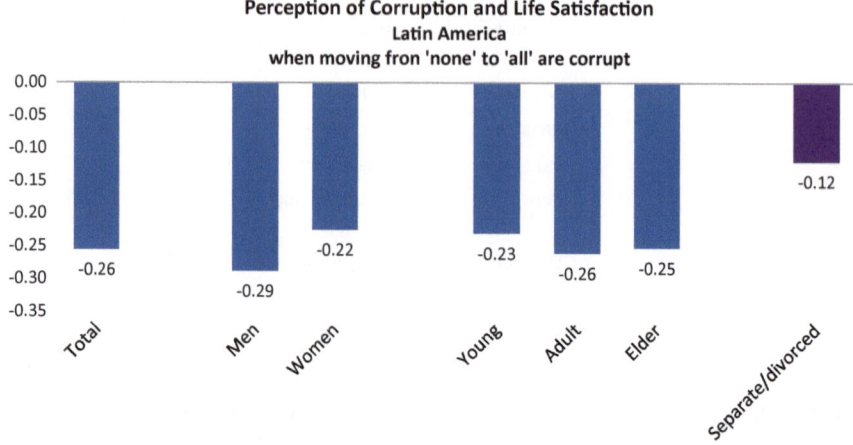

Fig. 11.3 Decline in life satisfaction associated to perceptions of greater corruption. When moving from None is corrupted to All are corrupted. From estimated coefficients from regression analyses; controlling by age, age squared, gender, education, subjective economic situation, marital status and country dummies. Life satisfaction in a 1–4 scale (not at all satisfied, not very satisfied, fairly satisfied, and very satisfied). Graph also incorporates the estimated coefficient for being separated or divorced rather than married. *Source* Latinobarometer 2016

11.3   The Complex Role of Bribes

11.3.1   Bribes Are Common in Latin America

The payment of bribes to public officers—and even to private ones—is common in Latin America. The Latinobarometer survey asked people whether they had being in contact with some public services in the past 12 months or not. The services under consideration were: Public Schools, Hospitals, ID document offices, Utilities Services, Police, and Courts. Those who were in contact where asked whether they paid a bribe or not. Figure 11.4 presents the percentage of users who report paying a bribe; it is clear that paying bribes is frequent in Latin America. About 22% of hospital users pay a bribe as well as 18% of public school users and 17% of those who have been in contact with police.

There are considerable differences across countries in the practice of paying bribes, with Mexico occupying an infamous first place (Fig. 11.5). About 44% of Mexicans report paying at least one bribe in relation to one of the six services under consideration (Public Schools, Hospitals, ID document offices, Utilities Services, Police, and Courts). Bribe rates are very high in Hospitals (39%) as well as in ID document offices (37%); about one third of Mexicans report having paid bribes to policepersons.

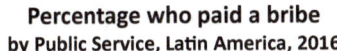

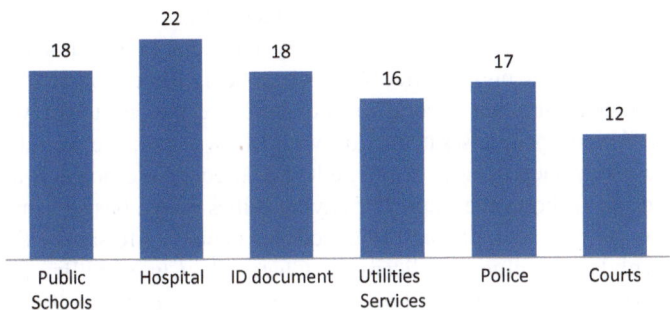

Fig. 11.4 Percentage who paid a bribe in the past 12 months, by public services. Percentage computed on the basis of those who made contact with public office. *Source* Latinobarometer 2016

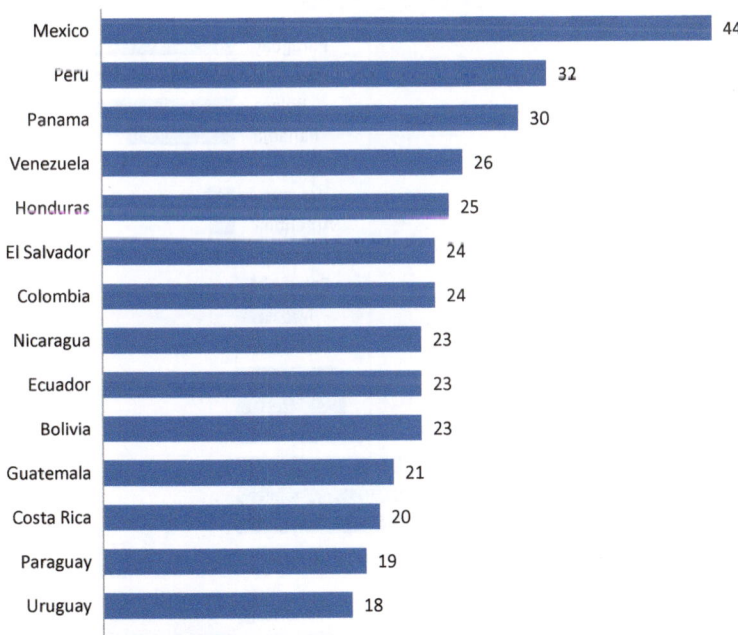

Fig. 11.5 Percentage who paid a bribe to any of the six services under consideration (Public schools, hospitals, ID document offices, utilities services, police, and courts) in the past 12 months. Percentage of total population. *Source* Latinobarometer 2016

11.3.2   Paying Bribes and Life Satisfaction

In general terms, one would expect for the payment of bribes to be negatively associated to people's well-being. There is not only a monetary cost but also a sense of
being openly robbed by public officers as well as being forced to pay for some services one has the right to have access to. A quantitative exercise to study the impact
of paying bribes on people's satisfaction with life was run; the exercise controls
for other variables such as age, gender, education, economic position and marital
status. Figure 11.6 shows the impact of paying bribes on the basis of this quantitative exercise. As expected, paying bribes reduces people's life satisfaction in most
countries, with large declines in Nicaragua, Guatemala, Chile and Brazil. However,
it is interesting to see that paying bribes is positively associated to life satisfaction
in Paraguay, Ecuador, Bolivia and Panama. This is an interesting result that requires
further research; it could be that in some societies bribes may work as enablers to

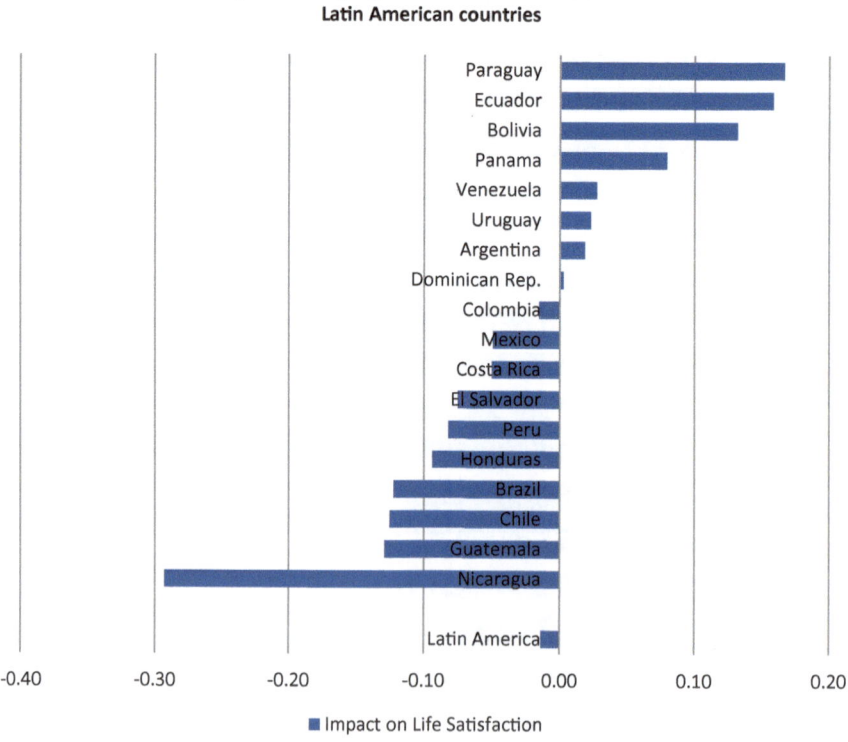

Fig. 11.6 Paying bribes and life satisfaction. Results from estimated coefficients from regression
analyses. Controlling by age, age squared, gender, education, subjective economic situation, and
marital status. Life satisfaction in a 1–4 scale (not at all satisfied, not very satisfied, fairly satisfied,
and very satisfied). *Source* Latinobarometer 2016

have (quick) access to services, it may also be that bribes allow people to 'solve' some 'wrong doings'—such as paying a bribe to a policeperson in order to avoid expensive fines. In all these cases a system of complex paperwork, fines, and discretional power has emerged which people consider being beyond their control; given this system people find that they are attaining a better solution by paying bribes than by not doing it, and their well-being increases. This is also important from a methodological perspective; the exercise presented in Fig. 11.6 is based on comparing the well-being of people who pay bribes with that of people who do not pay bribes even though they were users of the same services. It would also be necessary to compare the well-being of people who live in systems where they have access to services with no need of paying bribes with those who live in systems where the access to services required the payment of bribes; unfortunately, this kind of exercise is beyond the aims of this chapter.

11.4 General Policy Considerations

Corruption is a common practice in most Latin American countries; it takes place in many spheres of life: in people's relation with public officers, in their using of public services, when entrepreneurs want to open new businesses, in the allocation of public resources, in the hiring of public officers, in the payment of fines, and so on. Corruption practices seem to be entrenched in Latin American culture and to have historical roots.

Due to its nature, it is difficult to fully assess the scope of corruption in societies. It was shown in this chapter that the perception of corruption is negatively associated to satisfaction with life and that the magnitude of this association is large. In addition, it was shown that the payment of bribes is negatively associated to life satisfaction in most Latin American countries; however, a positive association in some countries poses interesting questions about the emergence of social systems that induce people to unilaterally pay bribes as an instrument that allows them to have greater well-being.

Corruption in Latin America goes beyond the bribes paid by citizens to public servants and politicians. Citizens do not observe a lot of the activities associated to corruption and only when major scandals emerge they realize that there are higher levels of corruption (Casas-Zamora and Carter 2017).

The payment of bribes is part of an intricate system that has emerged over decades and which has been created to make of bribes the best option citizens have to pursue their own objectives. Long delays, complex paperwork, hyper-regulation, discretional power, slow judicial system, little accountability, and many other practices are also part of the system that induces citizens and firms to pay bribes as their best unilateral decision.

References

Casas-Zamora, K., & Carter, M. (2017). *Beyond the scandals: The changing context of corruption in Latin America*. Washington DC: Inter-American Dialogue.

Granovetter, M. (2007). The social construction of corruption. In V. Nee & R. Swedberg (Eds.), *On capitalism* (pp. 152–172). Stanford: Stanford University Press.

Ionescu, L. (2011). Mexico's pervasive culture of corruption. *Economics, Management, and Financial Markets, 2,* 182–187.

Keefer, P. (2007). Clientelism, credibility, and the policy choices of young democracies. *American Journal of Political Science, 51*(4), 804–821.

Lavena, C. F. (2013). What determines permissiveness toward corruption? *Public Integrity, 15*(4), 345–366.

Licht, A. N., Goldschmidt, C., & Schwartz, S. (2007). Culture rules: The foundations of the rule of law and other norms of governance. *Journal of Comparative Economics, 35*(4), 659–688.

O'Donnell, G. (1999). Polyarchies and the (un)rule of law in Latin America: A partial conclusion. In J. E. Mendez, G. O'Donnell, & P. S. Pinheiro (Eds.), *The (un)rule of law and the underprivileged in Latin America* (pp. 303–337). Notre Dame: Notre Dame University Press.

Rotberg, R. (2019). *Corruption in Latin America*. Berlin: Springer.

Rotondi, V., & Stanca, L. (2015). The effect of particularism on corruption: Theory and empirical evidence. *Journal of Economic Psychology, 51*(Supplement C), 219–235.

Transparency International. (2017). *People and corruption: Latin America and the Caribbean*. Global Corruption Barometer.

Treisman, D. (2000). The causes of corruption: A cross-national study. *Journal of Public Economics, 76*(3), 399–457.

Treisman, D. (2007). What have we learned about the causes of corruption from ten years of cross-national empirical research? *Annual Review of Political Science, 10,* 211–244.

Chapter 12
New Development Strategy: Development as Well-Being

Abstract It is necessary to move from a paradigm of development as economic growth to one of development as well-being. It is vital to start thinking about development not in terms of greater income but in terms of people being satisfied with life. The paradigm shift needs to get rid of the notions of capital which are associated to the paradigm of progress as economic-growth; these notions must be supplanted by a narrative based on the drivers of well-being.

Keywords Well-being · Development · Progress · Beyond GDP · Happiness · Social capital · Relational wealth

In general, the concept of development makes reference to a journey from what is considered as an inferior situation to that which is considered as a superior one. Development refers to that path, not necessarily unique, towards the realization of those aspirations that have been established as desirable for, and preferably by, the members of society. The concept of development is intrinsically good and it is also necessarily vague, and it corresponds to each society to define what constitutes a superior situation and what is worthy of becoming a social aspiration.

The general concept of development plays an important role: it is used to assess the performance of societies over time and in comparison to others; it is also used to appreciate the benefits from different systems of social organization—such as the market and the central-planning systems. The concept of development provides insight on responding questions such as: Is the market system good for societies? Should countries implement pro-market reforms? Is government intervention convenient? What social regime is preferable? In addition, the concept is useful to judge the performance of governmental administrations: Was there development during the past administration? Is it convenient to reelect the official party?

It is important to distinguish between the concept of development and its specific conception in a particular moment and space. It is even possible for different conceptions to coexist—and compete—within a given society. The conception of development as economic growth was dominant during the 20th century; even at the beginning of the 21st century the main message sent by international organizations is still about sustaining high rates of economic growth and attaining ever increasing levels of per capita income. The development literature classifies countries on the basis of their per capita income; the path from underdevelopment to development necessarily requires countries to attain sustained rates of economic growth for many decades—or even centuries.

The turn of the millennium generated great interest in rethinking the conception of development; conceptions associated to well-being, quality of life and happiness have become more relevant. Well-being research has shown that the capacity of economic growth to contribute to people's satisfaction with life is limited. The concern for the sustainability of the planet has also exposed the deficiencies of a conception of development based on incessant economic growth.

During the 21st century a new narrative is emerging: Society's development is not about sustaining high rates of economic growth but about people having satisfactory lives that do not pose a threat to the planet and, in consequence, to the well-being of future generations. The recognition of the existence of environmental, social, and even human limits to economic growth calls for a reconsideration of the conception of development. The realization that there is not much well-being behind ever increasing levels of income makes it necessary to shift from a paradigm of development as economic growth to one of development as well-being.

It is within this paradigm shift that the Latin American case becomes of the greatest relevance. Some Latin American countries show that it is possible for people to enjoy high well-being levels for many years and to do it at a low cost to the planet. This is an important message to the development literature which for many decades has associated the idea of development to that of economic growth.

It is now possible to analyze how the conception of development as economic growth shaped policy making and development strategies in the 20th century. It is also possible to imagine and provide a new vision on how a paradigm of development as well-being would modify public policy and development strategies.

12.1   The Paradigm of Development as Economic Growth

12.1.1   Economic Growth and the Development of Societies

The last two centuries have been dominated by the paradigm of progress as economic growth. Within this paradigm the evaluation of the performance of societies is based on the behavior of the production indicators. The rate of growth of the Gross Domestic Product (GDP) per capita acquired central relevance as an indicator of development during the first decades of the 20th century. The paradigm benefited from economic theories backing the idea that people's well-being is closely associated to their income; this idea was promoted by economic theory. It was argued that the satisfaction of needs is crucial for people's well-being and that the abundance of goods and services contributes to the satisfaction of needs. The international community elaborated a discourse classifying countries as developed and underdeveloped; with the developed countries—those with high GDP per capita—becoming the model to follow. Modernization theory did also reinforce this view by dividing the world between modern and traditional societies—with the latter being associated to backwardness and underdevelopment. The paradigm of development as economic growth associates affluence—conceived as an age of mass consumption—to well-being and development, and it makes of this mass-consumption stage the final goal for all societies.

Therefore, within the paradigm of development as economic growth, international organizations and development-aid agencies focus on promoting the required trans-formations for underdeveloped and traditional societies to resemble the developed and modern ones, and the attainment of high per capita income levels becomes the main criterion to judge this endeavor's success. The study of the required transforma-tions constitutes a fundamental area of study in the history of economic development. The paradigm of development as economic growth had great influence in the con-struction of theories and models of growth during the 20th century. Many brilliant minds in economics became interested in identifying the factors that contribute to economic growth and which explain differences in per capita income across coun-tries. Factors such as institutions, values, human relations, geography, technology, security, education and health, and even religion have an instrumental function in these growth models; they end up being understood as factors that are relevant to generate growth. The development literature studies how these factors differ across countries and over time, but it assumes that income is equally desirable everywhere in the world and that the relationship between income and well-being is strong and universal.

12.1.2 Notions Associated with the Paradigm of Development as Economic Growth

Economists interested in modeling the process of economic growth keep proposing more sophisticated models which add new factors in order to explain the rates of growth and the differences in GDP per capita across countries. These models have evolved from the very simple ones based on physical capital and natural resources and which were developed immediately after World-War II to the highly sophisticated and mathematized models of the present. All economic growth models are inspired in the same assumptions upon which the paradigm of development as economic growth rests: they assume that income is a good proxy for people's well-being and that income is equally desirable everywhere in the world. These models end up transforming many aspects of people's lives into capital and positioning them as instruments to the service of economic growth. The following notions of capital are frequent in most economic-growth models:

Physical capital. The paradigm of development as economic growth approaches urban infrastructure, roads, means of transportation, machines, buildings, and many more as physical capital, and their value lies in their contribution to the country's

GDP. In most cases, technology is studied as a factor embodied into physical capital and its role is to generate qualitative leaps in the productivity of capital goods.

Natural capital. The paradigm of development as economic growth sees the environment mainly as a supplier of inputs for the production process. Therefore, the planet provides natural resources that become raw materials used in the production of goods and services; the value of these natural resources is measured in terms of their contribution to GDP. Furthermore, it is difficult to value those natural elements that have no use in the production process.

Human capital. The concept of human capital emerged in the 1960s to make reference to the contribution made by different attributes of the working force to the country's GDP. People are conceived basically as labor force and their main attributes are the skills and knowledge which are useful to the production process. Education, health, and even nutrition are valued in terms of their contribution to the productivity of the labor force and, in consequence, to the raise of income.

Social capital. More recently, the concept of social capital emerged to make reference to the contribution that interpersonal relations make to economic growth. Trust between unknown persons became important because it reduces transaction costs and allows for the expansion of markets and the division of labor. Networks are useful because they allow for people to find better jobs, and this contributes to a more efficient allocation of resources. Thus, within the paradigm of development as economic growth the value of interpersonal relationships is associated to their contribution in raising income. It is clear that the notion of social capital emphasizes instrumental relations where the focus of interest is not on the persons interacting but on the external benefits that can be obtained through this interaction.

There are other interesting features in the paradigm of development as economic growth:

Leisure as unproductive. The time people dedicate to leisure activities could be dedicated to productive ones; hence, leisure is considered as unproductive. This is also reflected in the national accounts system: leisure time does not contribute to GDP, but its alternative (work) does contribute. In fact, economic growth is not triggered by leisure time—unless this leisure implies greater expenditure, but research—and even common sense—shows that it is relevant for people's well-being.

Work as bad. Economic-growth models understand work as a sacrifice which reduces people's well-being. Economic theory assumes that work reduces utility and that people are willing to do it only because they receive a monetary payment which can be used to purchase commodities; and it is through the purchasing of commodities that people increase their well-being. Work is not conceived as a potential source of well-being but as a resource which is of value as long as it contributes to the production of goods and services. In this way, it is postulated that it is the income obtained by working and not work itself which allows people to increase their well-being.

Consumption as booster. Economic-growth models are full of consumers whose main activity is, essentially, to consume in order to generate the necessary demand to keep the production cycle going on. When consumers reduce their consumption or loss their confidence then economic growth suffers and it becomes necessary to implement measures to stimulate their expenditure. Persons have become mere consumers in this paradigm of development as economic growth, and their main role is just to act as consumption gadgets within a process centered in the rate of growth of GDP rather than on their well-being.

12.1.3   Income also Plays a Central Role in Related Conceptions of Development

Development is also associated with other conceptions that qualify or complement that of economic-growth, such as: poverty, inequality, and social mobility. These associated conceptions are also inspired the same paradigm that assumes a strong relationship between income and people's well-being. For example, the abatement of poverty is a common term in the political discourse as well as in the discourse of international organizations. The Millennium Development Goals initiative and the current Sustainable Development Goals initiative made of the reduction of poverty rates a global priority; however, poverty is conceived in income terms and its measurement relies on externally-defined income thresholds. Poverty lines assume that people with low income have low well-being and that people with income levels above the poverty line have socially acceptable well-being levels. The concept of multidimensional poverty argues for an expansion of the dimensions used to assess people's poverty situation; however, the other dimensions taken into consideration are highly correlated to people's income. This income-based conception of poverty implies for public policy to focus on economic growth as the main instrument to reduce poverty rates; hence, it is not only that the conception of poverty has an income-based substrate; it is also that it leads to the same recommendation of fostering economic growth.

The concept of social mobility is strongly associated to income; relative mobility is measured in the space of income deciles, while absolute mobility is conceived in terms of younger generations outpacing elder ones in the space of consumption and income. Economic growth becomes a basic requirement in the case of absolute mobility. Similarly, equity concerns focus on the distribution of income and material wealth while neglecting the distribution of many other drivers of well-being.

12.1.4   Doubts About Economic Growth as an Indicator of Development

The using of GDP growth as an indicator of the development of societies has not been free of criticism. One of the most common critiques states that GDP does not adequately measure what it is supposed to measure, this is: the production of final goods and services in a society. This critique points towards many measurement deficiencies of the GDP accounting system, such as: the non-incorporation of externalities, the difficulties to measure the production of informal and illegal sectors, the incorporation of some not-so-clear goods—such as weapons of mass destruction, the problems in measuring household production, and so on. The critique states that GDP does not adequately indicate the abundance of goods and services enjoyed by the inhabitants of a country.

There is another critique which can be considered as more insightful: It argues that even if GDP would adequately fulfill its function of measuring the production of final goods and services its role as an indicator of the development of societies is very limited. It is important to state that doubts about the capacity of GDP per capita to generate well-being have always being present. For example, John Maynard Keynes believed that the value of income does not go beyond what is required to have the material means to survive; Keynes thought that once the economic problem is solved human beings would have more important issues to focus on. In his preface to *Essays in Persuasion*—written in 1931—Keynes stated that *"the day is not far off when the Economic Problem will take the back seat where it belongs, and that the arena of the heart and head will be occupied, or re-occupied, by our real problems— the problems of life and of human relations. …"*. Hence, income is just a necessity but not something of major value.

In 1934, while he was leading the effort to construct the income and production accounting system, Simon Kuznets manifested that *"The welfare of a nation can scarcely be inferred from a measurement of national income"*. The economist Moses Abramovitz also expressed his doubts in 1959 by stating that *"we must be highly skeptical of the view that long-term changes in the rate of growth of welfare can be gauged even roughly from changes in the rate of growth of output"*.

Politicians have also been skeptical on the capacity of GDP per capita to be used as an indicator of development. In 1968 Senator Robert F. Kennedy delivered a well-known speech at the University of Kansas: *"But even if we act to erase material poverty, there is another greater task, it is to confront the poverty of satisfaction - purpose and dignity - that afflicts us all. Too much and for too long, we seemed to have surrendered personal excellence and community values in the mere accumulation of material things. Our Gross National Product. … counts air pollution and cigarette advertising, and ambulances to clear our highways of carnage. It counts special locks for our doors and the jails for the people who break them. It counts the destruction of the redwood and the loss of our natural wonder in chaotic sprawl. It counts napalm and counts nuclear warheads and armored cars for the police to fight the riots in our cities. It counts Whitman's rifle and Speck's knife, and the television programs which glorify violence in order to sell toys to our children. Yet the gross national product does not allow for the health of our children, the quality of their education or the joy of their play. It does not include the beauty of our poetry or the strength of our marriages, the intelligence of our public debate or the integrity of our public officials. It measures neither our wit nor our courage, neither our wisdom nor our learning, neither our compassion nor our devotion to our country, it measures everything in short, except that which makes life worthwhile."*

In fact, doubts about the capacity of GDP to measure development in societies were not rare in the 20th century; of course, these doubts extended to the capacity of income to generate well-being. The Movement of Social Indicators emerged in the 1960s and proposed measuring the development of societies on the basis of large sets of indicators. A few decades later the United Nations Development Program launched the so-called Human Development Index (HDI) as an alternative index to measure the development of societies. But the HDI is highly correlated with GDP per capita and it carries on with the deficiencies of 'top-down'-built indicators that neglect people's own well-being assessments.

12.2 Well-Being: A New Development Discourse

12.2.1 Paradigm Shift

Development as economic growth was the mantra of the 20th century, and it was postulated that societies should aspire to an age of high mass consumption. The Easterlin Paradox provided the first empirical evidence questioning the foundations of this development-as-economic-growth mantra by asking the following question: Does economic growth increase the human lot? The empirical answer showed that the contribution of economic growth to well-being in the second half of the 20th century was negligible.

At the beginning of the 21st century there are several social and academic movements asking for a reconsideration of what development is and what societies should aim for. Local and regional initiatives proliferate and call for new measures of development in societies; these initiatives propose to go beyond GDP in order to take into consideration the well-being of concrete people. Recent initiatives by the OECD (Measuring the Progress of Societies), the Government of the United Kingdom, and the President of France (the Stiglitz Commission for the Measurement of Economic Performance and Social Progress) raised the question of what should be considered as development in the 21st century; these initiatives also discuss what indicators are necessary to properly appreciate that progress of societies. In Mexico, the Initiative Measuring the Progress of Societies: A Perspective from Mexico conducted an extensive deliberation on the conception and measurement of progress in Mexico and the rest of Latin America. Some initiatives in South America aim at incorporating the traditional values of indigenous peoples into the conceptualization of the progress of societies. All these initiatives and many more that have proliferated at the local level recognize that production indicators are insufficient and even incorrect to appreciate people's well-being. Most of these initiatives also support a conception of development where people's experience of being well becomes a central criterion. In 2012 the United Nations General Assembly approved a resolution entitled *"Happiness: towards a holistic approach to development"* which explicitly stated that *"the pursuit of happiness was a fundamental human goal,* (and) *recognized that the gross domestic product (GDP) indicator was not designed to and did not adequately reflect the happiness and well-being of people*". A new conception of development as well-being is emerging. It is expected for this new understanding of progress to foster the development of a new national accounting system based on people's experiences of being well. A reconsideration of public policy and development strategies is also expected to take place once the final social aim shifts from economic growth to people's well-being.

The new paradigm states that society's development is not about abundance of material wealth but about citizens being satisfied with the life they lead. The paradigm shift in what is considered as the ultimate goal in societies implies a reexamination of the fundamental notions that have guided development strategies. The notions of physical capital, natural capital, human capital, social capital, work as a bad, leisure as unproductive and consumption as production booster, which emerged within a paradigm of development as economic growth, need to be reconsidered and modified.

12.2.2   From Physical Capital to the Livability of the Surroundings

The focus on people's well-being requires a different perspective on physical capital. The experience of being well people have depends on contextual factors such as the physical context; this is: urban infrastructure, roads, water systems, electricity, transportations services, public spaces, and others are important because the matter for the experience of being well people have. Hence, it is not about modern infrastructure, tall and taller buildings, fast and faster trains, large and larger harbors or the implementation of the most sophisticated and advanced technology in ever smarter cities; it is about people. The physical context has no intrinsic value; its value depends on how it influences people's well-being.

People live in communities, and communities are much more than agglomerations of houses where people sleep, commute, and work. Communities constitute the habitat where people live their daily lives and experience their well-being. Well-being research shows that policy makers should think about building communities rather than about providing housing solutions; this requires an emphasis on the habitability of the surroundings. The value of buildings, urban infrastructure, and transportation services is commonly assessed by their contribution to GDP but not by their contribution to people's well-being. The paradigm of development as well-being implies a different approach to the physical context, and it shows that there is high value in public spaces that promote interpersonal relations and which give sense of pride and belonging; there is also high value in public space that contributes to the enjoyment of life—by adults and children—as well as in urban infrastructure that facilities physical and mental health.

12.2.3 From Natural Capital to Our Home

The paradigm of development as economic growth approaches the planet as a source of resources and raw materials; the paradigm of development as well-being recognizes that the planet is our home—as a matter of fact, it is the only home human beings have at the moment—and it focuses on the global livability conditions which contribute to the life satisfaction of people in the present and in the future.

Most of the drivers of well-being are environmentally friendly; for example, the abundance of high quality interpersonal relations contributes a lot to people's well-being and has little impact on the environment. Leisure activities do not have to hurt the environment and, in fact, the combination of leisure and environment provides for highly gratifying activities at low cost. The paradigm of development as well-being allows for more room for policy makers to choose an environmentally-friendly strategy; within this paradigm policy makers have a larger arrangement of policies at their disposal to increase people's satisfaction with life and to do it at a low environmental cost.

The view of controlling and mastering nature is particularly dominant within the paradigm of development as economic growth, while the paradigm of development as well-being allows for a more harmonious coexistence with nature.

12.2.4 From Human Capital to Knowledge and Skills for a Satisfactory Life

The theory of human capital emerged during the decade of the 1960s within the paradigm of development as economic growth. It is a theory that focuses on the contribution of education, health and nutrition to economic growth; thus, it emphasizes the productive knowledge and skills acquired through education, as well as the importance of a healthy and well-nourished workforce. Education became the instrument to build a competitive and highly productive labor force, and educational programs were required to provide skills and knowledge to attain this goal. In the end, within the paradigm of development as economic growth, everything is about raising income and education—as well as health and nutrition—have no further role to play.

However, the contribution of education and health to the well-being of people goes far beyond their contribution to the generation of income. It is true that education is a means to acquire useful skills for the productive process; it is also true that education may allow access to a more comfortable economic situation. However, education can play a role that goes far beyond contributing to raising the productivity of people. People are much more than consumers and workers, and their life satisfaction depends on many factors beyond income. Education is a very good instrument to inculcate the skills and provide the knowledge and values that contribute to people's well-being; these skills, knowledge and values are not necessarily the same that contribute to people's productivity. For example, it is important to have skills, knowledge and values that favor gratifying interpersonal relations, that contribute to the rewarding use of free time and that promote the prevention of health-related problems.

Little kids at school are much more than future labor force; within the new paradigm of development as well-being education is no longer understood as an investment people make in order to attain greater income in the future. In economics the term investment is associated to a sacrifice people make with the expectative of obtaining economic returns in the future; but in the case of education people spend about a fifth of their lives at kinder gardens, schools and other educational institutions and these should be years of enjoyment rather than years of sacrifice. The few studies that exist on education and well-being show that happy children learn more and are less willing to desert. Educational programs should be as concerned about the well-being of little kids as about providing the knowledge and values and fostering the skills for these little kids to have a satisfactory life in the future.

An education that aims at providing knowledge and fostering skills for the labor market restrains its focus of attention on kids and young adults. On the other hand, an education that aims at providing knowledge and fostering skills for a satisfactory life is also important for adults and elder people; hence, these age groups should not be excluded from educational programs which provide knowledge and skills not to be productive but to have a satisfactory life.

12.2.5 From Social Capital to Human Relations

The paradigm of development as economic growth emphasizes a social-capital view of human relations. In this view human relations play an instrumental role in promoting economic growth; relations are useful to reduce transaction costs, to facilitate exchanges, and to promote an efficient allocation of productive resources; in addition, social networks allow people to find better jobs as well as good investment opportunities. The focus of the relation is external to the relationship itself; those interacting are more interested in attaining an external goal than in knowing each other. These relations may contribute to economic growth, but their well-being impact is limited.

On the other hand, person-based interpersonal relations constitute a main driver of people's well-being. These relations are close, warm and genuine; those who are interacting know and are willing to know more about each other. The relationship is not an instrumental one and well-being emerges not from the attainment of an external purpose but from the joint enjoyment of life; it is safe to state that the purpose of the relationship is the relationship itself. Person-based interpersonal relations have a large impact on people's well-being. If these relations are going well then it is very likely for life satisfaction and for positive affect to be high; of course, when person-based interpersonal relations are not going well they have a large detrimental impact on people's well-being.

Most person-based interpersonal relations take place with family, relatives, friends, colleagues and neighbors. Relations in the nuclear family are very relevant for people's well-being. In this type of relationships people approach others seeking to give and share rather than to receive and take.

Any development strategy that minimizes the importance of human relations or that makes of them an instrument for economic growth runs the risk of being inefficient in contributing to people's well-being. Hence, development strategies would do well in recognizing the importance of person-based interpersonal relations; there are many policies that can be implemented to strengthen these relations, for example: educational programs that provide the knowledge and foster the skills to have gratifying relations, urban space and public activities, neighborhood infrastructure, modifications in working shifts, and so on.

12.2.6 Leisure Is Productive

From a well-being perspective leisure is very productive. Free time allows people to practice own hobbies and pastimes and to pursue their own interests. Free time also allows people to interact with family, relatives, friends, colleagues and neighbors. Mental and physical health do benefit from the gratifying using of free time. In addition, free time allows for the presence of parents during the crucial years of child rearing; building attachment during the infant years and constructing close relationships between parents and children during the adolescent years is not only gratifying but also contributes to the formation of human beings with higher self-esteem, clearer sense of purpose in life and more life satisfaction.

The paradigm of development as economic growth led to a rushed pace of life in contemporary societies. There seems not to be enough time to get involved in leisure activities and less to relate with others. More free time and better infrastructure for its enjoyment is required; it is also important for people to have the knowledge for a gratifying use of free time. The administration of leisure, and not only business, is an important area of study in the new paradigm of development as well-being.

12.2.7 Job Satisfaction and Gratifying Work

People can enjoy and obtain satisfaction from their work. The view that work is a bad which people make in order to get some income to purchase commodities and attain well-being is very limited. It is also incorrect because there is not much well-being from additional income once some thresholds are surpassed; in addition, it is possible for work itself to be an important source of well-being. This implies a different perspective on the role of work. People spend a lot of their time at the workplace and doing work-related activities; holding satisfactory jobs is important for people's well-being. Research shows that job satisfaction is as important as economic satisfaction in contributing to well-being; in addition, wages are neither the only nor the most important determinants of job satisfaction. Holding a job contributes in many ways to people's well-being; for example: it provides the opportunity of building long-lasting relationships of friendship and companionship in the workplace; it also gives a sense of personal fulfillment, competence, purpose, belonging and identity.

The fact the work activities provide satisfaction goes against basic economics postulates and has important consequences for policy making. Job satisfaction does not come only from the income obtained but also from other attributes of the activity; hence, the loss of a job implies a well-being cost which is larger than the monetary wages not received; this is important information for unemployment and retirement policies. There are well-being losses in unemployment and—up to some degree—in retirement even when people are able of sustaining their income. The well-being cost of unemployment is larger than what monetary estimates suggest; unemployment has a large well-being cost and this justifies the implementation of policies aiming at its reduction. It is also important to develop alternative activities for retirees so as to mitigate their well-being decline due to retirement.

Of course, the main focus of public policy must be on how to increase job satisfaction, which goes far beyond the common goal of increasing wage rates.

While the paradigm of development as economic growth emphasizes the simplified figure of the worker, the paradigm of development as well-being speaks of human beings who work. This means that persons work, but that is just one of the many activities they do perform; they exercise as persons in many other areas of life; for example: they are human beings who also have family responsibilities—with their wife, children, parents, and others. Therefore, issues such as family-work balance acquire greater relevance within the new paradigm; and this balance of life is not important because it influences the productivity of people but, fundamentally, because it influences their life satisfaction.

12.2.8 Consumption Must Go Back to 'The Back Seat'

The pursuing of rapid economic growth has justified the implementation of policies that have dubious well-being impact but which are justified because they contribute to raise growth rates. For example, strategies such as easy money, rebates, coupons, personal credit cards, expansion of domestic markets, double mortgages, and so on are favored because they contribute to the dynamism of consumption, even when they are accompanied by higher debt rates and lower saving rates. The goal is for people to consume—or, at least, to shop—in order to boost demand and keep the cycle of growth going on. The obsolescence of products and the waste in consumption is accepted as long as this induces people to keep buying.

In 1931 John Maynard Keynes stated his prediction for the economic problem to *"take the back seat where it belongs, and that the arena of the heart and head will be occupied, or re-occupied, by our real problems—the problems of life and of human relations ..."*. The paradigm of development as well-being does not deny the importance of consumption, it has an important role to play in the satisfaction of human needs; however, its role is not to boost economic growth. It can be said that within the paradigm of development as well-being consumption takes the back seat—with evident environmental benefits—and 'the problems of life and of human relations' take the driver's seat in the definition of development strategies and in the design of public policies. People are no longer gadgets within a mechanism that emphasizes production and consumption, and people's well-being becomes the final aim of development.

Chapter 13
Well-Being: General Policy Considerations

Abstract The well-being approach expands the set of instruments policy makers have at their disposal; public policy is enhanced and precision is gained in attaining the final goal of increasing people's well-being. This implies a more efficient use of the scarce public resources.

Keywords Public policy · Well-being · Latin America · Social goals · Beyond GDP

13.1 Distinguish Between Intermediate Objectives and Final Goals in Public Policy

People's experience of being well constitutes a final goal. It is not only a personal goal—people want to lead lives they are satisfied with it is also a social goal—if social organizations and public policy is not useful in contributing to people's well-being then one wonders what policy is for. By clearly defining the experience of being well people have as a final goal societies can identify the relevant intermediate objectives and introduce some order and hierarchy in this space of intermediate objectives, which is very important for policy makers who are faced with decisions on the allocation of scarce resources.

Policy making takes place in the space of policy instruments and intermediate goals. Nevertheless, it is necessary to have a clear final goal which provides coherence to all policy actions and which allow policy makers to have a general view of the role that instruments and intermediate goals play.

Public offices and organizations specialize in the attainment of intermediate goals and have specific tasks to perform; this is fine from an operational perspective because expertise and focus are required for these tasks to go ahead. The well-being approach and the experience of well-being as a final aim imply for an integral, more holistic, people-centered perspective in policy making, which reduces the risk of making of intermediate goals a final one.

It is important for policy makers to have a dashboard full of indicators; however, what is relevant is to have a clear idea of what the destination is in order to know how to interpret the information provided by the dashboard indicators. The report

M. Rojas, *Well-Being in Latin America*, Human Well-Being Research and Policy Making,
https://doi.org/10.1007/978-3-030-33498-7_13

people make on their experience of being well allows pondering which information is relevant and what instruments should be used; without such report there is a high risk for the proliferation of intermediate objectives to introduce a lot of confusion to the design and evaluation of public policy. The space of public policy is full of intermediate goals and their indicators: employment, utilities coverage, soundness of the retirement system, investment in infrastructure, harbor capacity, health insurance coverage, life expectancy, housing construction, recreational areas, commuting times, road infrastructure, number of hospitals per population, anthropometric measures, income mobility, income distribution, income growth, inflation rates, civic participation, student desertion, enrollment rates, foreign investment attraction, rates of crime and violence, wage trends, political participation, urban regulation, cultural activities, subsidies and taxes, research and technology performance, and so on. All these indicators are probably relevant and they constitute legitimate areas of public-policy concern; however, working with so many indicators and specific objectives would lead to a compartmentalized view of public policy which cannot address important policy issues such as facing trade-offs, taking advantage of synergies, establishing priorities and hierarchies, and considering intertemporal decisions.

It is important to recognize that most of the indicators and objectives mentioned above are not final goals, this is: they are not pursued for their own sake but because it is believed that they contribute to people's well-being. Hence, by directly incorporating people's well-being into the design of public policy and by keeping track of well-being indicators it becomes possible to design a more efficient public policy.

In addition, the absence of a global criterion to prioritize the instrumental objectives increases the exposure of public action to the lobbying of pressure groups. By relying on the report people make regarding their well-being experience public policy ends up being guided by and for the interest of citizens rather than by the lobbying capacities of particular groups.

13.2 Expanding the Scope of Instruments. Complexity and Opportunity

People's well-being depends on many factors; such as: the state of their family relationships, the relationships with friends and relatives, the economic situation, the conditions in their community, the security they perceive, their education, their working conditions, their health and the health of their loved ones, the availability of free time, the infrastructure and activities to carry on leisure activities, their values, goals and standards of evaluation, and many more. The importance of these factors may change across population groups and over time.

There are multiple drivers of life satisfaction and this implies for a lot of instruments that policy makers have at their disposal to increase people's well-being.

Hence, the well-being approach broadens the scope of public action and allows policy makers to be creative in finding policy combinations. For example, most poverty-abatement programs aim at increasing income; a raise in people's income could be one way to increase their well-being, in particular when income is low; however, this is not the only instrument that policy makers have to raise the well-being of those in income poverty. Considering the lack of success of many poverty-abatement programs to raise income and the existence of some chronic conditions that make it difficult to attain this intermediate objective—at least in the short and mid run—it may be interesting to explore alternative instruments to raise people's well-being even when their income is not increasing. For example, strengthening community bonds or enhancing the community's recreational facilities and activities may have a large impact on the well-being of people in income poverty; similarly, eradicating domestic violence could generate a well-being which is much larger—and probably more reachable—than the impact of increasing household income.

The possibility of thinking about alternative ways to increase people's well-being is very useful and allows for public action to be more effective; the increase in well-being may be larger and there is no need to wait years—and even decades—for the impact to take place. In addition, it does not require from governments to spend more, it is just about spending wisely once the final goal is identified. In addition, by broadening the scope of policy instruments each country can find the appropriate policy combination that better fits its particular situation; some countries may find it more effective to pursue an increase in people's income through economic growth while others may find it more effective to focus their policy in community building, leisure activities, public safety and others.

Poverty-abatement programs constitute just one example; many other possibilities arise. For example, there is great loss in people's well-being as a consequence of chronic and terminal illnesses. If doctors were successful in reversing terminal and chronic illnesses then it could be justified for policy makers to focus on their reversion; however, it is not only that reversing chronic and terminal illnesses is very expensive, it is also that the degree of success could be very small. Hence; from a well-being perspective there may be other policies that raise people's well-being even when the illness condition is not reversed; for example, some countries are implementing work-absentee permits that allow relatives and friends to be close to terminally ill persons. Another example: changes in the demographic pyramid and the increase in life expectancy make it very difficult—almost impossible—for people to sustain their income flows after retirement. The drop in income associated to retirement may threat people's well-being in the future, and it could make sense for some organizations to think about ways to substantially raise retirement income; however, once it becomes clear that the final goal is not income but well-being it is possible to think about alternative policies that raise elder people's well-being even when their income is not increasing.

The consideration of the multiple factors that influence people's well-being as well as of the full spectrum of instruments that policy makers have at their disposal allows for designing better policies that have greater impact and even at a lower cost. It addition, it allows for having the complete picture on the direct and indirect

impact of particular policies. For example, it could happen that a program focused
on reducing income poverty is successful in achieving the intermediate objective
of raising household income—let's say, by opening opportunities for one partner to
migrate to a city with higher wages—however, this program is also impacting on other
well-being drivers. In this particular example, a focus on income would imply for the
spouse's opportunity of finding a job that pays higher wages to be considered as good
policy to increase household income and get the family out of poverty. However, the
raise of income is just an intermediate goal which needs to be pondered in terms of
its well-being consequences; policies that promote for one of the spouses to migrate
and to show up at home only occasionally could have detrimental consequences for
family satisfaction and for the present and future well-being of children who are
growing up without one of their parents. It could be that the family is out of poverty
but that their well-being is not increasing—or that it is even declining.

Policy makers have more instruments at their disposal when they realize that
well-being and not income is the ultimate goal.

13.3   Greater Efficiency in the Use of Scarce Resources

For decades, cost-benefit analysis has been used to guide public and private policy
and to make recommendations regarding the best course of action. The methodology
compares to monetary benefit from some actions to their monetary cost. In those cases
where it becomes impossible to have a direct monetary valuation the methodology
relies on indirect valuations based on contingent or hedonic valuation methods. The
basic principle is that everything must be valued in monetary terms and that policy
makers should opt for those actions that provide the greatest net benefit, with some
distributional considerations taken into account. The approach is consistent with
the paradigm of development as economic growth, it is based on evaluating the
contribution different actions make to the generation of income and opting for that
action that contributes the most; in principle this implies an efficient allocation of
resources and the implementation of the best policies to promote economic growth
and for people to have more income.

The main problem with this approach is that it makes of income the final aim
of public policy rather than an intermediate goal. Everything is valued in terms of
money but nobody knows what the value of money is. The well-being approach
allows measuring the value of money in terms of its contribution to people's well-
being and it also allows comparing the contribution money makes to the contribution
of alternative actions; hence, income becomes an instrument rather than a final aim
and its productivity in generating well-being can be empirically measured.

In the absence of well-being information policy makers would need to rely on
income as well as on other indicators of instrumental goals. The focus on particular
instruments makes it difficult to keep track of all the benefits and costs which social

programs and policies imply. For example, a program could be successful in raising people's income but it also implies a cost in terms of enjoyment of free time; well-being information allows policy makers to find out what the hidden costs and hidden benefits from social programs and policies are; in fact, this information provides a complete and holistic assessment of the well-being benefits and costs as people experience them. The appreciation of these impacts and their incorporation into the design and evaluation of social programs would allow for a better use of scarce resources.

In addition, it is now possible to study how different paths to raise household income end up impacting on people's well-being. The well-being approach recognizes that different ways of increasing income may have different effects on people's well-being; in other words, well-being is sensitive not only to the attainment of a goal but also to the way in which this goal was attained. For example, household income could increase in 1000 euros and this may be important for the well-being of family members; but from a well-being perspective it may not be the same that the extra 1000 euros are obtained from farming the own land than from becoming an agricultural laborer. Income indicators are not sensitive to the process leading to its raise but well-being indicators are and, in consequence, provide a more complete picture of what is happening to concrete people.

13.4 Construction of a System of National Well-Being Accounts

The Commission for the Measurement of Economic Performance and Social Progress provided a report which states that what is measured matters and it provides illustrations on how public policy has been misled by measurement problems. It is true that what is measured matters, just as it is also true that for policy making it is necessary to measure what matters: the experience of being well citizens have. Fortunately, during the past decades there has been progress in the measurement of well-being as people experiences it. Nevertheless, it is necessary to go one step further in order to elaborate a well-being national account system that provides information not only on the well-being of citizens but also on the behavior of drivers and explanatory factors.

This well-being national account system would allow policy makers to visualize other drivers beyond the economic one. The system should incorporate information on the explanatory factors of these drivers and should distinguish between those factors that are within the influence of some policy instruments and those which are not influenced by policy makers.

Those factors that can be influenced by policy instruments constitute the main focus for policy making. They will require further research on the relationship between instruments, factors, drivers and well-being. Models need to be developed and tested.

There are also some factors that are beyond the scope of policy making; this may happen because there are no instruments under the control of policy makers that can influence those factors or because society considers that government intervention in these areas is beyond the scope of public policy. In any case, keeping track of all indicators would provide a complete picture of how people's well-being is evolving and why and it would allow for better policies to be designed.